FULLY UPDATED & REVISED FOR 2015

COMPLETE GUIDE TO INTERNET PRIVACY, ANONYMITY & SECURITY

How to prevent online tracking and profiling; be safe from hackers, snoops and surveillance; avoid censorship; and be anonymous online

Matthew Bailey

www.cogipas.com

Contents at a Glance

Table of Contents

Chapter 18: Getting Rid of Other Kinds of Trace Information Left Behind on Your Devices.. 187

Chapter 19: Permanently Deleting (Wiping) Your Sensitive Items and Data 209

Chapter 1: Introduction

Why You Need this Book

There is no question that the Internet is an amazing tool providing you with many benefits. But it is all too easy to forget that using the Internet also poses a number of risks to your privacy and security.

This book is about how to manage those risks. You will learn how to protect yourself from a range of people and businesses that may have malicious intent and that could not care less about trampling on your privacy for their own benefit or profit.

Overall, the trend is towards the Internet becoming less private and less secure too. It is also becoming increasingly difficult to be anonymous online.

Therefore, it is important for you to know the risks and to know what is needed to face and counter them. Even if you cannot entirely eliminate the risks, it is important to be able to reduce them and protect yourself against the worst-case scenarios.

In that spirit, this book, the Complete Guide to Internet Privacy, Anonymity and Security (or "COGIPAS" for short) and its companion website http://www.cogipas.com/ contain all the unbiased and independent information and recommended services and apps that you will ever need. It outlines the very real risks you face and provides appropriate strategies for reducing them and for maintaining your privacy, anonymity and security while enjoying everything the Internet has to offer.

Your reasons for wanting to keep your online activities private are entirely your own and may vary. For example, perhaps you are motivated by:

- keeping your personal information and habits out of the hands of firms tracking your activities and building profiles about you
- shielding yourself from the prying eyes of elements that may be monitoring what you are doing online such as your ISP, overzealous government authorities, hackers, snoops, spammers, identity thieves and other troublemakers
- protecting your most intimate secrets, activities and downloads from being discovered by people having access to your devices or accounts
- safeguarding yourself and your loved ones from online trolls, predators and scammers
- the list goes on and on – you only need to read the technology headlines in the daily news to see the multitude of risks we all face.

Whatever your reasons for wanting to keep your activities private, this book can really help. The more you implement the measures described here, the more your privacy and security will be protected.

About this Book and How to Use it

This book tries to achieve the delicate balance between explaining what you need to know and how it all works. In the end, this is a manual that must be accessible to both relative beginners and advanced users alike. This is not always an easy task.

Each chapter in this book starts with the most fundamental concepts and then gets more advanced as it unfolds. If you are a beginner, you may wish to stop once the materials start getting too advanced. As your interest in these topics grows, you can always revisit the materials and expand your knowledge.

More advanced users may wish to do just the reverse: flip through the start of each chapter as a refresher and then pay closer attention to the materials that are new or less familiar.

Top Tip - Throughout this book, I'll use the generic term *device* to mean desktop computer, laptop, tablet or smart phone. Similarly, the term *storage device* refers to hard drives (internal and external), USB memory sticks and flash cards, as applicable. I'll also use the term *apps* to mean applications and software that run on devices.

How this Book is Organized

The contents of this book are divided into three main parts:

Part I covers *the basics* ensuring that you are secure in your online activities and when using your devices.

Part II covers *enhanced methods* for increasing your privacy and security. It also covers in detail how to be *anonymous online*.

Part III covers areas of *special interests* through a number of handy annexes.

The book concludes with an all-encompassing *Quick and Practical Checklist for Protecting your Internet Privacy, Anonymity and Security* summarizing the principles, apps and services recommended in the book. This checklist can also be found at http://www.cogipas.com/privacy-protection/.

About the Companion Website

The website www.cogipas.com complements the book with up-to-date materials, news and links to tutorials, as well as to the COGIPAS Facebook page. In particular, should any recommendations change, the updated information will be reflected as much as possible and as soon as possible on the companion website.

Top Tip - When you see in the book URLs (website addresses) to other websites starting with www.cogipas.com or goo.gl, these are simply ways to make long URLs more manageable by shortening them. The first address is via my own website, while the second is via Google's URL shortening service.

Please note that some website addresses appearing in the book begin with https, a special type of secure website address. Don't forget to type in the 's' at the end of https.

About the Symbols Used in this Book

To highlight or expand on certain points, various text boxes are used.

! Warning ! - related warnings, dangers or risks to be aware of

More About - additional facts, figures or technical explanations

Top Tip - helpful tips and tricks to enhance your experience

When explaining menu choices, either for using apps or for navigating websites, the selections will be separated by the symbol '>'. For example, to print a document in most word processing software you would select the following menu choices, *File > Print*, which means you first choose the *File* menu item and then select *Print*.

When this book suggests search terms to use, either in an Internet search engine or in apps on your device, the search terms will be surrounded by "double quotes". When entering the suggested search terms in the search engine or app, you should *omit* the quotes, unless the instructions expressly tell you to include them.

About the Screenshots Used in this Book

Please note that the screenshots in this book reflect the most recent versions of apps and websites at the time of publishing. Of course, as apps and websites are updated or changed, your screens may vary somewhat from the screenshots presented. As always, consult www.cogipas.com for updates.

You may notice that some of the screenshots in this book have portions *blurred* or *smudged out*. This has been done merely to remove any identifying information, such as trademarks or personal data that are not necessary to illustrate the techniques shown in the screenshots.

About Windows 8 & 8.1

Since its launch in October 2012, the take-up of Windows 8 by consumers has been poor to say the least. In particular, the response to Window 8's *Metro* interface has been almost universally negative. Even among people who did upgrade to Windows 8, many people chose to change the settings to make it look and feel as close to Windows 7 as possible. For these reasons (and not because I'm lazy) the screenshots in this book are shown more in the style of Windows 7.

If you haven't already done so and want to make Windows 8 (or 8.1) look and feel more like Windows 7 you only need to take a few steps. This will bring the desktop to the foreground, helping you bypass the Windows 8 Metro start screen.

You will need to change a few settings in the *Taskbar Properties*. You can access these settings either by typing "taskbar" in the Windows Search or by right-clicking on any empty space on the Taskbar and then selecting *Properties*. Either option will open up the *Taskbar and Navigation Properties* dialog box. Choose the option that allows you to bypass the start screen at login. Under the *Navigation* tab, you'll see a section called *Start screen*. Under this tab, tick the option *Go to the desktop instead of Start when I sign in*. Other good options to tick are *Show the Apps view automatically when I go to Start* and *Search everywhere instead of just my apps when I search from the Apps view*.

While this won't completely transform Windows 8 into Windows 7, it will do a lot to make Metro recede into the background.

~ ~ ~

Right, let's get started!

Top Tip - The topics of Internet privacy, security and anonymity are not always easy. To help you when coming across any unfamiliar terms, please consult the detailed definitions relating to these topics at http://www.cogipas.com/glossary

* * *

Each chapter of the book will end with a link to the companion website where you can find updates and additional information related to the chapter's subject matter.

PART I - THE BASICS

In this part, you will learn the most fundamental aspects of protecting your privacy and security on the Internet. These are the *minimum* measures that you should take.

~ ~ ~

Chapter 2: Risks at a Glance

The risks to your Internet privacy and security come in various shapes and sizes, but let's try to outline some broad categories to help make managing them easier.

Cracked Passwords

Weak passwords are a major source of security breaches. Poor passwords are more easily cracked, even by novice hackers using tools widely available on the Internet. To make matters worse, if one of your account passwords is cracked, this can lead to your other accounts being compromised as well. For example, once a hacker gains access to one of your accounts, he or she could gain access to a number of other passwords contained in confirmation emails or by making *forgotten password* requests at other sites, resetting passwords or obtaining instructions on how to create a new password. And once your account is hacked, the first thing the hacker will usually do is change the password, locking you out.

Online Tracking

As aspects of people's lives increasingly migrate online, it is becoming easier for big business, governments, hackers and other snoops to track in great detail your online activities, behavior and personal preferences. Traditionally, this online tracking was done with *cookies*, small text files downloaded to and shared with your device from visiting a website. While these cookies helped the website identify you and learn about your earlier activities on the site, cookies can also track you across *other* websites. Today, apart from traditional cookies, other means of tracking are widely used such as *super cookies* (cookies difficult to get rid of), *flash cookies, beacons*, as well as hidden *third party elements* (TPEs) embedded in websites and other sophisticated means of *device fingerprinting*. Taken together, these instruments can be used to track virtually everything you do online.

Online Profiling

By matching, aggregating and cross-referencing individual pieces of your Internet activities – usually through the fingerprints you leave behind from your *IP address* (see *More About* box) – vast, accurate and potentially intrusive personalized profiles are being amassed about you. It is a lucrative business to collect such information, build profiles and sell them to advertisers, other commercial organizations or anyone else interested in acquiring them. You have probably already noticed that websites display eerily accurate ads for products or services that you may have recently purchased or been researching. But this is just the tip of the iceberg - tailored ads are only the most visible aspect that your profile is being used for. Your profile can just as easily be used to tailor website content, even prices, or be used for other nefarious purposes such as a secret screening tool for loan applications, insurance coverage, memberships or job applications.

More About: *IP address* - IP address stands for *Internet Protocol address* - a unique numerical label, such as 123.456.78.90, that identifies every device connected to the Internet at a given time.

Malware

In this book the term *malware* is used to cover any threats emanating from software or apps that have been designed with a malicious intent. These include viruses, worms, Trojans, rootkits, adware and spyware. The lines between these variations of malicious programs are blurring all the time, so the comprehensive term malware will be used. In one way or another, they are all intended to harm your devices, varying from the mildly annoying (freezing your display), to the troubling (tracking your activities) to the downright criminal (capturing your credit card or banking login details).

Unsecure Wireless Networks

As wireless Internet connections (Wi-Fi) become available almost everywhere, there is a real risk of sharing your connection with strangers. If the network you use (whether at home or elsewhere) or the devices you use are not set up properly, third parties may be able to access or piggy-back on your connection and devices, perhaps even launching attacks on other victims under your guise. Sophisticated hackers can take advantage of this, mining your wireless connection for banking information, passwords or other valuable data.

Scams and Frauds

Everyone thinks that they are too smart to become a victim of online fraud. But it really can happen to *anyone*. Nowadays, scammers use sophisticated technologies as well as old tricks to get at your money or personal information. Crooks may use methods ranging from email, online ads, web browser pop-up windows, search page results to malware. Usually crooks try convincing a victim to transfer money or provide important information in a short timeframe, sometimes wrapping it in an attractive proposal to make a quick buck or obtain some other benefit. For example, scammers may offer you an attractive home-based job, discounted loan rate, "miracle" medicines or amazingly priced products. Other popular themes for scams include lotteries, investment schemes and online dating. Although some scams are simple and maybe even obvious, too many people fall victim to scams, even smart people such as you.

Phishing

Phishing (pronounced "fishing") is when fraudsters send you emails that appear to be legitimate asking you to provide personal information, such as passwords or financial data. A common tactic is that the phishing email says that there has been suspicious activity on your account and asks you to update and verify your details such as your name, address, birthdate, username, password, social security number, etc. If you fall for this bait the fraudsters will have the information they need to access your account. Phishing attacks are not usually aimed at one particular person; rather they are conducted through mass email distributions. *Spear phishing* is targeted phishing applying a more sophisticated and tailored attack aimed at a specific individual, perhaps referring to you by name or referencing some recent activity you undertook, thus adding credibility to the message and increasing the likelihood of you taking the bait.

Spoofing

Spoofing is where a malicious website tries to pass itself off as a legitimate site - sometimes with a similar-looking website address and sign-in page - in an attempt to fool you into providing your username and passphrase, or perhaps even your credit card details, address, or other personal information. Typically, an attacker sets up a false copy of a legitimate website to deceive you into entering your personal data or financial information. This is often, but not always done, to look like a login page. Spoofing is often used in conjunction with phishing: you receive a seemingly legitimate email that directs you to a seemingly legitimate website login page. Spoofing also exists *offline* too when, for example, fake banking machines are used to capture your banking PIN code.

Identity Theft

Identity theft is an illegal act which involves the theft or misuse of your personal data, such as your name, birthdate, social security number or any other personally identifying information. Identity thieves acquire and use your information for financial fraud such as incurring credit card charges, taking out loans or receiving government benefits, all in *your* name. Identity thieves often use online phishing, spoofing, or malware to help them achieve their goals. Identity theft is becoming more common with 7% of US households falling victim to it every year. Victims of identity theft can have their credit ratings destroyed, be held responsible for financial compensation, be pursued by debt collectors, be blacklisted from receiving future benefits and even far worse nightmarish scenarios!

Physical Security

Millions of devices – especially laptops, tablets and smart phones - are stolen every year, often containing mountains of personal information. Why should an identity thief go to all the trouble of trying to infiltrate your Internet connection or device with complex methods when he or she can simply steal your laptop, tablet or smartphone when you let your guard down at the local coffee shop? Believe it or not, there are also less widely known privacy risks posed by photocopiers and printers as well as little spying devices called *keyloggers* that can be connected to your devices and used to monitor your activities.

Spam

Spam is usually associated with unsolicited commercial email, but spammers are now expanding their techniques to all corners of the Internet including the web, social media, chat rooms, torrent file-sharing and Usenet newsgroups. Spam is usually more annoying than dangerous unless it contains or transports malware, but even "harmless" spam wastes your time and bandwidth.

Adversaries

Much of the attention in this book is focused on attacks on your privacy by big business, government, hackers, snoops and identity thieves. However, there are far more potential adversaries out there that may be interested in your online activities or in accessing your devices for their own benefit or even to harm you. These people could include online trolls or predators, jilted lovers, ex-spouses, rival co-workers, ex-business partners, or any person who has a perceived grudge against you. In addition, lawyers often advise clients or hire private investigators to collect emails, social media posts, transcripts of online chats, and smartphone messages as part of the preparations for legal proceedings (for example, employment claims, divorce or civil suits).

~ ~ ~

Even this brief outline should illustrate that it is not all smooth sailing on the Internet. But don't despair! You can address and lessen *all* of these risks with the information you will find in the pages of this book.

* * *

For updates and additional information about these risks in general, please visit http://www.cogipas.com/risks-at-a-glance/.

Chapter 3: Importance of Good Passwords (Passphrases)

Introduction

Everyone is already well aware about what constitutes a good password and how to compose them. Right? Well, statistics and daily news headlines consistently tell a different story.

In order to reinforce the techniques outlined in this chapter, the term *passphrase* (instead of password) is used as much as possible throughout the book. The term pass*word* denotes using a single word to protect your accounts from unauthorized access. To better protect your accounts, you should use longer, more complex constructions – in other words pass*phrases* – to safeguard your accounts from unauthorized access by hackers and other troublemakers.

On that note, this chapter will use the term *hacker* for anyone attempting to access your accounts without your permission. While that term may generate images of a faraway shadowy figure, the person trying to hack into your account could be any of the adversaries I mentioned in chapter 2.

What Makes a Good Passphrase

Rather than lecture you page-after-page about passwords - whoops, I meant *passphrases* - instead I simply recap the best practices you should adopt.

Simply stated: you must construct strong passphrases that are difficult for hackers to crack. This is one of the most fundamental aspects of your Internet security. Your accounts, information, devices and apps are only as secure as the passphrases you use to protect them.

This means using *longer*, more *complicated* and even *random* passphrases. As general rules:

- Passphrases should be *at least* 8 characters long, but the longer the better.
- Passphrases should use a mix of at least 3 character types (uppercase letters, lowercase letters and numbers). Ideally, you should also use symbols (! – +), if supported.
- Passphrases should *not* contain your name, username, birthdate, license plate number, phone number, favorite movie or any other personal information, including similar details for your spouse, partner or children.
- Passphrases should *not* contain any nouns (the names of persons, places or things).
- Ideally, passphrases should not contain words found in any dictionary of *any* language.

The last point is often ignored but important as it further protects your accounts from *brute force* dictionary attacks.

More About: *Brute Force Dictionary Attacks* - A brute force dictionary attack is a method that hackers use to crack passwords by applying all possible words found in dictionaries (and not only English-language dictionaries). Hackers use apps to enter every word as well as combinations and variants of words, to gain entry into your accounts. This hacking method can be surprisingly simple and fast.

When generating passphrases, pick something random and even ridiculous. If you follow these guidelines, it will simply take too long for hackers to crack your passphrases and they will move on to an easier victim.

Automatically Generating Strong Passphrases

If you have trouble coming up with your own good passphrases, there are plenty of websites and tools to help you. These are some of my favorites (all free):

- MakeUseOf's Secure Password Generator http://passwordsgenerator.net/
- Norton Identity Safe Password Generator https://identitysafe.norton.com/password-generator/
- Ultra High Security Password Generator https://www.grc.com/passwords.htm

You can also check the strength of a passphrase with a number of resources:

- Microsoft's Password Checker https://www.microsoft.com/security/pc-security/password-checker.aspx
- The Password Meter http://www.passwordmeter.com/

A Single Weak Password Can Be Your Undoing (You Should Always Use Different Passphrases)

Although inconvenient, you should *never* use the same passphrase for different accounts, no matter how unimportant you may think any single account. Use a *unique* passphrase for each and every one of your accounts. Otherwise, the security of *all* your accounts may only be as good as your weakest passphrase.

Top Tip - I'll say it again, don't repeat passphrases. Use a different passphrase for each and every account you have.

Formulas and Patterns are Bad Too

Similar advice is do *not* use a formula or pattern for generating passphrases. If an attacker discovers that you always use the same formula or pattern to generate otherwise "unique" passphrases, he or she will soon be using it to breach your accounts.

An example of such a pattern or formula would be using the first and second letter of a website's name (with the second capitalized) and then adding 123456 to the end. Using this formula for the website www.example.com would make your password eX123456. While this password might look strong, once the pattern or formula is discovered, it becomes useless and leads to only more account breaches.

Hackers similarly exploit the fact that many people repeat the same passphrase or only alter them slightly each time. Similarly, professional snoops are also trained to crack the easy passwords first because many people use the same or similar passphrases for all of their accounts. In addition, your employer or colleagues may have access to some of your passphrases at work; if you use this same passphrase (or pattern) for your personal accounts, you will be exposing these other accounts too.

The Domino Effect of a Single Bad Passphrase

Such *knock-on security risks* can also arise when a hacker gains access to a non-sensitive account and then uses the information he or she finds to correctly guess or crack your more sensitive accounts. As already mentioned, once a single one of your accounts is compromised, the hacker may be able to find confirmation emails or other details helping them breach *other* accounts.

Even if the breached account doesn't contain password confirmation messages for other accounts, it may still contain plenty of personal information enabling the attacker to answer 'Forgot your password?' security questions or to gain access a number of other ways.

In cases where the password reset is protected by additional security questions, the hacker could try answering them using little more information than your birthdate, your mother's maiden name or the name of your pet. Perhaps the hacker has gleaned this information from the initially hacked account or even posts you or a friend made to social media.

And of course, the first thing a hacker will do after compromising your account is change the password, locking you out. And it is no easy task to reclaim an account once it has been *hijacked.*

It is because a single account breach can quickly lead to others that you need to follow and take seriously the passphrase guidance in this chapter. Despite all the sophisticated hacking methods available, the simple breaching of weak passwords remains by far and away the biggest threat to your security. Just ask the celebrities victimized by the *Frappening*. The good news is that this risk is easily addressed.

Using Tools to Keep Track of Your Passphrases

While it may be a pain to keep track of many complicated passphrases, there are plenty of tools to help you quickly generate strong ones and to keep track of them. Many apps even help you automatically login to your stored accounts.

I highly recommend *LastPass Password Manager* ¢ (free) http://www.cogipas.com/lastpass as a handy passphrase management tool for all your online accounts. With LastPass, you set up one master passphrase and it keeps and manages all of your account passphrases. LastPass helps you construct strong passphrases with an easy wizard that automatically appears when you are creating a new passphrase. The underlying data is kept on LastPass' encrypted servers - hence, using this service requires a degree of trust in the provider and confidence that they won't be a victim of a widespread hack - but storing your data in the cloud this way also allows you to access your passphrases remotely from any device connected to the Internet.

RoboForm ¢ (premium) http://www.cogipas.com/roboform is a popular and reliable premium passphrase manager. RoboForm also includes a feature called RoboForm2Go that lets you securely save and manage all your passwords from a USB memory stick.

* * *

For updates and additional information about protecting yourself with strong passphrases, please visit http://www.cogipas.com/importance-of-good-passwords-passphrases.

Chapter 4: Minimizing your Online Digital Fingerprints (Learn about Online Tracking & Profiling)

Introduction

Whatever you do online is *your* business and nobody else's. At least, that's the way it *should* be. Unfortunately, there is money, BIG money to be made at every turn by those who want to profit from your privacy. For this reason alone, it is important to be informed about what the online trackers and profilers are up to and how to keep them at bay.

Plenty of people may deny it, but there *are* some potential benefits to being "profiled": you are served up information and ads tailored to your past behavior which, after all, is usually the best predictor of your future wants and needs. However, we may not want these sometimes helpful technologies applying to *all* our activities. So, cherry pick if you like. The techniques available are *not* all or nothing in nature. When indulging in activities you prefer to keep private, go off the radar. When you are not, you can stay on the grid if you like. This approach can provide you with the best of both worlds.

Top Tip - Although Google is the most popular search engine, consider using alternative search engines that better respect your privacy and don't track you, such as DuckDuckGo https://duckduckgo.com/ and Ixquick https://www.ixquick.com/.

There will always be people who don't trust the powers that be, who think that Big Brother lurks behind every corner, and who want to stay off the radar as much as possible. That's fine. At the end of the day it is a *personal choice* you can make based on your own situation, preferences and comfort level. The trouble is, most people have no clue about just how invasive or potentially invasive the profiling and tracking is, can be or may become.

All Your Activities are Being Tracked and Profiled

The most evident way you are being tracked shows up in the online ads served to you. It can be embarrassing when showing a mainstream website to a friend, colleague or your partner only to have it display lots of invasive or even inappropriate ads.

Sometimes the ads displayed are directly related to the websites you have visited, the searches you have conducted or the products and services you have researched or purchased. This happens because the online advertisers and their multitude of digital minions know very well what you are spending time watching, searching, playing, and purchasing.

Other times, it is simply because the ads fit your *general* characteristics. For example, maybe you have been categorized as a single, upper income, 30- to 40-something. In such a case you may be targeted for ads thought to appeal to this target group even though *you* have no interest in them.

The accuracy of the tracking and profiling is getting downright scary. Although the tracking and profiling firms are not supposed to have data that identifies you by name, your name hardly matters anymore. The profilers may know far more about you than most of the people who *do* know you by name. In short, the profilers know your online secrets. This is why the ads you get can be so specific and accurate.

The oft-quoted example is the one about these profiling firms knowing that a woman is pregnant before her own family knows. The profilers gain this insider knowledge based on the websites that the mother-to-be is browsing, the health-related articles she's reading, the baby products she's looking up and the research she is conducting about what she can expect during pregnancy and childbirth. The exact same analogy applies to someone investigating a medical condition, researching an addiction, exploring their sexual identity, looking into how they might go about getting divorced, have an affair, quit their job, declare bankruptcy or any other private matter.

This tracking and profiling also means that those invasive ads tend to follow you. The boss may not be so impressed when you show her a work-related article and the ads displayed side-by-side the article provide a little too much of a glimpse into things you would rather keep private. Or when you are showing your partner a recipe online and the site is also serving up embarrassing ads based on little more than your general profile or on an errant or ill-advised click you made while mindlessly browsing the web a few days earlier.

How Do They Do This?

IP Address Tracking

Your Internet connection leaves a trail of sorts that becomes imprinted on all of your online activities. This fingerprint is foremost your *IP address*. Browser web page requests (and your browser's cookies), web search history, email messages, social media posts, chat sessions, torrent file-sharing traffic and Usenet newsposts will normally all leave behind remnants of your IP address in one way or another.

Once someone has your IP address and has linked you to it, they can easily target you for purposes that range from the annoying, such as building a profile about you that marketers and data miners can track and exploit, to the alarming, such as snooping on what you are downloading or making targeted hacking attempts against your devices.

Cookies, super cookies, flash cookies, bugs, beacons and a variety of third party elements (TPE) can be used to determine your IP address and then be cross-referenced and linked to your email address(es), social media profiles and other accounts.

To see how you are tracked by your IP address, go to http://www.cogipas.com/whats-my-ip/. The sites listed there demonstrate what is just the tip of the iceberg about the kind of hidden information that your web browsing activities reveal. Increasingly, your online digital fingerprint is being determined by other factors too.

Device Fingerprinting

The technology used for tracking you online is already moving away from IP addresses to other more sophisticated means. This trend is on the rise because the trackers and profilers (and other snoops) want to follow you across *all* your devices as most of us are now using more than one and many of us are using three or more devices.

In addition, some of your devices, such as smartphones, don't rely as much on IP addresses. But even on IP-driven devices like desktop computers, laptops and tablets, the tracking is no longer relying on IP addresses alone. Now, the combination of the browser, plugins, apps and fonts installed on your device can themselves make for as unique an identifier as your IP address. This technique is called *device fingerprinting*. When combined with more traditional IP address tracking, the results are even more accurate.

The Electronic Frontier Foundation's Panopticlick website at https://panopticlick.eff.org/ aptly illustrates this point.

They are Following You Too

The tracking has become so smart and pervasive that you are now tracked across your different devices (your desktop computers, laptops, smartphones and tablets, both at home and at work). The tracking also works across all the operating systems your devices use (whether Windows, Mac O/S, Linux, iOS or Android).

It used to be that the activities you undertook on your different devices were tracked independently and sealed off from one another. So, maybe it was okay to use your home desktop computer for more sensitive web browsing activities. But that's no longer the case. Now the trackers and profilers are so good at cross-referencing the data that all of your activities, even across different devices, locations, operating systems and platforms, is all merged and combined into a mightily accurate and comprehensive profile.

This is also why potentially invasive ads now *follow* you from your desktop computer to your laptop, to your tablet to your smartphone, whether at home, work, in transit or on vacation.

Add it all up and the trackers and profilers can follow you across all your devices all the time, anywhere, and they don't have to rely solely on your IP address.

But It's Even Worse Than You Think

I'm afraid the reality is far worse than that. Even if targeted ads are the most *visible* use of your profile, they probably represent its *least* intrusive use. If advertisers are able to use your profile to serve up extremely personalized ads and calls to action, imagine what else is being done or can be done with your profile that you never even see?

Also, a little voice should be telling you: if the tracking and profiling firms have this information and are providing your profile to online advertisers, who *else* are they offering it to? And for what purposes?

There's a fear that governments, insurance companies, financial institutions, employers, or any third party might also be making use of such information for their gains. For example, your profile could be used to determine:

- whether you represent a subversive risk to your government
- whether you might pose a risk for drug or alcohol abuse or whether you may not be quite the "right fit" for a potential employer
- whether you qualify for a loan or insurance coverage
- the *variable price* you are charged for goods or services (different prices being displayed to different people for the same products or services)
- whether you should be accepted as a member to a club or society
- whether you are a suitable match for a potential mate
- the possibilities are endless

In fact, it may only be a slight exaggeration to say that our profiles and the data used to build them are becoming a substitute for blood, urine, and genetic testing. However, unlike the tightly regulated testing of these substances, how and by whom your online profile is used is still the Wild West; anything goes.

A related symptom of this phenomenon is the alarming trend of employers asking job candidates for their social media passwords. Currently this takes the form of the potential employer asking for the password directly and poking around your social media account or by asking the job candidate to login with the scrutinizing employer taking a look. An entire chapter in this book is dedicated to social media (see chapter 6).

The Shape of Things to Come

Furthermore, building on the example above, any kind of physical presence is probably already unnecessary. Now, the potential employer (or whoever) need only send a link or app to the target subject and, upon them providing consent by a simple click (if you don't accept you cannot be considered for the job) or perhaps even without any express consent (such as a *beacon* embedded in the job application page itself), the target's metadata and profiles are near instantly accessed and cross-referenced allowing the employer to make a decision on the candidate's suitability. This could happen just as easily for medical insurance coverage, financial products, dating websites, any goods or services; it's all coming folks.

The richness of the profile information being harvested, cross-referenced and bundled is staggering and can already provide a good predictor of who would be a reliable employee, insurance customer, borrower, customer, client, mate and perhaps even citizen. Never mind a sample of your blood, urine or genetic material for testing, you may be evaluated based on your online profile.

Top Tip - To get a sense of this check out sites such as Cambridge's *Apply Magic Sauce* http://applymagicsauce.com/ and MIT's *Immersion* https://immersion.media.mit.edu/. These sites analyze your Facebook likes and email metadata, respectively, and present you with sometimes very interesting results. These demonstrations give you a *small* glimpse into how online trackers and profilers may be using the same information.

What's worse, if you are rejected or discriminated against on the basis of your profile (information that, I hasten to add, may be based on completely wrong information), you may never know it, let alone have an opportunity to correct it. This could translate into a lost job opportunity, being rejected for insurance or a loan, paying a higher price for goods or services, being deemed ineligible for a membership etc.

The current reality may not be this bad yet, but sooner or later all of your online habits might find their way into your profile(s) and have consequences that you may *never* have appreciated or even became aware of.

Do you really need any more reasons to keep your online activities as private as possible?

The good news is that these risks are mostly preventable. The bad news is that though the basic steps to reduce these risks are easy, the tracking is difficult to *completely* prevent and will only get harder to prevent in the future.

How Not to Leave Obvious Fingerprints in the First Place (Browsing in Private Mode)

The easiest, quickest and most basic action you can take is to use your Internet web browser app in its *private mode*. This provides only a bare minimum of protection, but for some people this may be enough.

Browsing in private mode safeguards you from being tracked by the sites you visit and by the tracking elements they use, such as cookies, beacons and social media icons.

Each of the major web browser apps has a feature enabling you to browse in private mode. Sometimes this feature is euphemistically referred to as "porn mode" but it has many uses other than this label would suggest. As a general rule, you can enter private browsing mode whenever you want to temporarily disable your browser's cookies, its record-keeping features (visited website and search histories) and its plugins (add-ons and extensions).

Chrome calls its private browsing mode *incognito*, Internet Explorer calls it *InPrivate Browsing* and Firefox calls it *private browsing*. Though generally the same, each browser's privacy mode has its own peculiarities.

In Chrome, you can start a private browsing session by accessing its main menu button (the three horizontal lines, ≡) and selecting *New incognito window*. You can also do this with the keyboard shortcut *Ctrl+Shift+N*. To open a link in private browsing mode, right-click on the link and select *Open link in incognito window*.

Top Tip - Some websites only let you access a limited amount of material in a given time, blocking further access until you pay a subscription or sign-up. For example, many news sites will limit the number of free articles per month you can read after which they will block your access until you pay a monthly subscription fee. This blocking is usually enabled by cookies. Sometimes you can side-step this blocking by accessing the materials while browsing in private mode. In your browser, simply right-click on the link to the article you want to read and select the private browsing feature for your particular web browser.

Apart from browsing in private mode to cut down on a certain amount of tracking, it also helps keep your habits under wraps from anyone that may have physical access to your device. This is because private browsing mode also temporarily disables a number of features in your web browser app such as the history records of your recent searches, website visits and downloads which, though usually helpful, are also ways that your privacy can be breached. This is all discussed in great detail later in the book.

As I mentioned at the outset, the protection private browsing mode offers against online tracking and profiling is very basic. That's because, though browsing in private mode is helpful and easy, your online behavior may still be detected and tracked in all kinds of ways including with flash cookies and the device fingerprinting I talked about earlier. However, don't worry as I will show you everything you need to know about overcoming these risks too.

Another potential downside of browsing in private mode is that it generally disables most if not all of your web browser's plugins, add-ons and extensions because these items can also be a potential source of tracking risk. However, this disabling also means a number of plugins that can help *prevent* tracking in the first place – including those I recommend below - won't work. These include using specialized plugins for your web browser that enhance your privacy by not only blocking cookies, but other kinds of tracking elements too.

Best Web Browser Anti-Tracking Plugins (Add-ons and Extensions)

Whatever web browser app(s) you use, consider installing the following plugins to counter online tracking. Best of all, these plugins are absolutely free.

- *Disconnect* https://disconnect.me/disconnect
- *Ghostery* https://www.ghostery.com/ (but ideally *skip* the "GhostRank" opt-in during setup)
- *AdBlockPlus* https://adblockplus.org/
- *Privacy Badger* https://www.eff.org/privacybadger
- *HTTPS Everywhere* https://www.eff.org/https-everywhere

~ ~ ~

Although browsing in private mode and using privacy-enhancing plugins with your web browser represent a good start, they are only the most basic and bare bones way to protect you from online tracking and profiling.

You can also use techniques to make your web browsing *anonymous*. You can achieve this using tools called web proxies, The Onion Router (Tor for short) and virtual private networks (VPNs for short). They can make your entire Internet connection seem to originate from somewhere else thereby keeping hidden your true presence. These more advanced techniques are discussed in upcoming chapters. But first, let's return to security for a moment to discuss malware.

* * *

For updates and additional information about minimizing your online digital fingerprints to help prevent online tracking and profiling, please visit http://www.cogipas.com/online-tracking-profiling/.

Chapter 5: Protecting Yourself from Malware

What is Malware?

As used throughout this book, malicious software (or *malware* for short) collectively means viruses, worms, Trojans, rootkits, adware and spyware.

Malware spreads in many ways including by email (both as links and attachments), websites (whether as pop-up windows or code embedded in web pages) and, of course, downloads (whether obtained from the web, social media, chat, torrent file-sharing or Usenet newsgroups).

In addition to being disruptive and a nuisance, malware can be used to steal your personal data or turn your device into a *zombie*. A zombie is a device that has been taken over and is controlled remotely, sometimes used to perform illicit activities such as to launch attacks against others.

Below, each category of malware is described in more detail. However, the lines between these categories are increasingly blurring as the malware and their creators get more sophisticated in their methods.

What is a Virus?

A *virus* is a software program (a piece of executable computer code) that is capable of replicating itself and wreaking havoc on your devices and data. Such programs are usually created with malicious intent. A typical virus operates on your device without your knowledge or permission. It first attaches itself to a file or app on your device. When the infected file is opened, the virus multiplies itself and infects other files or apps on the same device as well as on other devices connected to it over a network.

Viruses can take any form in email attachments, but are typically sent as images, games, greeting cards, screen savers, audio files or videos. When you open an infected attachment, it secretly infects your device. Many viruses are also capable of using email to spread themselves to other devices (see 'What is a Worm' below). Viruses can also be spread through the web, social media, chat, torrents and Usenet as well as through removable storage media such as a USB memory stick, portable hard drive and CD, DVD or Blu-Ray discs.

The damage caused by a virus can be serious. It can corrupt or change data or delete everything stored on your device. It can forge your email address and send mails to all the contacts in your address book. Sometimes, it may only multiply itself without causing any damage to your data, but even in such minor cases, it still degrades the performance of your system by using up memory or storage space. Once infected, your device may run slowly, often lock up, have corrupt apps, or become unstable and crash.

Viruses come in all shapes and sizes and given the emerging *Internet of things*, they can be expected to infect *all* Internet-enabled devices, even your refrigerator or home thermostat.

What is a Worm?

A *worm* is very similar to a virus in that it is also a malicious software program. However, worms differ from viruses in that worms reproduce and spread *automatically* from device to device.

Similar to other malware, worms can make their way into your system through email attachments, links to websites with malicious content, or executable *scripts*. The moment you select the attachment or link, or otherwise activate the malicious content, the worm installs itself on your device.

Once a worm is installed, it usually locates your address book (email) or list of friends (social media) and, without your knowledge, sends every one of them a message with the same attachment or link to the worm. The worm then sends similar messages to everyone listed in *their* address books and friend lists and so on. The process can go on for some time!

A worm usually makes your device slow or unresponsive. A worm may also open network security holes on your device through which hackers and snoops can install backdoors. Your device could then become a zombie under an adversary's control.

Apart from creating network damage, a worm can also damage your device much like a virus. It can corrupt or delete crucial system files and even stop some critical apps from working.

What is a Trojan?

Similar to the legendary horse given by the Greeks to the people of Troy, the term *Trojan* describes a malicious software program that poses as a legitimate app.

A Trojan may arrive as an email attachment, be part of a download from a website or torrent file-sharing network, or arrive any other way you obtain downloads. For example, a Trojan may introduce itself by posing as an anti-malware app that you are enticed into downloading and opening.

Most Trojans are in the form of an *executable* item (meaning a file that you can run), but may be disguised and named to look like a game, movie or a music download. Because your operating system may hide the true nature of some files, you may be tricked into thinking that the download is innocuous (see later in this chapter). However, the moment you open it, it installs and begins its malicious action without you knowing. In contrast to a virus, generally a Trojan does not replicate itself or infect other files. When detected, Trojans should be deleted.

What is a Rootkit?

A *rootkit* is a collection of undetectable programs, often riding piggyback on other apps to look legitimate, that gain a high degree of access to your device. A rootkit modifies specific code in the operating system and essentially becomes part of it, thus preventing your anti-malware apps from detecting the rootkit. The rootkit could conceal itself from detection on your device, making it difficult for you to ever know about it. Rootkits can be acquired from infected web content, malicious email attachments and links, as well as from storage media.

A rootkit usually creates a *backdoor* into your device that can be used by hackers and snoops to gain full, unfettered access to your device and to execute all manner of malware as well as access logs, monitor your activities, change your settings and even attack other devices connected to the Internet under the cover of your device and Internet connection.

If you detect a rootkit on your system, you may have to completely start over, deleting your device's storage, clear its memory and reinstall the operating system.

What are Adware and Spyware?

Adware and *spyware* run in the background of your device, sometimes constantly, eating up its memory, bandwidth and power, all the while tracking your activities, either in real-time or at regular intervals. Adware and spyware are not always easily spotted and sometimes make their way onto your device because they are often bundled within "legitimate" apps.

Adware is usually installed with your agreement (though sometimes you are tricked into it) and can usually be *un*installed like any normal app. Usually adware is more annoying than anything else, serving up ads that you don't want or that are too frequent.

Spyware is installed more stealthily without your knowledge or agreement, sometimes disguised entirely as something else and may be difficult to uninstall. Spyware is very undesirable as its sole purpose is to monitor your activities and send that information back to unknown parties for unknown purposes. Who knows what they are tracking and why.

Using Anti-malware Apps

The single best way to protect yourself from malware is to have an up-to-date anti-malware app. Some apps come as a comprehensive package covering viruses, adware / spyware and website screening, while other packages may be available in separate modules. It is inexcusable not to use these apps as many good products are free for personal use.

Because malware and the hackers that use malware are always adapting and changing, you should always keep your defenses up-to-date by regularly updating the latest *virus definitions* for your anti-malware app. These definitions are the databases that help your app identify malware and malware-like activity or symptoms in the first place. Keeping your definitions up-to-date can usually be set automatically and the more frequently you update them the better.

Recommended Anti-malware Apps

AVG Anti-Virus (free) http://free.avg.com/ is a good anti-virus (and anti-adware/spyware) package that deserves its popularity. AVG is a good combination of simple, powerful and hassle-free.

Kaspersky Internet Security 2015 ¢ (premium) http://www.cogipas.com/premium-anti-malware is award-winning malware protection from one of the most trusted names for decades in online security. This app offers runtime protection as you would expect and also alerts you to potentially malicious web sites and has a host of other industry-leading features.

Are You Infected?

The symptoms of your device being compromised by malware vary. Sometimes your device will begin acting strangely, run more slowly or start to freeze and crash regularly.

If you think your device is infected with malware, the best thing to do is to perform a *full scan* of the device with a fully up-to-date, reputable anti-malware app. If your device has a large amount of storage data (for example, a desktop computer with a Terabyte drive) a full scan could take hours so consider running it overnight.

Top Tip - Some Windows-based malware loads up at the earliest stages of your device's start up, so to be extra cautious, you can run your anti-malware check after booting into Windows *Safe Mode* by pressing F8 just before Windows starts. Booting into Safe Mode ensures that a minimum of processes are running when you perform a malware scan.

In addition to scanning your device regularly with an anti-malware app, you can also use a number of free malware detection and removal tools which are regularly updated. For Windows, check out Microsoft's tool at http://www.microsoft.com/security/malwareremove/default.aspx.

Suspicious Attachments and Links

To help avoid falling prey to malware, pause and reflect before opening unfamiliar links or attachments. This is true whether they are contained in emails, webpages, social media messages or chat sessions, even when the messages come from trusted sources. Shed the risky habit of routinely opening attachments and links as this makes you susceptible to malware and hacking attempts.

Scan all attachments for malware before opening them. Even if your email service has built-in malware scanning, you should scan message attachments after saving them to your device, especially if they were sent to you from unknown or seemingly suspicious sources.

For links, if your email and web browser app supports it, hover your cursor above a link before clicking on it and see if the actual URL matches the displayed text. When supported, the URL of a link is usually displayed either in a small, pop-up display or in the status bar at the bottom of the app's window. If the URL doesn't match the link text, be extra careful.

In fact, the safest practice (though not always practical) is to manually type web addresses into your web browser rather than clicking on links. Of course, this is a pain for long link addresses. In addition, many subscriber-based emails will have links with long complicated URLs as they are often redirected through the subscription management service (such as Aweber).

Manually typing link addresses into your web browser is especially recommended - even mandatory – when contained in emails you were not expecting or that are from unknown sources. It is easy to be fooled into clicking on a link that sends you to a fake or spoofed website. These links can look convincing. However, if you type the link into your browser, you will never be tricked into visiting www.amazon.com or www.facebok.com when you wanted www.amazon.com or www.facebook.com. (As it happens, both of these misspellings will take you to the proper sites, but that is not always the case.)

Using Spam Filters

Spam filters - filters that prevent you from receiving unsolicited junk email - are widely available for most email apps and webmail providers. Enabling these filters and spending some time with the settings should help prevent a lot of malware (and spam of course) from reaching your inbox in the first place. Gmail and Yahoo both have excellent built-in filters.

Keeping your Device's Operating System and Critical Apps Updated

Always keep your device's operating system and other critical apps up-to-date. This means activating any automatic update features on your device to ensure that any flaws or vulnerabilities that are found are patched as quickly as possible.

In the Windows Start menu type "Windows Update" (no quotes) and select *Change Settings*. In the 'Important updates' radio bar select *Install updates automatically (recommended)* and then select *OK*.

Apart from your operating system, it is equally important that you keep critical apps up-to-date too, such as those apps protecting you from malware, viruses and spyware. Each app will have its own automatic update setting, but it shouldn't be too hard to find. The automatic update setting is often enabled by default in any event.

Don't Hide Your File Extensions

When you open an item, Windows knows the app to open it with because of its *extension* (usually three letters after the last dot in the filename, such as .DOC). Depending on your settings, Windows may hide your file extensions which means that the extensions of items associated with an app will not be displayed.

Hiding extensions can be risky because this makes it easier for attackers to masquerade malicious items as innocuous ones. Some malware distribution techniques take advantage of this. If you ensure file extensions are displayed you will be less likely to be tricked into opening files containing potential (hidden) threats. For example, KISS_ME.JPG.exe will look like a harmless image file if the extension is hidden, but it is actually a potentially dangerous executable file. Please look at it again.

Another example would be BEAUTIFUL.AVI.vbs. If your device's settings were set to hide extensions, the item would display as BEAUTIFUL.AVI. You might be tempted to click on it (especially if it was sent by a friend) and expect to see a video. However, the extension is actually .VBS, an executable script (mini program) that if opened could harm your device.

There are dozens of executable file types (comprehensive listings can be found by typing "executable file types" in your favorite search engine), but the most common are .BAT, .COM, .EXE, .PIF, .SCR, .REG, .VB and .VBS.

In Windows, to make sure that your file extensions are *not* hidden follow these steps. Access *Folder Options* by selecting the Windows Start menu and typing "folder options". Alternatively, in Windows Explorer, select from the menu *Organize > Folder and search options.*

Either way, once the Folder Options dialogue box opens, choose the *View* tab and ensure that the *Hide extension for known file types* option is *unchecked* (*not* enabled), and select *OK* (see screenshot).

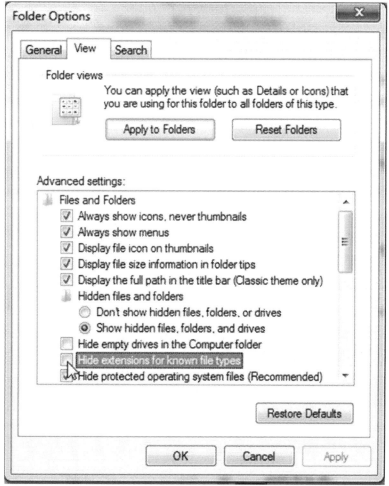

Figure: Making sure the hide extensions option is *unchecked*

Once selected, Windows should always display item extensions and *not* hide them. This will help ensure that you are not fooled into opening dangerous attachments that are camouflaged to look like other items.

What's Running on Your System? (Processes and Services) (Advanced Users)

It is not always easy to determine if something suspicious is running on your device, especially if it is something running in the background. In Windows, you can investigate using *Task Manager*. Type "task manager" in your Windows Start menu and select the item *View running processes with Task Manager* (see screenshot).

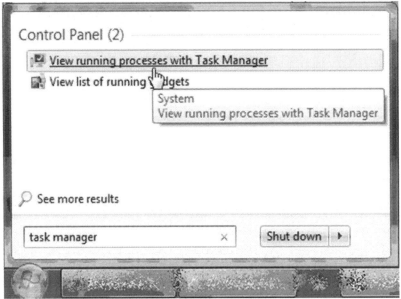

Figure: Starting Windows Task Manager

Once in Task Manager, you can view what apps, processes and services are running on your device by selecting the appropriate tab.

To see the processes running on your system, click on the 'Processes' tab (see screenshot). Then click on the 'Memory' column to sort the processes by those using the most amount of memory. These are not always easy to understand, but may provide clues about what is hampering your device's performance. If any process looks suspicious or out of place, including by the amount of memory it is using, perform a search about it in your favorite search engine, but only rely on the information you find from *reputable* sources. You should never "kill" a process (by selecting the *End Process* button) unless you are confident about what you are doing.

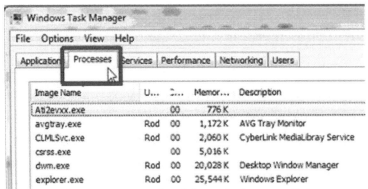

Figure: The Processes tab of the Windows Task Manager

Similarly, the next tab, *Services*, is a bit more complicated. Services are not always easy to understand but, in combination with some Internet research using your favorite search engine, may also provide clues about any issues you may be having on your device. In essence, services are mini-apps that run quietly in the background of your device.

Once under the Services tab, you can explore them in a little more detail by selecting one and selecting the *Services...* button at the lower right.

Some services are rarely, if ever used, and others still may be completely unnecessary for your purposes. There is plenty of reputable advice about what services are unnecessary - just type "which windows services should I disable" into your favorite search engine. Of course, what services are appropriate to disable varies from user to user and will also depend on the version of Windows you have.

For example, some thoughtful analysis can be found at http://www.howtogeek.com/139028/which-windows-services-can-you-safely-disable/ and http://www.blackviper.com/service-configurations/black-vipers-windows-8-service-configurations/.

Disabling a Service

To disable a service, select the service in the list (as above), right-click and select *Properties*. In the menu that appears, choose *Disabled* under *Startup type:* and then select *OK*. *Manual* is a kind of middle (safer) setting.

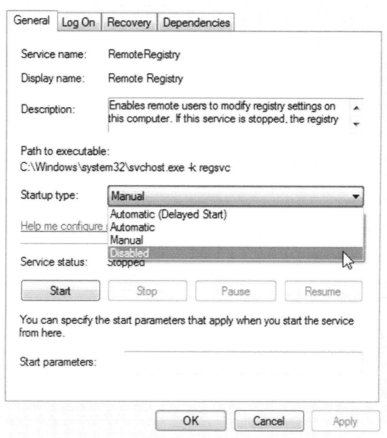

Figure: Disabling the service *Remote Registry*

If after disabling a service you are experiencing any problems, follow the same instructions above to return the service to the same state as before you disabled it.

* * *

For updates and additional information about protecting yourself from malware, please visit http://www.cogipas.com/protecting-yourself-from-malware/.

Chapter 6: How to Protect Your Privacy and Security on Social Media

Introduction

Nowadays everyone and their parents (make that grandparents even) seem to be on Facebook, Twitter, LinkedIn, Instagram, Pinterest and Google+. Social media sites (also known as *social networking* sites or *social networks*) are a great way to make new friends, get back in touch with people, help you find a job, and to learn and play as well as to discover music, products or brands.

The same still holds true for more classic online forums and discussion areas on websites (which used to be called *bulletin boards*). These remain fantastic resources to get information, read fan fiction or engage in discussion with people from across the globe that share the same interests as you.

Social media is immersive and fun, but also fraught with privacy risks. This chapter focuses on Facebook, the largest social network with over 1.11 billion users. However, the principles discussed here also apply to the other social media sites mentioned above as well as to yet others such as *VK* (the "Russian Facebook") and *RenRen* (the "Chinese Facebook").

Risks of Being Social

It is easy and tempting to share aspects about your personal life on social media, but the information you post may spread beyond your control. Your likes, shares, tweets, posts, blogs, tags, photos, friend requests and simply your clicks and views can be used to further track and profile you. In combination with other methods I already discussed - such as IP address tracking, device fingerprinting, web bugs, super cookies, beacons and other third party elements used to track your online activities – an astonishingly detailed profile about you can be amassed. Further, these profiles can be used, shared with other parties, and built upon for years to come.

It is often said that if an Internet service is free, you are not the customer, you are the product. It is wise to keep this maxim in mind especially for social media. The entire business model of these sites revolves around your information so they will do whatever they can to engage and even entice you to enter, post and share as much of your personal information as possible.

In addition, you have little control over what is shared about you by *other users*. Have you experienced someone tagging something on Facebook with your name? These posts can be narratives mentioning your name or images containing your picture, sometimes in circumstances that are not flattering.

Worst of all, the risk of people sharing information about you exists even if you do not have an account on the social media site! It is a fallacy to think you are immune from these problems merely by staying away from and never opening an account on Facebook, Twitter, Google+ or other sites.

Other risks include phishing attempts, Trojans and worm-like hazards that are specifically designed to target social media (Koobface was one such example). While Facebook and other social media operators have become better at acting quickly in the face of such threats, you should still do all you can to protect yourself.

Scarier risks, though thankfully more remote, include being targeted by trolls, bullies, stalkers or worse.

What Facebook Collects About You

Facebook is not a charity. It is a large, publicly-traded corporation listed on the stock market with shareholders to please. Yet, using Facebook is free. The reason Facebook is "free" is that it collects a mind-boggling amount of information about you and makes money from it.

It does this by tracking and collecting every aspect of your activities on its site, amassing enormous amounts of information about you, your preferences, your activities, and those of your friends. Of course, this information is not limited only to that which you (and your friends) voluntarily post and share. In fact, you don't even have to be on Facebook for the tracking and profiling to work.

Every time you visit a website containing a Facebook icon of any kind, your activities are reported back to Facebook, even without you selecting the icon and even if you do not have a Facebook account. In essence Facebook's own website and the tracking elements it uses all around the Internet act like the super cookies I discussed in chapter 4 tracking people and their activities. Facebook uses your IP address (and device fingerprinting), comparing and matching it to millions of other data points representing your online visits and activities, in an attempt to track and examine what you do online.

To illustrate this point take the case of a law student that recently went to court to compel Facebook to provide a full copy of the personal information it had collected about him. He received 1222 pages from Facebook for just three years of activity. The information covered all aspects of his online life and was roughly organized into 57 categories, including deleted posts, private messages, friends, contact information, previously used profile names and his searches as well as more customary information about the date, IP address, location and timestamps of his Facebook usage.

You may also be surprised to learn that Facebook collects your *biometric data*. You probably noticed the *suggest tags* prompt whenever you upload a photo of someone. Facebook is able to match photos with names of your friends by a complex analysis of biometric data. This process converts a person's face into a unique numerical identifier. The calculation of this identifier is based on the distance between a person's eyes, nose and ears as well as face shape. After calculating the identifier, Facebook tries to match it with one already in its database containing tens of millions of others. This allows Facebook to automatically detect the faces in any photos you upload, *whether or not* you actually choose to apply tags. When you do tag photos, you help Facebook increase the accuracy of its biometric identification technology.

In fairness, Facebook does alert you when someone has tagged you in a photo and you are provided with an opportunity to *untag* it. But whether you are tagged for people to see or not, Facebook's ability to link photos to your likeness still exists.

Advertisements and Profiling

You pay for Facebook with your personal information and thus your privacy. Information is valuable; collecting, bundling and selling it is a very profitable business. Social media is a powerful way to gather rich information about users. When you select an advertisement, post a status update, upload an image, friend someone, like an item or follow a page, this is all recorded. Such records contain information about your preferences and are primarily aimed to help Facebook's advertisers target you as a consumer. However, the information can also be used by Facebook (and its partners) for a whole host of other purposes.

After you or your friend likes something using a Facebook icon, this information will be used to help determine which advertisements you and your friends will be served. If you are friends with someone who brought product X, advertisers are willing to bet that you are also more likely to buy that same product given that friends usually share some common interests. This is valuable information that advertisers are willing to pay for in order to target you with effective ads.

But it's not only you and your friends' likes that generate valuable information for the targeting of advertisements. Your profile and activities (and those of your friends) are also *data mined* for further patterns and behaviors. For example, information about your family status, age, location, and education level as well as the web browsing activities of you and your friends, as picked up by Facebook's ubiquitous tracking elements, can all be used to build on the profiles.

Even if you provide a minimal amount of personal information to Facebook, you will still be tracked and profiled as your friends' information will be used to fill in any gaps. Combined with the personal information and online behavior of your friends, this will be more than a sufficient basis to build a rich profile about you.

More About: *Offline Tracking* - Interestingly, social media providers are also using information about your *offline* activities too. That's right, offline. Increasingly, social media providers cooperate with data collection companies which have information about you through various client cards, loyalty programs, mailing lists maintained by retailers as well as from public records. You can imagine just how detailed and rich a profile emerges about you when all the online and offline information is cross-referenced and combined. This is why advertisers are pleased to spend fortunes obtaining this information.

Advertisers know just how effective the targeted ads are. In addition, the demand and profits from this information only continues to grow. In other words, from a privacy perspective things will get worse, perhaps a lot worse, before they get better.

Basic Facebook Privacy

Introduction

You are not powerless in the uphill struggle to protect your privacy when using social media. Due in part to pressure brought by consumer groups, social media providers have been paying more attention to privacy settings and giving their users more control over them. But it is incumbent on you to learn about and implement the best settings to protect your privacy.

Facebook understands the risks faced by its hundreds of millions of users and makes efforts to reduce these risks, including *security* measures to prevent fraud and hacked accounts. At the same time, arguably Facebook stands to benefit from you being lackadaisical about your *privacy* and from encouraging you to post and share as much information as possible on their platform.

Settings and Good Habits

Facebook often revises its privacy policy and settings. Therefore, it is recommended that you closely follow new features introduced by Facebook and keep your privacy settings up to date and for you to tailor those setting to your specific needs.

If your privacy settings are weak, an unlimited number of people could have access to your information on Facebook. The general public may be able to view your photos, read your posts, review your personal information, as well as further share, comment on or tag your posts.

It is recommended that you limit access of third parties to your account and make sure that only your friends can see your profile and posts. Below you will find first some general principles and related tips followed by more detailed instructions on how to maximize your privacy settings in Facebook.

First and foremost, make a habit of regularly checking the privacy settings for your social media accounts to ensure that your profile is *not* shared with the public at large. To check this, make sure you are logged out of your social media account and then type your name in your favorite search engine. Do not be surprised if your social media profile turns up in the search results - click on it and check what information is displayed. Everything you see is generally available to the public. This is the information a virtual stranger anywhere on the globe can access about you. If all your contact information, personal photos and wall posts are visible, it's time you changed your privacy settings.

Check that Your Most Basic Privacy Settings are Right

The name and profile picture of your account are public, you cannot hide them regardless of any settings you choose. But you can follow the lead of many people by using fake information (a pseudonym) for your account. You can also use a photo that is not of your personal likeness such as that of a cartoon character.

In order to ensure your basic information is not public, go to your profile page (by selecting your name and then selecting *About* or by going directly to https://www.facebook.com/me/about). Each item under your *Work and education* will display a privacy icon allowing you to select who can see the item. Your choices are broad, shown below and include Public (which means everyone), Friends, Only me, Custom (which allows you to limit some of your friends from seeing your posts) and any custom lists you may have created.

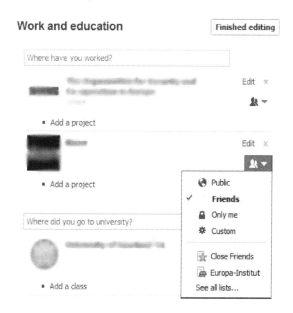

Check How You Look to Other People

If you want to check what information other people can see, click on the lock icon in the upper-right portion of Facebook's menu bar and select *Who can see my stuff?* Under that heading you will see the sub-item, *What do other people see on my Timeline?* and a *View As* prompt. Facebook will emulate the display of your information based on the selections you make.

So, if you want to see how your account looks from the perspective of a specific user, select *View as a specific person* and type his or her name (for example, your ex or a work colleague).

If some information is displayed that you would prefer to keep hidden from the audience you selected, change your overall privacy settings, or change the privacy setting for any specific posts and keep repeating these steps until all the impugned items disappear from the particular view you had selected.

Going Through the Privacy Menu

As mentioned, your privacy settings in Facebook are something you should check every now and then. You can access your privacy settings by selecting in the upper-right corner of the menu bar either the lock icon or the downward arrow icon together with *Settings* and then *Privacy Settings*.

Privacy Settings and Tools

Who can see my stuff?	Who can see your future posts?	Friends	Edit
	Review all your posts and things you're tagged in		Use Activity Log
	Limit the audience for posts you've shared with friends of friends or Public?		Limit Past Posts
Who can contact me?	Who can send you friend requests?	Everyone	Edit
	Whose messages do I want filtered into my Inbox?	Basic Filtering	Edit
Who can look me up?	Who can look you up using the email address you provided?	Everyone	Edit
	Who can look you up using the phone number you provided?	Everyone	Edit
	Do you want other search engines to link to your Timeline?	No	Edit

Figure: Facebook's Privacy Settings and Tools menu is a handy one-stop shop for many important privacy settings

Either way, you arrive at options that let you choose who can see your *future* posts and limit the audience for *past* posts you have already shared with friends of friends or the general public. You may choose between Public, Friends, Only me or Custom. Make sure that 'Public' is *not* selected.

If you edit "Who can see your future posts" your selection will become the default for all your future posts (but of course you can select a different setting each time you post).

You can also change the setting to restrict *everything* you have ever posted in the past, so that they can be seen only by your friends. To do this, edit "Limit the audience for posts you've shared with friends of friends or Public".

Who Can Find You?

Other options under the same *Privacy Settings and Tools* menu let you select who can find you using your email address or phone number. To make your selection, look for the Edit near *Who can look you up using the email address or telephone number you provided?* Some people don't mind being discoverable on Facebook by 'Everyone' as this makes it easier for old friends and colleagues to find them, while other people would rather remain undiscoverable.

Figure: Choose the 'Who can look me up' setting that is right for you

Accepting Friend Requests

Although having hundreds of friends or followers on a social network might be a nice stroke to your ego, you should only accept friend requests *sparingly*.

Accept friend requests only from people that you actually know because accepting friend requests from people you don't know or don't know well comes with risks.

First, sometimes it takes only one "friend" with poor privacy settings to result in *your* data being shared even more, whether through apps, games or social logins (discussed in the pages ahead). Many of your friends may be unaware that, depending on their privacy settings, they may be granting access to their friends' data (including your data). This can happen *regardless of your own settings*. So the more friends you have, the more likely it is that you will have a weak link in this privacy settings chain.

Second, all sorts of other people may be trying to friend you in order to gain access to your more detailed information. Imagine a stalker or troll disguising themselves as an innocuous "friend" or wannabe follower in order to determine where you live or your movements, or to obtain controversial posts or photos for the purposes of leaking them in an attempt to harm you.

Be aware that friending is sometimes used as an investigative technique by government agencies, private investigators, debt collectors, process servers, commercial interests or even data gathering robots. All these parties and more may try, while disguised, to friend you in order to gain access to personal information.

Keep your group of friends small and tight. When in doubt, do not accept a friend request.

It is better to err on the side of caution and keep your circle of friends as small as possible. Some people get a kick out of having hundreds of friends displayed on their profile, but unless you really do have hundreds of genuine admirers this is probably a mistake. Be selective with your acceptances and your invites, and focus on quality over quantity.

Even if you have limited to a small number the people who can see your posts, it is usually still not necessary that *all* of them should be given access to the same amount and detail of information. Most social media networks, including Facebook and Google+, have handy tools that let you filter who can see what posts and photos, even among your friends. Use these settings to create different lists or circles of people to further manage their ability to access your posts.

The easiest sub-groupings to imagine are those between your close friends and your mere colleagues. But nothing prevents you from making all kinds of different sub-groupings representing the different types of posts you make. You can even tailor for each post exactly who can access it.

What Never to Post

Given the open and fun nature of social media, it is all too easy to let your guard down with the kind of information you post. Regardless of how careful you are with your privacy settings and limiting access to your profile and posts, you should *never* share the following information on social media:

- your full date of birth
- your address
- your phone number
- your middle name(s)
- your picture
- your vacation or away plans *in advance* (it's OK *after* you've returned)
- any personally-identifiable information that could be used to help someone pose as you
- any similar information about friends and family

In official speak this category of information is sometimes referred to as *sensitive unclassified information*. If you have uploaded and made public too much of your personal information, this may facilitate identity thieves and similar crooks.

Identity thieves could use such details to reassemble and assume your identity. Offline thieves could use your away plans to conduct a hassle-free robbery.

Yet other troublemakers could use the above information to set up realistic fake pages or accounts under your name or cause other mischief. For example, they could create a fake account using your name (or a variation of it) and photo, and communicate with people from your openly visible friends list.

Or the information may enable hackers to correctly guess answering your forgotten password questions for other accounts, as was discussed in chapter 3.

Some people find the recommendation not to post your picture difficult to accept, but with the introduction and growing use of *facial recognition* technology by social media operators, this recommendation is more important than ever.

You should do everything you can to make sure that the gold nuggets of personal information listed above do not enter the public domain. Once "out there" you never know who may be collecting and trading or sharing in your personal information or when or how this might come back to haunt you. As you will see in the pages ahead, most identity theft victims take 12 months to realize they have been wronged (see chapter 7).

Pause and Reflect Before You Post

Regularly there are stories about people sharing information on social media that later implicates them in a scandal. This can lead to workplace discipline, academic sanctions, matrimonial agony, risking a security clearance, and overall reduced future prospects in your professional and personal life. So always keep in mind that information you post, tweet, pin or blog could come back to haunt you.

It is no longer difficult to imagine a job applicant or political candidate being probed about a post on social media from earlier days. More employers and educational institutions also harvest personal information from the Internet about potential and current employees and candidates. You have no way of knowing what is being recorded in databases and by whom.

Some users also have a habit of sharing too much about their employer online - information about reorganizations, hirings or firings, products or projects. This can lead to consequences for you and your employer - ranging from mere embarrassment to legal problems. If you're the spouse of an employee and you tweeted about the long hours your spouse is spending on Project X, this too can lead to unintended consequences.

A general rule that is too often ignored is to *pause* and *use common sense* before posting anything potentially controversial, regardless of how few people have initial access to it. Keep in mind that it may be virtually impossible to un-do a post. Even if you manage to have the information removed, it may already have been re-posted, re-tweeted, further shared with others, picked up by automated feeds, cached in search engines or *screen captured* (tip: this is when someone takes a picture of their device's display). This makes it nearly impossible to get the genie back in the bottle and your information can soon take on a life of its own, perhaps even turning *viral*. So make sure you can live with *all* of your posts for *years* to come.

Also engage in occasional *wall scrubbing*. This can take many forms including when you try to undo or delete your own posts, request others to do the same with their posts, or ask the social media site itself to remove the information (sometimes you can *flag* a post as inappropriate). The time and difficulty involved in these efforts increases in the same order as they are listed. But if the post has already been further shared as described above, no amount of wall scrubbing will help.

Frequently Review Your Facebook Activities (View your Activity Log)

Every now and then, look back over your Facebook activities to ensure that you haven't overshared or shared something by accident. Remember, there are lots of websites and apps that use deceptive or misleading practices that can trick you into sharing information on your Timeline. It is becoming increasingly common that posts people think they are reading in private are being broadcast on their Timelines, leading to embarrassment or much worse consequences. This is described in detail a little later.

To review your Facebook activity, explore your *Activity Log*. You can access your Activity Log in three ways: directly by visiting https://www.facebook.com/me/allactivity, by selecting it from the triangle icon in the main dropdown menu (see screenshot) or by visiting your profile page (*not* your default Timeline stream page) and select the View Activity Log button floating atop your cover photo.

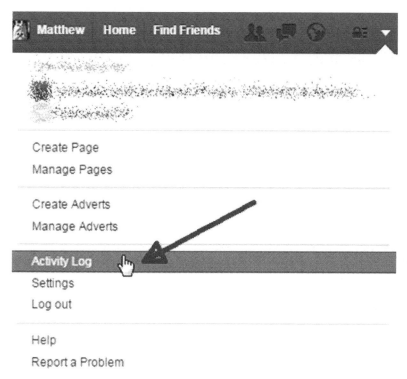

Figure: Checking your Activity Log in Facebook

Top Tip - Think before selecting links. Hoaxes and fake messages that lead to pages and apps trying to sell you something abound on social media. Such links could purportedly come from friends, but remember: malware and hackers can get into social media accounts and send fake or malicious messages to everyone in their victims' lists of friends.

Monitoring your Public Online Presence

A quick, easy and effective technique for monitoring and alerting you to when you may have been over-sharing information is to set up one or more Google News Alerts. This works great whether the source of the over-sharing is by you, friends, adversaries or apps. This tip takes 30 seconds to setup and could save you from lots of future headaches.

Go to Google News, https://news.google.com/ and enter your name in the search box. If you do not get meaningful results enter your name in quotes ("Alex Freely") and/or add something a little more personalized such as the city in which you live or the name of your school or workplace.

Once you are satisfied that the search is turning up (or would turn up) public information about you, scroll to the bottom of the search results page until you see the prompt,

Keep up to date with these results:
Create an email alert for [your search will be shown here]

Click on the link and follow the instructions to set up the News Alert. For the widest coverage, select *Everything* for 'Result type' and *All results* for 'How many'. Also enter the desired frequency of alerts and the email address you want the alerts sent to.

Now, whenever any items appear on the Internet matching the search criteria you entered, you will receive an email alert. It is also easy to adjust the settings later if you find the frequency or scope of the results unsuitable.

If you are worried about your name surfacing only with a certain kind of information (drunk, bikini, whatever), add the relevant search term(s) during the setup to limit the news alert's results.

Of course, this technique only picks up *public* online information. As such, it does not help you monitor non-public information including information online trackers and profilers may have on you. But this tip is better than nothing and easy to perform.

Recommended Web Browser Plugins to Prevent Facebook Tracking

Depending on the web browser you use, a number of plugins are available to prevent Facebook from tracking your Internet activities. Remember, through its Like buttons, other tracking elements and its partnerships, Facebook can track much of your online activities when you are not on Facebook and even when you are completely logged out of your Facebook account. Use these web browser plugins to block Facebook tracking.

Facebook Disconnect (free) https://disconnect.me/disconnect stops the flow of information that is sent to Facebook every time you visit a webpage containing Facebook elements (such as the Facebook Like icon).

Ghostery (free) https://www.ghostery.com/ detects the third party tracking elements on webpages you visit and lets you block them or find out more information about them (in case you want to temporarily allow or permanently whitelist them). During the setup, ideally skip the

"GhostRank" opt-in.

DoNotTrackPlus (free) http://www.abine.com/dntdetail.php protects you from targeted advertisements.

Social Logins and Single Sign-ons (SSO)

A *social login* (sometimes called a *single sign-on* or *SSO*) is when you log into an account using your *credentials* from a different account, usually a social media site, instead of having to setup and use a new, different password. So, using your name and password for account A, you login to account B, thus saving you the hassle of having to set up a separate username and password combination for site B. And if you are already logged into site A, usually it's just a matter of a single click to log in to site B. You might be able to use your credentials from account A to sign in to dozens of other accounts this way.

Most commonly this occurs when you are already logged into Facebook, visit another website and are asked to "Sign in using Facebook" with a single click. But the credentials of all sorts of accounts can be used such as Google, Twitter and Yahoo!, not just Facebook.

On your first attempt using a social login, you'll be prompted with a screen asking you whether the two sites can share certain information. This notice will make sense to you, so you go ahead and select OK. But ask yourself, what information will be shared and *why*?

The downside of using social logins is that you will be sharing *even more* of your information. By agreeing, information will now be shared between the credential-granting site (Facebook in our example above) and the credential-receiving site.

The credential-granting site will tout the benefit of you being spared from having to remember multiple passwords. So, if you use your Facebook credentials to login to your Yahoo! account, you only need to remember your Facebook password. This may be true, but there are other ways of accomplishing the same thing without all the information sharing this entails such as using a password management app as was discussed in chapter 3.

By using the social logins, the credential-granting site may now have access to additional information, in some cases much more, about your activities in the *credential-receiving* site. Depending on what you do in the credential-receiving site, the credential-granting site may now be accessing your contacts, the contents of messages, the documents and news articles you read, the songs you listen to, the websites you visit, the stocks you track, the items you buy, the images you download, the games you play, the videos you watch, etc.

Social logins mean more sharing of more information which means more tracking and more detailed and intrusive profiles. It all equals less privacy. The trackers will learn even more about your online habits.

So skip the social logins in the first place to reduce the amount of sharing between the sites that you use. Instead, use a password management app to save you from having to memorize all your accounts and their associated usernames and passwords.

Auto-Posts and Auto–Shares (The Risks of Broadcasting)

In addition, if you are not careful, sometimes when you agree to a social login or agree to use an app, game or service, you may be giving it permission to *broadcast* your activities. For example, you might be agreeing to allow them to post actions or activities to the wall, Timeline or stream of your social media account. Of course, the broadcasting site is delighted with this social posting and sharing to occur because it is like free advertising for them ("Alex has just read/watched/listened to/bought XYZ...").

Because of the tangible benefit this free publicity brings to the broadcasting site, app, game or service, they are not always as up-front as they could be about the fact that your activities will be broadcasted upon you agreeing to its terms.

It doesn't take much imagination to realize how the public broadcasting of web pages, articles, images or videos you are accessing or the items you purchase could cause headaches or come back to haunt you, whether professionally or personally. Imagine reading a controversial article or viewing a steamy video only to learn later that your activities were broadcasted! This troublesome post could then be further shared and quickly get out of your control as described earlier.

If you see these kinds of potentially worrying broadcasts on a friend's social media account that you think they would be unhappy about, don't assume that they are aware of it. Quickly send them a message letting them know about it. In most cases they will have had no idea and will appreciate you giving them a heads up.

If these broadcast, auto-post or auto-share features are enabled, disabling them may take some poking around in the settings of *both* sites (the broadcaster's and social media site's settings). To prevent any automatic broadcasting of this kind, adjust your privacy settings as described later in this chapter. You may also need to search the help files or in your favorite search engine for terms such as "disable auto-posting".

And these are only the *visible* use of your information. Even if your activities are not being shared publicly or you disable the auto-posting and auto-sharing features, the broadcasting site can still collect, harvest, cross-reference, bundle, use and share your information quietly in the background, resulting in you being tracked and profiled even more closely and further wrecking your privacy.

This is yet another reason to regularly check your Activity Log in Facebook. Occasionally checking it will help you detect any automatic posting of this kind or other surprising posts. It is an especially good idea to conduct this extra check after you have been interacting with potentially sensitive sites or apps.

A Few Words about Facebook Security

Facebook garners a lot of attention when it comes to privacy, but don't neglect your Facebook security either. While no measures are ever going to provide 100% guaranteed protection from hackers and other troublemakers, if you follow the few easy tips below, your Facebook account will be as secure as possible.

Enable Double Authentication with your Mobile Phone

A surprisingly large number of people do not opt to link their mobile phone to their Facebook account. On the one hand, doing this provides Facebook with yet another piece of your personal information but, on the other hand, it will significantly help protect your account from unauthorized access. If you don't want to provide Facebook with your mobile phone number, you can link another device (such as a tablet) to your account to provide the necessary login approvals.

<u>Linking Your Account to a Mobile or Other Device</u>

Here's how to link your mobile phone (or other device) to your Facebook account.

Go to your *Settings* by clicking on the down arrow icon at the upper-right corner of your Facebook page. The page that is displayed will have a number of items listed on the left, select *Mobile*. Follow the prompts and add your mobile phone number.

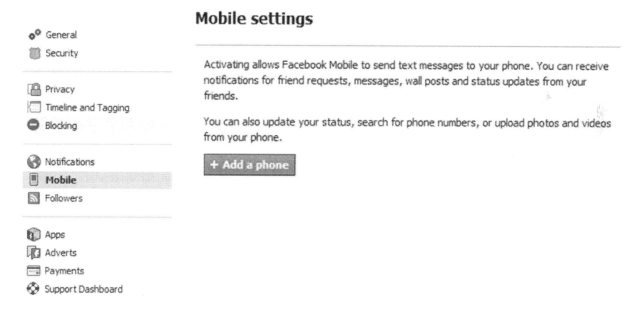

Mobile settings

General

Security

Activating allows Facebook Mobile to send text messages to your phone. You can receive notifications for friend requests, messages, wall posts and status updates from your friends.

Privacy

Timeline and Tagging

Blocking

You can also update your status, search for phone numbers, or upload photos and videos from your phone.

Notifications

Mobile

+ Add a phone

Followers

Apps

Adverts

Payments

Support Dashboard

<u>Enabling Login Approvals</u>

To enable login approvals, access the menu from the downward triangle found in the upper-right corner of the Facebook tab, selecting *Security*.

From the menu that appears select *Login Approvals and then Require a security code to access my account from unknown browsers.*

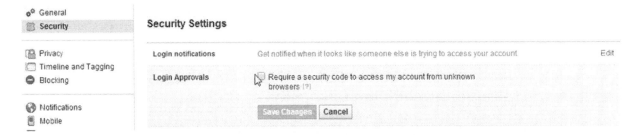

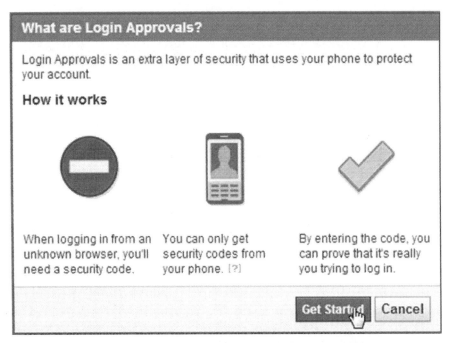

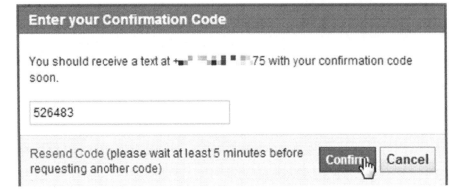

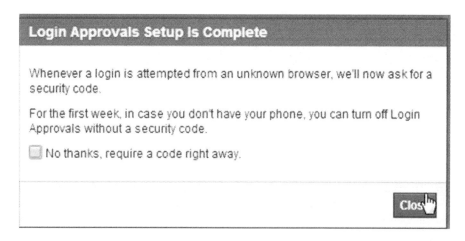

Now, should anyone try accessing your Facebook account from a web browser or device that is different from what you normally use, they will be prompted to enter a security code sent as a text to your registered mobile phone number (or generated by an app on your linked device). While this means you will occasionally have to enter a code when accessing Facebook from a different web browser or device (while travelling etc.), this is a simple and effective way to really enhance the security of your Facebook account.

Enable Login Notifications in the Security Settings

Building on the security measures above, you can also choose to receive an alert every time your account is accessed from an unknown device. When selected, Facebook will send you a warning by email or text that someone has tried to access your account, further helping to protect your account from unauthorized access.

To enable these alerts, go to Privacy Settings and select the second option displayed at left of the page, *Security*. Look for *Login notifications* and select whether you want to receive alerts by email or text message. Select *Save Changes* when you are happy with your settings.

Detailed Walkthrough of Other Facebook Privacy Settings (Advanced Users)

Facebook's privacy settings, features and menus are changing all the time. The instructions and screenshots that follow were current at the time of publishing. However things may have changed in the meantime. If instructions or screenshots are not exactly the same they should be similar enough to help enable you to navigate through the settings and options. The online version of these tutorials found on the companion website at www.cogipas.com will reflect the latest information.

How to Limit People's Access to your Facebook Photos

Facebook lets you choose the audience for *each* of your photo albums. Go to your Profile, select *Photos* and then *Albums*. For each album *except* Profile Pictures and Cover Photos you can configure the allowable audience by selecting the privacy icon (at the lower-right for each album) and applying your desired setting.

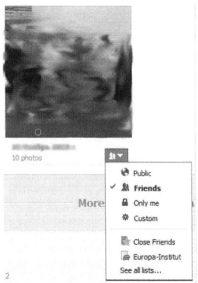

Figure: It's easy limiting or changing people's access to your Facebook photo albums

You can also select an audience for each and every *individual* photo in your albums by opening a photo and selecting the privacy icon found in the upper-right corner. Your last privacy selection will have been retained for your next choice, so remember to change it if needed.

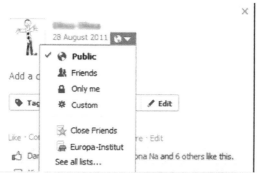

Figure: Facebook lets you change the privacy setting for each and every photo in your albums

Preventing Yourself from being Tagged

As mentioned earlier, you can be tagged in photos without your consent and this means photos can appear on Timelines without your approval. While you can exert some control over photos you are tagged in from appearing on your *own* Timeline, you can exert less control over them appearing on other Timelines.

Unfortunately, you cannot totally prevent yourself from being tagged. Facebook users can tag you without your permission. The options available to you are to ask the person who tagged you to *untag* you or, failing that, to report the tagged item to Facebook in the hopes it will be removed. However, even when you try taking these steps the damage may have been done already, with the tagged items *screen captured* or further shared, copied, picked up in feeds, etc.

To change the tagging settings for your Timeline, access Facebook's main privacy settings page at https://www.facebook.com/settings/?tab=privacy and select *Timeline and Tagging*. In the menu that appears, settings are available about who can post things to your Timeline (including photos), who can see things on your Timeline and how tagging is managed.

For items you are tagged in appearing on your Timeline, Facebook lets you review posts your friends tag you in *before* they appear on your Timeline (see screenshot). If you do *not* set this up, all items in which you are tagged will appear automatically on your Timeline, without your prior approval.

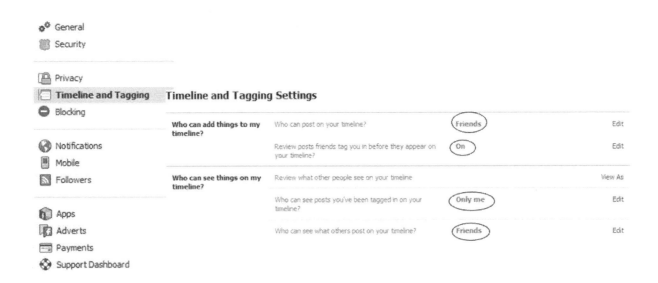

Figure: Enable the option, Review posts friends tag you in before they appear on your Timeline

A little further down in the available options, you can also enable the prior review of tags that people add to *your* items (for example, when a friend wants to tag himself in a photo you added to your own Timeline). Make your selections in the section, *How can I manage tags people add and tagging suggestions?*

If you want to be untagged from a specific item, go to the item, select its *Options* (usually at bottom-right), then select *Report/Remove tag*. After that, a new window will appear letting you untag yourself and/or ask the person who posted the item to remove it.

As mentioned, friends can tag you in photos and in posts. Although Facebook offers you the option of reviewing tags before they are applied, this consent only applies to items appearing on *your* Timeline. This previewing feature does not prevent you from being tagged in photos or posts appearing in other places, such as a friend's Timeline, unless you take the active steps necessary to expressly *untag* yourself. Because it's easy to miss these notifications, you may not be aware of items in which you are tagged.

Check and Control your Likes

You can also edit the audience that can see your *Likes*. To access your Likes go directly to the page, https://www.facebook.com/me/likes or go to your profile page, then select *More* and then *Likes*. Then select the Edit icon (it looks like a pencil) and *Edit Sections*. In the menu that appears you can select specific categories of Likes you wish to hide. Alternatively, you can also *Unlike* any page you previously Liked.

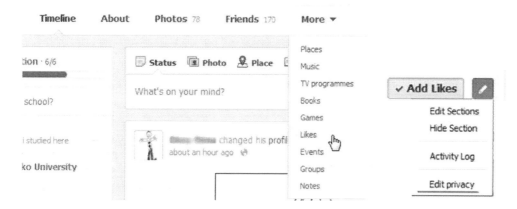

Protect Yourself (and Your Friends) from Targeted Advertisements

Unless you opt out, Facebook will use *your* information to also help it target *your friends* with advertising. Of course, the advertisements your friends see will be based on many things but, by default, this will include information you have shared with Facebook, such as your likes and pages you share.

Opting out will not only help prevent your friends from being profiled in even more detail, but it will also help keep your information from a wider audience.

Go to Facebook's Setting menu at https://www.facebook.com/settings and select *Adverts* from the sidebar. In the *Third-party Sites* options, use *Edit* to select *No one* and save your changes. Do the same for the next section too, *Adverts & Friends*, to disable Facebook's Social Adverts features.

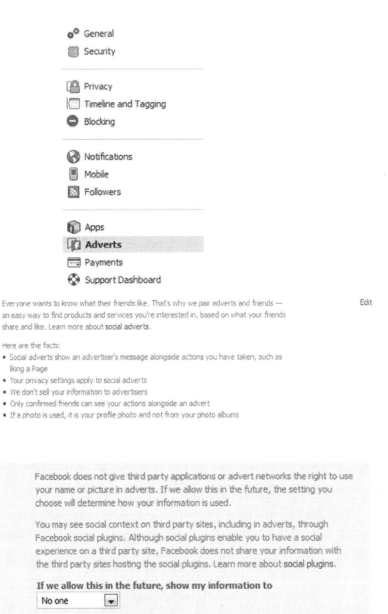

Top Tip - If you wish to prevent Facebook from using information about your *offline* shopping habits for their targeted advertisements, you should exercise your right to opt-out from the three major data collecting companies that co-operate with Facebook, Acxiom, Datalogix and Epsilon. See chapter 7 for more details on how to do this.

Risks Posed by Apps and Games

Even when you make your Facebook information accessible only to your friends (as opposed to *friends of friends* or the public at large), Facebook apps that you or your friends use may undermine these efforts and facilitate the sharing of information to third parties.

Facebook apps and games may contain weaknesses that leak your personal information. Basic information, such as your name, gender, profile photo and friends list, is usually deemed needed by apps and games on Facebook. Certain apps may even wish to have access to the information your *friends* share with you and vice versa. The risk can be minimized through your privacy settings, but it cannot be completely eliminated especially when, in your rush to install the app or game, you blindly accept its terms of access.

It is relatively easy to create and make available an app on Facebook (a "developer" needs only to have a verified Facebook account and phone number or credit card). With this level of arguably loose quality control, it's no wonder there are risks of your data being misused.

Limit the Access your Facebook Apps Have to your Account

As mentioned earlier, many apps can expose your private information to third parties (some apps may even have access to the information your friends share with you and vice versa). To protect yourself from apps that leak information (whether by poor design or with overreaching privacy settings), use only trusted apps and tweak some of your Facebook setting as follows.

To limit the access apps have to your private information start by going to the *Settings* menu and selecting *Apps* from the sidebar or go directly to https://www.facebook.com/settings?tab=applications. Look for the heading *Apps others use*, select *Edit* and deselect the information items that you do not want your friends' apps to be able to "bring with them" (in other words, your personal information that your friends' apps can access and use for goodness knows what). When finished making your selections, *Save Changes*.

General

Security

Privacy

Timeline and Tagging

Blocking

Notifications

Mobile

Followers

Apps

Adverts

Payments

Support Dashboard

Apps others use	People on Facebook who can see your info can bring it with them when they use apps. This makes their experience better and more social. Use the settings below to control the categories of information that people can bring with them when they use apps, games and websites.

☐ Bio	☐ My videos
☐ Birthday	☐ My links
☐ Family and relationships	☐ My notes
☐ Interested in	☐ Hometown
☐ Religious and political views	☐ Current location
☐ My website	☐ Education and work
☐ If I'm online	☐ Activities, interests, things I like
☐ My status updates	☐ My app activity
☐ My photos	

If you don't want apps and websites to access other categories of information (like your friend list, gender or info you've made public), you can turn off all Platform apps. But remember, you will not be able to use any games or apps yourself.

Save Changes Cancel

* * *

For updates and additional information about how to protect your privacy on social media, please visit http://www.cogipas.com/how-to-protect-your-privacy-on-social-media/.

Chapter 7: Preventing Identity Theft and Fraud

Introduction

You've probably read stories about *identity theft*, a crime that Gallup says is more prevalent in the US than burglary, mugging, car theft and physical assault *combined*. This chapter explains what identity theft is and how you can avoid falling victim to it.

Identity theft is an illegal act which involves the theft or misuse of your personal data, such as your name, birthdate, social security number or any other personally identifying information. This information is used to impersonate you – whether online or offline – with the ultimate goal of withdrawing your money, taking out a mortgage or loans, or signing up for services, government hand-outs or credit cards, all in *your* name.

On average it takes more than *twelve months* for a victim to realize that their identity has been stolen. By then, much damage may already have been done to your credit rating, financial position and reputation. It can also take a long time to undo the damage caused by identity theft, so it's important to take *proactive* steps to protect yourself from this rising crime.

Protecting Yourself from Phishing and Spoofing Attacks

Identity thieves try obtaining your personal information through scams called *phishing* (pronounced fishing) and spoofing. Both scams involve fraudsters pretending to be an organization such as your bank or retailer and using a fake email (phishing) or a fake web page (spoofing) to trick you into providing your username, passphrase or personal information. *Spear phishing* refers to highly targeted phishing attempts where, for example, the fake emails are specifically addressed to you and therefore seem all the more legitimate. Sometimes phishing and spoofing scams are easily spotted, but other times it is almost impossible to tell the difference between fake and legitimate solicitations.

Phishing messages will often include part of a legitimate website's name in the link they want you to click on (such as, http://cogipas.example.com/) so take a close second look. To make matters worse, the URL you see in an HTML-based email message or on a web page is not necessarily the true destination of the link. Follow the techniques I outlined earlier by hovering over links without selecting them to see what address is displayed. Make sure that the true link looks valid before you select it or, better yet, type URLs directly into your web browser. Manually typing in the address of the website you want to visit in your browser ensures that even if you receive a phishing message and react to it, you'll always end up at the real website, so no damage will be done.

Also look out for the tone of the message. Many phishing messages attempt to scare you into accessing your account immediately, so that you won't take the time to notice the spoofed site you were sent to is a fake. They'll often threaten to deactivate your account, suggest you've got a large unexpected bill to pay, or say your account has been hacked.

Many web browsers, email apps and webmail services offer *phishing filters*. These work similar to spam filters in preventing phishing messages from reaching your inbox. Although the filters are not foolproof, they are yet one more layer of protection in your lines of defense, so use them.

Note in particular, that *banks* do not include any links in their messages to you. Instead, their messages will ask you to use your browser and type in the domain name, which you can check on your bank statement or any official paperwork from the bank.

You should use the same technique of typing website addresses directly into your browser rather than selecting links even if a friend or other trusted source sends you a link to a website you know. The email may have come from a trusted source, but perhaps *they* have fallen victim to malware or were hacked. It's always better to be safe than sorry.

Otherwise, you may not notice that the link is to www.cogipas.com or to cogipas.example.com (rather than to www.cogipas.com) and that you are falling for a fake, spoofed site. To make sure you are dealing with a legitimate website, pay close attention to the website address displayed in your web browser's address bar.

If You Get Phished In

If you do fall for a phishing message and provide your details to a spoofed website, go to the legitimate site and change your passphrase *immediately*. If the hackers beat you to it, he or she could lock you out of your own account, *hijack* it and perhaps attempting to breach your other accounts with the information they now have available.

If your account is hijacked, reclaiming it can be very difficult. You can't just solve it with an email to the site's helpdesk saying your account was hijacked and you want it back. If it were that easy, this is a technique that the hackers would use to seize control of your account in the first place.

To help ensure that others do not fall for the same phishing attack, you could also report the incident to the Anti-Phishing Working Group (APWG) at http://www.antiphishing.org/. There may be no immediate personal benefit in reporting a phishing attempt, but it will help in the overall fight to reduce the number of people getting swindled.

If you do become a victim of outright identity theft, you should also report the matter to the FTC at https://www.ftccomplaintassistant.gov/. While the FTC will *not* resolve your individual consumer complaints, they will use the information to help in the pursuit of prosecutions and investigations as well as to detect patterns of unlawful activity.

As you can probably detect, you may have a long, hard, lonely slog to reverse the damage caused by the identity thieves. This is why *prevention* is so important.

Safe Online Shopping

Another potential security vulnerability you face is when making payments online. Online shopping offers consumers a host of advantages compared to traditional shopping: there is no need to fight for a parking spot, you can travel from store to store with just a few clicks or taps, and it is easy to compare prices and styles - all from the comfort of your chair. In addition, online shopping lets you find great deals on the Internet while you browse and socialize at the same time.

However, it is easy to become complacent and neglect the real risks to your security posed by online shopping. After all, it is estimated that someone is victimized every seven seconds by online scams. To avoid being one of the victims, follow these tips when shopping online.

Know Your Merchant

Always spend a few minutes doing some research about the website that you are thinking of transacting with. That slick new product for half the best price you've seen anywhere else may just be too good to be true after all. The web is certainly a great retail equalizer, a place where an entrepreneur can have a website as good as much larger competitors, but a polished and slick website may not always be backed up by a legitimate, reputable business.

If you are buying from an online vendor or an e-store on a larger site such as eBay or Amazon, make sure that the vendor has excellent feedback scores based on many transactions.

On other sites, the presence of seals of approval like BBBOnline http://www.bbb.org/online/ may also provide you some comfort that there is an actual business behind the website and that it meets some level of proper business conduct.

Dealing with reputable vendors is also important because your purchase data will be on file with them. Many people don't think about this, but if the vendor's systems or customer databases are compromised by hackers, the hackers may gain access to your banking or credit card details together with personal data such as your name, address, telephone number and even birth date, all a gold mine for identity thieves.

Ironically, the information you have been trying so hard to protect from hackers could be disclosed by the sloppy business practices of a third party you entrusted with the same data. Even if the hackers "only" obtain your username and passphrase for that particular account, we have already seen how this can enable them to infiltrate your other accounts, leading to more of your accounts being breached.

'S' for Safe

Only engage in financial transactions on websites using a *secure* connection (sometimes called secure socket layer or SSL). This means that when it comes time for the online transaction, make sure that your web browser's connection to the ecommerce site is encrypted and that the address starts with https:// (note the 's'). Depending on the web browser app you use, a lock icon may also appear either in the web bar or in the status bar at the bottom of the window (see screenshot). An encrypted connection between your device and the merchant's site helps to ensure that credit card and other details cannot be intercepted in transit.

Figure: These highlighted elements displayed in a web browser's search bar give you confidence that a secure (SSL) connection has been established

Protecting Yourself from Keyloggers

Keylogging is another way identity thieves can steal your personal information. This technique involves the adversary, without your knowledge (sometimes via malware), installing software on your device that captures the information and keystrokes you enter on your device and sends them to the adversary. Needless to say, in no time they will have the usernames and passphrases for a number of your accounts.

Top Tip - Some employers use keylogging software to monitor their employees. In addition, computer forensic experts are trained to install keyloggers as part of investigations, including in advance of a device being seized, in order to capture as much information as possible, including account passphrases.

There are also *hardware* keyloggers which can avoid detection by anti-malware apps. Hardware keyloggers can take many forms. They can be a small device secretly installed between the end of your keyboard cord and its port at the back of your desktop computer. Keyloggers can also be a separate device that looks similar to a small USB memory stick plugged into one of your available USB ports. See http://www.cogipas.com/keylogger-examples to check what keylogging devices can look like.

You can thwart the risk posed by keyloggers with a number of tools, including *SpyShelter* ¢ (14-day free trial) www.cogipas.com/spyshelter. It detects if any keylogging software or any keylogging type activities are present on your device and will purge them for you.

Understanding Credit Reports and Data Brokers

Credit reports provide a central repository of your financial health, so that when you request a loan, a bank can see what other loans you already have and can make sure you can afford a new loan. These reports are used legitimately by banks (to approve loans), potential employers (as part of background checks), or lawyers (for due diligence checks).

Clearly, there can be important consequences to any erroneous information appearing in these databases. For this reason, you should check the most important ones (see below) regularly - annually for example - and tenaciously correct any errors you find. Periodically checking your information in these files is also a good way to detect any strange activity that suggests you may have been a victim of identity theft in the recent past.

In many jurisdictions, you are entitled to access your credit report (sometimes for free or for a nominal fee) and to correct any errors you find. This sounds easy. The *requesting* part of the process usually is straightforward, but *correcting* erroneous information can be an uphill struggle at times. So be prepared to be persistent.

Each reporting agency has its own policies regarding how you access and correct the information they have on file about you. Follow their directions meticulously; otherwise, they may use the slightest excuse not to comply with your requests.

Checking Your Record with Credit Reporting Agencies

There are three main credit reporting agencies. You should request and check the information held by *all three* because the information on file may differ between them. You can start checking your record by visiting their websites:

- *Equifax* www.equifax.com (in the UK, www.equifax.co.uk)
- *Experian* www.experian.com (in the UK, www.experian.co.uk)
- *TransUnion* www.transunion.com (in the UK, www.callcredit.co.uk/consumer-solutions)

Checking Other Sources (US Only)

Although not among the 'big three' credit reporting agencies above, you may also want to check what *Innovis* and *PRBC/Microbilt* have on file about you as they too keep credit reports. If you find an error in their reports, both websites contain information and contact details about how to correct errors.

To access your credit report from *Innovis*, go to https://www.innovis.com/InnovisWeb/pers_orderCreditReport.html (or go to www.innovis.com > Personal Services > Order Your Innovis Credit Report)

For *Microbilt*, go to http://www.microbilt.com/consumer-dispute.aspx (or go to http://www.microbilt.com/ and type "disputes" in the Search box)
The *MIB Group* also maintains consumer files, but related to health- and medical-insurance information. At the time of publishing, to request your consumer file for free from MIB go straight to http://www.mib.com/html/request_your_record.html (or go to www.mib.com > Consumers > Request Your MIB Consumer File)

Another large source of database information is *Lexis-Nexis* which caters to attorneys and related industries. Lexis-Nexis does permit you to *opt-out* from their database (your ability to opt-out may vary). For information about this, visit http://www.lexisnexis.com/privacy/forconsumers/opt-out-of-lexisnexis.aspx (should this address change type "lexis nexis opt-out" in your favorite search engine).

More Resources

Entire books have been written on the subject of identity theft alone so I won't pretend that this chapter covered everything. However, it has provided enough information and self-help techniques to give you a great start.

If you want to learn more, excellent sources of information about identity theft include the US government's central website, http://www.ftc.gov/bcp/edu/microsites/idtheft/ and the UK's Internet crime reporting center at http://www.actionfraud.police.uk/fraud_protection/identity_fraud.

The US Federal Trade Commission also maintains information about how you can obtain your credit report for free from each credit reporting agency once per year. See http://www.ftc.gov/freereports and http://www.ftc.gov/bcp/edu/pubs/consumer/credit/cre34.shtm.

For similar information in the UK, again consult the information at http://www.actionfraud.police.uk/fraud_protection/identity_fraud.

A book I can recommend on the subject is '50 Ways to Protect Your Identity in a Digital Age', available both in the USA ¢ http://goo.gl/fDPyL1 and in the UK ¢ http://goo.gl/c1pQCp.

* * *

For updates and additional information about preventing identity theft and fraud, please visit http://www.cogipas.com/preventing-identity-theft-and-fraud/.

Chapter 8: Risks and Dangers of Wireless Networks and "Hotspots"

Introduction

Wireless networking, whether at home, your workplace or at a public Internet connection (called "hotspots"), often makes the task of hackers and other troublemakers much easier. Hotspots represent a particular security and hacking risk because your Internet traffic is easily intercepted, including any sensitive information you send while using a hotspot, such as passwords or credit card details.

Similarly, you want to avoid sharing your home Internet connection with strangers. People have had their front doors kicked down by authorities because a hacker or even just the neighbor had hijacked their Internet connection to conduct abusive or illegal activities.

It is not difficult to securely set up your Internet connection and wireless *router* (the box with blinking lights that is plugged into the wall and that makes your wireless Internet connection possible). The steps include:

- Protecting your router from unauthorized access by using a *non-default password*. Too often people don't change the default username and password for their router making it that much easier for hackers to breach.

- Hiding your wireless connection from nosy neighbors and other snoops by deactivating your router's automatic broadcasting feature.

- Enabling stronger encryption for your wireless connection.

- Making sure that only *your* devices can access your wireless connection by hiding your connection from other devices.

These steps may sound complicated, but are all explained below. But first, let's talk about hotspots.

Using Hotspots Securely

Hotspots or public wireless networks are becoming pervasive, available in almost all cafés, airports, restaurants and bars. While offering convenience, you must appreciate that you are sharing an unknown network with an unknown number of strangers.

The risks of using hotspots fall into two broad categories: spoofing/phishing and sniffing.

Beware of Spoofers and Phishers

Although it sounds obvious, you should make sure that you are connected to the actual hotspot (!) rather than a decoy, fake or *spoofed* site. For example, there are apps that allow a hacker sitting nearby to make you think you are logging on to a legitimate site (for example, the login page for the hotspot or for a popular webmail, social media or shopping site) when, in fact, you are entering your username and passphrase into a fake portal.

The spoofing app enables the hacker to create a replica of the legitimate login page and fool you (phish you) into providing the hacker with your username and passphrase, sometimes even your credit card details.

To make sure that you are on the correct sign-in page look carefully at the URL in your browser bar. Remember my earlier examples about phishing tricks such as posing www.cogipas.com as www.cogipas.com. In addition, most legitimate sign-in pages will be through a *secure* connection, so look for the https (note the 's') at the start of the URL and a lock icon displayed in your browser bar (see screenshot).

Figure: These highlighted elements displayed in a web browser's search bar give you confidence that a secure connection has been established

Beware of Sniffers

There are other apps that hackers and snoops use called *sniffers* which capture data over unsecured networks. When using an unsecured wireless network, adversaries can capture *all* the traffic you send over the Internet including your emails and passphrases or any other data, such as credit card information, you are transmitting. This is one reason you should never do any online shopping or access any sites requiring your usernames/passwords over an unsecure public hotspot.

To help protect yourself, use only verified https connections (again, note the 's') as this means the data sent to and from your device is *encrypted*. This way, even if the data is intercepted by a hacker or snoop, it will be completely unintelligible to them.

Always trust your instincts and have a look around to make sure that you do not have any overly curious neighbors sitting close to you. That said, adversaries employing sniffing methods do not have to be in your immediate vicinity and could even be sitting in a car parked outside (discussed more in the pages ahead).

You can ensure your connection is secure on public hotspots by using something called a *virtual private network* (VPN). A *VPN* creates an encrypted tunnel of your Internet traffic, no matter where you are, fully protecting you from the risks above. As VPNs are an important tool for protecting your online security *and* privacy an entire chapter is dedicated to them later in the book (see chapter 12).

For solid protection specifically tailored for using public hotspots, you can use a tool such as *HotSpotShield* (free) http://www.hotspotshield.com/ or its premium *Elite* version ¢ http://www.cogipas.com/hotspotshield. It is an immensely popular app (200+ *million* downloads) which encrypts all of your web browsing activities end-to-end, making it ideal for protection when using public Wi-Fi hotspots. The free version displays ads.

Top Tip - When using a device in a public place *without* needing access to the Internet, turn off your device's wireless connection. For example, on most laptop computers a quick key press will disable your wireless networking. Similarly, most tablets and smartphones can quickly be put in airplane or flight mode. Why leave your device unnecessarily open for attack?

Don't be Blasé about Your Home Internet Setup

Wireless routers allow devices within a specified range to access your Internet connection without all the messy wires running from each device to the router box. If your wireless network has not been properly set up, adversaries can find your openly accessible connection and exploit it. In fact, if your wireless network is set up poorly enough, it's not only sophisticated hackers or snoops you have to worry about but also regular people, such as your neighbors, piggybacking on your connection.

How to Check if Your Home Internet Connection is Vulnerable and Open to Attack

You can double-check this risk by asking a friend to come over with their wireless Internet-enabled device (for example, their laptop, tablet or smartphone) to see if your wireless network is visible and, if so, whether it allows them to access your Internet connection. Even if your friend is prompted for a password, a risk remains (though only from more sophisticated adversaries) because wireless passwords may be easy to crack and anyway are no harder to crack than other passwords as already discussed in chapter 3.

But someone piggybacking on your wireless Internet connection is just the tip of the iceberg. Sophisticated hackers can do much more damage by exploiting your connection, ranging from capturing sensitive data you send over the Internet to hijacking your device without your knowledge.

Your connection could be taken over and used to launch attacks on other victims from *your* device. Hackers could route spam or launch Trojans or DDoS distributed denial of service attacks (see box) using your connection and devices. In these cases, it will be *your* IP address showing up in any logs. In other words, the local authorities could be knocking on your door to ask questions.

More About: *DDoS and Zombies* - A *distributed denial of service* attack (or *DDoS attack*) occurs when an Internet website becomes overloaded under a barrage of web page requests. Other people trying to access the same website will be denied access to it. Sometimes these attacks are launched from an army of enlisted *zombie* devices, devices secretly taken over by hackers and used to launch unwitting attacks on others.

About War Driving

Wireless equipment can now operate over a long range extending to the home or office next door and even to the roadside. Professional hackers known as *war drivers* are in search of unprotected wireless networks, sometimes posting the details of the open networks they find, along with GPS coordinates, and sharing the information with fellow hackers.

In their war driving quest, these hackers employ a variety of equipment, apps and tools to detect open wireless networks. Hackers will move around, either on foot or in a car, with a wireless Internet-enabled device trying to gain access to open wireless networks.

To protect yourself whether from professional war drivers, hackers or just nosy neighbors, follow the security precautions discussed next especially as your wireless network could be inadvertently open and accessible from a surprisingly large distance.

How to Properly Configure Your Wireless Internet Connection

There are a few key things to keep in mind about setting up your wireless Internet connection. Although these tips are straightforward, many people do not apply them, leaving themselves open to attack. Following in detail are the precautions you must take to properly configure your wireless network.

For the precise details related to your specific brand of router, consult its manual for everything you need to know. There are also plenty of good online tutorials you can find by typing the model of your router into your favorite search engine. You should spend some time reading these instructions as it is important to understand your router's features and take steps to secure it.

Changing the Default Username and Passphrase

The first thing you should always do, right from the start, is change your router's default password. For example, many home wireless routers now come with a web interface with the default username "admin" and the password "admin". If these are left unchanged, it's easy for hackers to guess these default username and passwords. This is especially true because default passwords are widely available online, including in user manuals. Even an amateur could gain access to your wireless router in this way.

Here's a short sample video for a popular brand of router (remember, the instructions for your router may differ), https://www.youtube.com/watch?v=Mop2Hrlj6_o.

When setting a new password for the router, as always, make it a strong one. If needed, see chapter 3 for a refresher on how to create strong passwords.

Disabling your Router's Automatic Broadcasting Feature - Service Set Identifier (SSID) Settings

It is also important that you disable your router's automatic broadcasting feature by changing its service set identifier or *SSID* setting. This may sound complicated, but it isn't. Taking this step will help ensure that your wireless network is not being announced to the world at large. A wireless router *automatically* gives off a signal on a regular basis, broadcasting its ID number. This enables nearby devices to "see", find and connect to it.

You can easily set up your router so that it does *not* automatically broadcast its SSID number. Rather, it is better that you manually enter the SSID number into each of your devices so that hackers or snoops cannot easily find (and then exploit) your wireless connection. If your router's broadcasting is turned off, the availability of your router will not be advertised to war driving hackers, snoops or your neighbors. In fact, disabling broadcasting means third parties will not even be aware of your wireless Internet connection, though some sophisticated adversaries may still be able to detect it in some circumstances.

Please check the manufacturer's manual on how to turn off your specific router's SSID broadcasting function. It is usually a matter of finding the correct option in the menu and simply disabling it. Easy!

Here's a short sample video for a popular brand of router (remember, the instructions for your router may differ), https://www.youtube.com/watch?v=3NbIfo9XIAo.

Enable (Stronger) Encryption for Your Wireless Connection

Technology is changing all the time and wireless Internet routers are no exception. For this reason, routers are usually *backward compatible* meaning that they will still support older technologies. Otherwise, your older devices wouldn't be able to connect to your wireless network.

Without getting into the entire mumbo jumbo, simply make sure that your router is configured to use the latest encryption method which is *WPA* or *WPA2*. The older technology, *WEP*, can be cracked much more easily. So double-check to make sure that your router is configured to use WPA/WPA2.

Here's a short sample video for a popular brand of router (remember, the instructions for your router may differ), https://www.youtube.com/watch?v=k_7SukJNToc.

Preventing Stranger's Devices from Accessing your Wireless Connection - Using Media Access Codes (MACs)

One of the best means of protection is to restrict your wireless network on the basis of *media access codes* (MAC). A *MAC* is like a social security number that uniquely identifies a wireless-enabled device or piece of equipment. Each wireless device has its own MAC address.

You can set up your wireless network to work only with the MAC numbers you permit by entering these MAC addresses into your router's settings. It's kind of like having a bouncer guarding your wireless connection: if your name isn't on the list, you don't get in. If the device's MAC address isn't on your router's permitted list, it will not be permitted to connect to your wireless Internet connection.

Your router's presence will go undetected to other devices whose MAC numbers have *not* been entered in the router's setup. The process varies for each model of router, so check your router's manual for details. While this method does mean you will have to enter the MAC addresses for each new device you buy, that is a small inconvenience for the significant security benefit that it brings.

How to Determine Your Device's MAC

The advice above begs the question, how do I find out what my device's MAC number is? To determine the MAC address for your Windows-based device, type *command* in the Start menu, and select *Command Prompt* (see screenshot).

Figure: Starting the Windows Command Prompt from the Start menu

An old-fashioned DOS-like window will open. If you type IPCONFIG /ALL a list (usually not too long) of your relevant settings and configurations will be displayed. Look for your *Wireless Network Adapter* and note the long series of letters, numbers and dashes beside *Physical Address*.

Voila! You have now determined your Windows device's MAC address (00-13-CE-3C-39-BA in the middle of the next screenshot).

```
Microsoft Windows [Version 6.1.7600]
Copyright (c) 2009 Microsoft Corporation.  All rights reserved.

C:\Users\Rod>ipconfig /all

Windows IP Configuration

   Host Name . . . . . . . . . . . . : AcerLaptop
   Primary Dns Suffix  . . . . . . . :
   Node Type . . . . . . . . . . . . : Hybrid
   IP Routing Enabled. . . . . . . . : No
   WINS Proxy Enabled. . . . . . . . : No
   DNS Suffix Search List. . . . . . : kabsi.at

Wireless LAN adapter Wireless Network Connection:

   Connection-specific DNS Suffix  . : kabsi.at
   Description . . . . . . . . . . . : Intel(R) PRO/Wireless 2200BG Network Conn
ection
   Physical Address. . . . . . . . . : 00-13-CE-3C-39-BA
   DHCP Enabled. . . . . . . . . . . : Yes
   Autoconfiguration Enabled . . . . : Yes
   Link-local IPv6 Address . . . . . : fe80::f9a8:69c7:9805:9ede%14(Preferred)
   IPv4 Address. . . . . . . . . . . : 192.168.1.101(Preferred)
   Subnet Mask . . . . . . . . . . . : 255.255.255.0
   Lease Obtained. . . . . . . . . . : 11 July 2010 10:49:00
   Lease Expires . . . . . . . . . . : 12 July 2010 10:49:00
   Default Gateway . . . . . . . . . : 192.168.1.1
   DHCP Server . . . . . . . . . . . : 192.168.1.1
   DHCPv6 IAID . . . . . . . . . . . : 369103822
   DHCPv6 Client DUID. . . . . . . . : 00-01-00-01-12-90-E5-17-00-C0-9F-E4-B2-5C

   DNS Servers . . . . . . . . . . . : 195.202.128.2
                                       195.202.128.3
   NetBIOS over Tcpip. . . . . . . . : Enabled
```

Figure: Displaying the MAC address with the `IPCONFIG /ALL` command

Once you have the information you need, exit the command window by typing *Exit*. You will now need to enter the relevant MAC address in your router's settings.

How to Disable File Sharing

Years ago, this was a greater risk when sharing files on devices was enabled by default. Unsuspecting users were leaving their systems open to Trojan backdoor and other malware attacks. Now, the default setting for newer operating systems, including Windows 7, 8 and 10 is to have file-sharing *disabled*. This is a good thing.

Sharing files on your device is especially risky over a public network, such as a hotspot, but also on your home connection unless you have followed the techniques earlier in this chapter.

It only takes a moment to check and confirm that your shared file settings are disabled in Windows. Perhaps someone has changed the settings without telling you or you are using an older operating system.

In the Windows start menu, type "manage advanced sharing settings". Or, type "control panel" and then select the relevant Control Panel items until you reach *Network and Sharing Center > advanced sharing settings* (see screenshot).

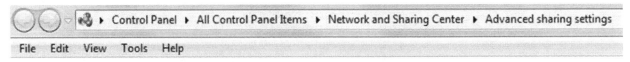

Control Panel ▸ All Control Panel Items ▸ Network and Sharing Center ▸ Advanced sharing settings

File   Edit   View   Tools   Help

Figure: The Control Panel path where you can find Window's shared file settings

From here, you can verify that file sharing is already disabled or, if not, you can disable it (see screenshot).

Change sharing options for different network profiles

Windows creates a separate network profile for each network you use. You can choose specific options for each profile.

Home or Work (current profile) ⌃

Network discovery

When network discovery is on, this computer can see other network computers and devices and is visible to other network computers. What is network discovery?

◉ Turn on network discovery
○ Turn off network discovery

File and printer sharing

When file and printer sharing is on, files and printers that you have shared from this computer can be accessed by people on the network.

○ Turn on file and printer sharing
◉ Turn off file and printer sharing

Figure: Making sure that file sharing is turned off, as above

* * *

For updates and additional information about the risks and dangers of using wireless networks and "hotspots", please visit http://www.cogipas.com/wireless-networks-and-hotspots/.

Chapter 9: Securing Your Devices

Introduction

This chapter outlines the remaining essential steps you should take to have a basic level of *security* protection for your *devices*. Many people will not take even these easy steps so by doing so you will already be ahead of the majority.

Lock and Password Protect your Devices

A very simple, but often overlooked, strategy for protecting your device is to enable its lock or screensaver protection. Too many people are lazy and don't enable these features. But entering a password or PIN merely takes a second each time and comes with a number of benefits.

Enable password protection on all your devices and always *lock* devices even if they are out of your sight for only a short time. This habit prevents unwelcome (snoops) or unannounced persons ("honey, I'm home early") from gaining access to your device should you happen to be away from it. This applies equally for devices both at work and home.

In Windows, this is just a matter of holding down the Windows logo key (on some keyboards it may look like a cloverleaf) and pressing the 'L' key to invoke the lock immediately. Alternatively, simultaneously hold down the *Control+Alt+Delete* keys and, once the menu appears, select *Lock*.

Locking your device is a simple tip that you should get in the habit of doing whenever you leave it unattended. This is not the most advanced of techniques, but will protect you from casual or passer-by snoops whether at home, at the office or travelling. An unauthorized person only needs a few seconds to gain access to your device. In this short time, an adversary could delete or copy data, read or forward emails, or install malware or a keylogger without your knowledge.

User Accounts and Privileges

In order to best protect your device, you must also understand the basics of *user accounts* and *privileges*. Most operating systems will let you set up different user accounts on a device so that multiple people can use it but with each person able to keep intact their own tailored menus and settings.

When you set up a new user account on your device, part of the process will involve selecting the privileges that will apply to it. Privileges is a fancy term for nothing more than 'what can this user do on this device'. Some privileges are full, allowing the user to do anything and everything on the device (sometimes called *administrator* privileges), while other privileges are more limited.

An account with full privileges acts as a 'super user' account. A user logged on to an account with full privileges is permitted to change security settings, install apps and hardware, access all files on the device, and can also make changes to *other* user accounts on the device. Accordingly, when attacking systems hackers target accounts with full privileges.

Windows comes with a default *Administrator* account with full privileges. If you keep and do not change the default settings for the Windows administrator account, you make it that much easier for a hacker to find and breach. By renaming the administrator account, you add a small barrier for hackers that may be enough to discourage and convince them to move on to an easier target.

The user account settings in Windows are reached by typing "user accounts" in the Windows Start menu or selecting these menu choices, *Start > Control Panel > User Accounts and Family Safety > User Accounts* (see screenshot).

Figure: Windows user accounts menu

Select your current administrator account and then select *Change your account name*. Enter the new name you want for the administrator account, and that's it. Easy!

You can even set up a decoy, fake or dummy administrator account to replace the renamed one. This is a good idea because if a hacker does infiltrate your device and sees that the customary administrator account is missing, he or she will know that it has been renamed and will look for it. Setting up the decoy, fake or dummy administrator account is also easy.

Once you have renamed the administer account by following the instructions above, set up a new (the decoy, fake or dummy) administrator account in name only as it will have *limited* privileges (a standard, non-administrator type user account).

In the Start menu type "user accounts" and select *Add or remove user accounts*. From the page that appears, select *Create a new account* (see screenshots).

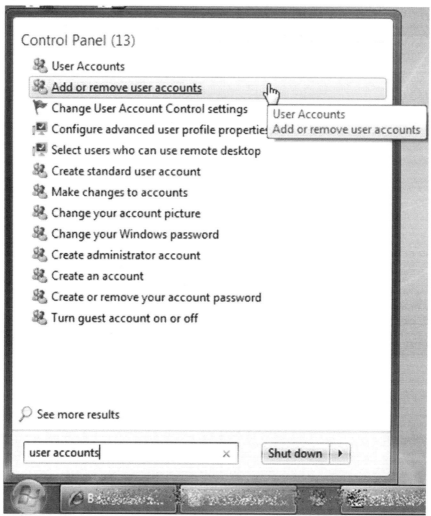

Figure: Accessing user accounts through the Windows start menu

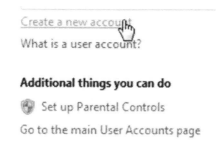

Ideally, you would want the name of the new account to be "Administrator". Unfortunately, not all versions of Windows support this so you may have to settle for "Admin". For account type, choose *Standard user*. Do *not* choose Administrator for the account type, because this is the whole point of setting up the decoy administrator account! Then select *Create Account* (see screenshot).

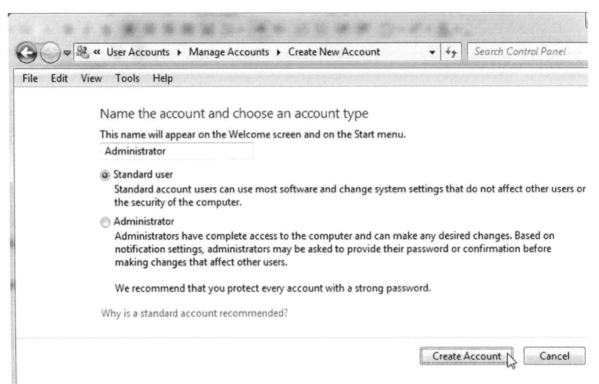

Figure: Creating the decoy administrator user account in Windows

Now, when any hacker pokes around your device and finds what they think is the administrator account they will be much more limited in any harm they can cause.

Some people don't pay any attention to these user accounts. Some people use an account with full privileges for all of their tasks and never set up other accounts. They may even use the full privileges account without setting up a password for it.

Do not be complacent like this! Think of the scenario where your device needs servicing and you bring it to a repair shop or to a friend or colleague for assistance. The person now has complete administrative access to your entire device, your data and apps - a scary thought if your device holds financial, medical or other sensitive personal information.

Using a Limited User Account to Browse the Web

This tip may not appeal to advanced users, but it is an especially good idea to use a more limited *user account* for browsing the web.

If you set up a limited user account *without* administrative privileges and use it for your web browsing activities (see screenshot) this will, similar to above, restrict the damage posed by a *drive-by hack* (when you visit websites that contain malicious software code). The extent of the damage that could be caused by a drive-by hack will be significantly reduced by using a more limited user account.

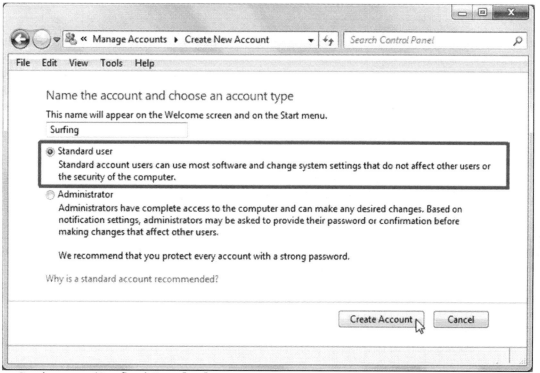

Figure: Setting up a 'Surfing' Standard user account to maximize your protection while browsing the web

Even if this tip does not appeal to you personally (for example because you want the ability to install apps) you should still consider setting up limited accounts for your children or any guests using your device.

Disabling the Windows Guest Account

Because some operating systems, notably Windows, also have a Guest account, hackers also sometimes attempt to hack through it. Disabling the guest account is straight-forward in Windows. First, go to the User Accounts menu (see the earlier instructions and screenshots).

Follow the relevant menu items to get to the guest account and then select *Turn off the guest account* (see screenshots).

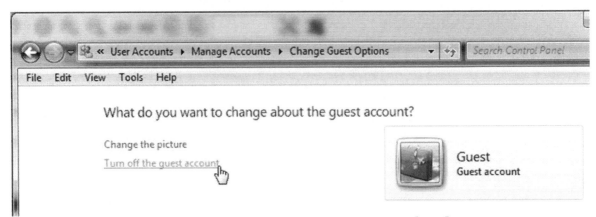

Figure: Disabling the guest account is quick and easy

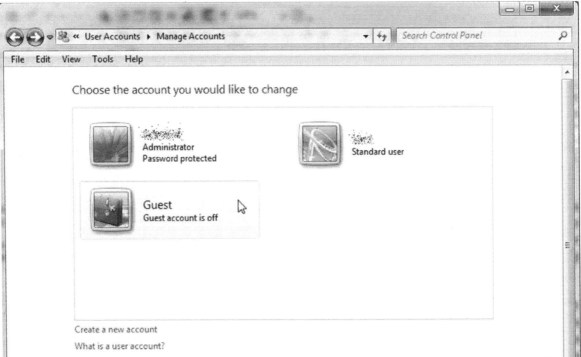

Figure: Confirming that the guest account is now disabled (Guest account is off)

Recap

The above all bears reiterating - at the very minimum, do the following on your device, whether you are the sole user of the device or one of many:

- Protect your user account with a strong passphrase
- Lock your device using its screensaver or password protection
- Rename the Windows Administrator account
- Create a decoy 'Administrator' or 'Admin' account
- Disable the Guest account
- Create an account with limited privileges for web browsing or for use by your children or guests

Protecting Your Ports (Advanced Users)

As mentioned in chapter 4, Internet communications are based on the interaction of *IP addresses*. *Ports* are a similar but different concept altogether. References to ports and port numbers appear in a number of places in the book so let's introduce them now. You can think of ports like radio or television channels. Each port carries a different "show" your device can tune into.

There are 65536 ports available to your device for network traffic. Some ports are fixed and reserved for certain types of Internet traffic such as web browsing, sending and receiving emails and chatting. The first 1024 ports (0-1023) have been designated for specific types of Internet traffic. Full port listings can be found easily online, though they can be dry and technical. However, some of the most commonly used ports are listed below.

> port 21 = FTP file transfers
> port 25 = SMTP email
> port 43 = WHOIS lookup information
> port 80 = HTTP web browsing
> port 110 = POP3 email
> port 119 = NNTP Usenet newsgroups
> port 194 = IRC chat
> port 443 = HTTP_S_ secure, encrypted websites using SSL (note the 's')
> port 5010 = IM (Instant Messaging) such as Yahoo! Messenger

Outside the first 1024 ports, those remaining have not been designated for a specific purpose and are therefore available for other uses. Ports 1024 to 49151 are registered and not used arbitrarily, but are transient in nature. The upper range, 49152 to 65535 are considered private or dynamic ports. Sometimes, these upper range ports set off alarm bells, in your anti-malware app for instance, because Trojans, malware or backdoor apps sometimes use them.

If you used a tool to monitor your ports, you would see dozens of ports establishing connections, sitting idle, closing, or listening and waiting for a connection (see screenshot).

Process Name	Process ID	Protocol	Local Port	Local Port Name	Local Address	Remote ...	Remote Port Name	Remote Address	Remote Host Name	State
firefox.exe	5144	TCP	62444		127.0.0.1	62445		127.0.0.1	AcerLaptop	Established
firefox.exe	5144	TCP	62445		127.0.0.1	62444		127.0.0.1	AcerLaptop	Established
firefox.exe	5144	TCP	62453		127.0.0.1	62454		127.0.0.1	AcerLaptop	Established
firefox.exe	5144	TCP	62454		127.0.0.1	62453		127.0.0.1	AcerLaptop	Established
iexplore.exe	2748	UDP	58877		127.0.0.1					
iexplore.exe	4692	UDP	62445		127.0.0.1					
RIMAutoUpdate.exe	2752	UDP	54200		127.0.0.1					
Skype.exe	3268	TCP	64080		10.0.0.99	10490		189.69.114.75	189-69-114-75.dsl.tel...	Sent

Figure: A screenshot from CurrPorts, a port monitoring utility

More About: *TCP and UDP* - You will also see references to protocols TCP or UDP. *TCP* is a two-way type of connection whereas *UDP* is a one-way or push broadcasting type of connection. TCP is used to enable two Internet hosts to establish a connection and check that the recipient received all of the data sent from the source. As a result, TCP is more resource intensive than UDP. UDP is often used for more 'quick and dirty' type connections, such as media streaming, which do not use robust data verification.

Testing Your Ports

To test your device's ports from the outside world, emulating a hacker's probing to some extent, visit:

- http://ww.grc.com/ > from the top menu, select Services > ShieldsUp and then select the 'Proceed' button >. From the choices displayed the new page select 'Common Ports' (or 'All Service Ports')

- http://www.auditmypc.com/ > select Firewall Test

- http://www.pcflank.com/ > from the choices, select Exploits Test

Very cool! If your operating system's protections are working well, the ports on your device will appear closed or, even better, non-existent (which is sometimes called stealth mode). This means that hackers trying to sniff and probe around your device's ports will not even be able to find you in the first place - a good thing.

In fact, there are tools available that prevent undesirable IP addresses such as those of spammers and known government snoops from connecting to your device. *PeerBlock* (free) http://www.peerblock.com/ is available for Windows and comes with default libraries of undesirable IP addresses which it keeps up-to-date automatically. At the same time, the block lists are fully user-configurable should you need to tweak the settings, for example, to temporarily or permanently allow an address. In a kind of peer reviewed way, PeerBlock is an effective tool for protecting your device. I talk more about PeerBlock when discussing torrent file-sharing in chapter 16.

* * *

For updates and additional information about securing your devices, please visit http://www.cogipas.com/securing-your-devices/.

Chapter 10: Keeping Your Children Safe Online

Introduction

For children the Internet is a wonderful, expansive place. However, parents know that their children can be harassed, bullied, groomed, stalked or targeted by savvy marketers. Children can also come across inappropriate materials such as websites or apps with themes of a pornographic, racist, violent, gory, hateful, disturbing, bizarre or otherwise offensive nature.

If you are a parent, below are some techniques that you can use to help keep your children safe online.

There is No Substitute for Attentive Parenting

The same parenting rules you should use in the real (offline) world also apply for the online world. This means trying to get to know what your children are doing online, participating as appropriate, and taking the necessary time to coach and mentor them.

Check-in periodically on your children when they are online and ask them about what's going on and, if they are chatting, with whom. You do not need to conduct an inquisition but rather to show interest. As in the offline world, you want to know what your children are up to after school in their free time.

In a nutshell, spend time with your children and take an interest in what they are doing online.

The SafeKids.com's Family Contract for Online Safety http://www.safekids.com/family-contract-for-online-safety/ is a great way to start the process. There is a "pledge" that children (of different ages) and parents can take. This is a good way to get the issues on the table and start the dialogue.

Children Online Security Basics

As always, the operating system and anti-malware app on your children's devices should be up-to-date and properly configured. Chapter 5 covered all of this.

If possible, consider having your children's computer (especially for younger children) in a *common area* such as the family room or living room. This alone can prevent a lot of potential mischief.

It is also a good idea to configure the *user accounts* and *profiles* on the devices that your children use to have *limited privileges* (see chapter 9). This limits both the inadvertent damage they can do on the device as well as the damage hackers or malicious websites can inflict should they infiltrate your child's device.

In addition, just as you would in the real world, introduce a *curfew* on how long your children can stay online. Most wireless Internet connection routers can be programmed to automatically stop Internet access between certain times. This can be a very effective way to automatically enforce the curfew; for example, at 9 pm the router simply stops working until the starting time the next day. No more arguments about when Internet time is over!

Web Browsing Protection

On the Internet, inappropriate websites are a mere keyword search and selection away. It is also possible for children to stumble on these materials quite innocently and accidentally. For this reason, consider using *site blocking apps*. These prevent your child's device from connecting to and displaying such content. Though not always foolproof, a site blocking app can be a powerful tool to help protect your children.

The site blocking app that is best for you will greatly depend on your specific needs and the age of your children. It is recommended that you browse the offerings and read the various reviews to determine what is most suitable for you and your family (and your budget). You can check these sources for the latest offerings:

- for free apps, check resources such as CNet http://download.cnet.com/windows/ > *Security Software > Parental Control* (check the box 'Free')

- for premium apps, check resources such as Amazon ¢ (premium) via http://www.cogipas.com/parental-control-apps or navigating Amazon's categories as follows, *Software > Antivirus & Security > Parental Control*

Social Media Safety

The safety tips in chapter 6 especially apply to children. Instill in your children the good sense that they should not disclose their personal information on social media. They should also never set up meetings in person on the basis of online friendships unless you participate.

Interestingly, it is not just bullies, predators and hackers that you need to be wary of for your children. Increasingly, *online profilers and trackers*, including savvy marketers, are targeting children. This sometimes takes the seemingly innocuous form of games and contests which entice children to submit personal information. This information is later used to build brand recognition as early as possible or to peddle products and services, sometimes directed at the parents through their children.

Children love to chat on social media and this may be the most difficult sort of Internet activity for you to take an interest. You *could* completely block your children from performing these activities, but this is probably not feasible or even desirable. You could also use a *monitoring app* (see below) to keep tabs on them, but that may be somewhat ethically troubling and do you *really* want to know *everything* your children are doing and chatting about online?

In the end, it may simply be best to trust your children and instill in them the principles in this book most relevant to them. At a minimum, try making sure your children:

- don't give out personal information
- don't share their pictures or personal details with strangers
- don't set up meetings in person without a parent being present
- don't select links or accept attachments in messages from unknown sources
- don't install apps without your supervision and help
- understand that people they interact with online may be disguising, exaggerating or misrepresenting their true identity or masquerading as someone else entirely
- tell you about any troubling or upsetting incidents that do occur

Monitoring the Online Activities of Your Children

There are plenty of monitoring apps available if you want to keep tabs on what your children are doing online. Monitoring apps are different from the parental control apps mentioned earlier. Parental control apps *prevent* your children from accessing certain web content whereas monitoring apps actually *record* and can *alert* you about your children's online activity based on criteria of your choosing. Monitoring choices could cover web page visits, email messages, chat exchanges, items downloaded, apps launched, torrents shared and, if you want, even every single keystroke they make.

Usually these apps will alert you by email or text message the moment any potentially inappropriate behavior is detected. Some of these apps will even let you play back everything your child did on their device, similar to an instant replay.

Popular child monitoring apps include *Family Cyber Alert* ¢ (premium) http://www.cogipas.com/family-cyber-alert-app and the more expensive, but industry leading, *Spector Pro* (premium) http://www.spectorsoft.com/products/SpectorPro_Windows/.

* * *

For updates and additional information about keeping your children safe online, please visit http://www.cogipas.com/keeping-your-children-safe-online/.

~ ~ ~

Congratulations on reaching the end of Part I. Now you should have a good grounding in the *basics* of Internet privacy and security as well as safeguarding your devices. Next, it's time to explore these topics in even more detail and explain how to be *anonymous* too.

PART II – ENHANCED METHODS FOR INCREASING YOUR PRIVACY & SECURITY AND HOW TO BE ANONYMOUS ONLINE

In this part, you will learn more advanced techniques for protecting your online privacy and safeguarding your devices as well as how to mask your identity and achieve (or maximize) online anonymity.

~ ~ ~

Chapter 11: Getting Rid of the Trace Information Left Behind by your Web Browser

Introduction

As we already learned in Part I, a great deal of information is recorded by your web browser and remains on your devices.

Recall that when you visit a website, conduct a search, watch a video, add a bookmark, install an app or download an item, your web browser automatically retains a potentially long-lasting record of that activity on your device. Anyone with access to your device could find these records and perhaps use them against you.

Obviously, these sorts of privacy risks could lead to a number of problems from the relatively minor (potential embarrassment from activities and interests you'd rather keep confidential) to the serious (workplace discipline, matrimonial problems, identity theft, forms of blackmail or worse).

Records your Web Browser Keeps and How to Remove and Prevent Them

Let's look at the sources of these trace data risks from your web browser in more detail.

Web Browser History

Your web browser *history* is simply a list of websites that you visited in the past *x* number of days, depending on the options and preferences set in your browser. To see your browser history in most browser apps, look under the Settings or Preferences menu for a History item or tab.

For example, to see your browser history in Chrome, select the *Customize and control* menu button (three horizontal lines at upper-right, ≡) and select the menu item *History* (see screenshot). Or you can use the keyboard shortcut *Ctrl+H*.

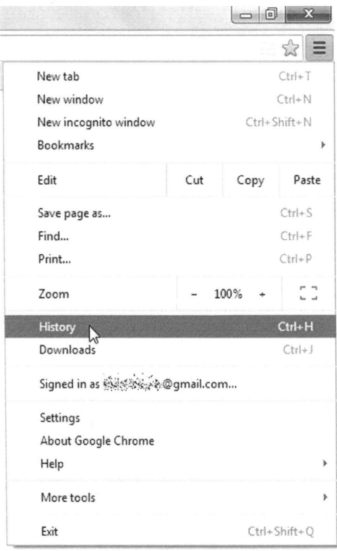

Figure: How to access Chrome web browser's *History*

Thankfully, it is easy to clear this history. At the same screen you can delete individual entries appearing in your browsing history. You can also choose to clear your *entire* browsing history for a certain period of time.

To delete individual entries, check the selection box in front of each entry you wish to clear and, after making your selections, select the button *Remove selected items*. You can also select the small down facing triangular icon after each entry and choose the option *Remove from history*.

To clear your entire browsing history for a certain period of time, select the button *Clear browsing data....* A menu will appear asking you what categories of items you want to clear together with a dropdown menu for the period of time to apply (hour, day, week, 4 weeks, beginning of time). To clear your web browsing history, make sure the box *Browsing history* has a tick in it. When all your selections are made, press the button *Clear browsing data.*

Top Tip - You can also directly reach the menu for clearing your entire browsing history at any time with the keyboard shortcut *Ctrl+Shift+Delete.*

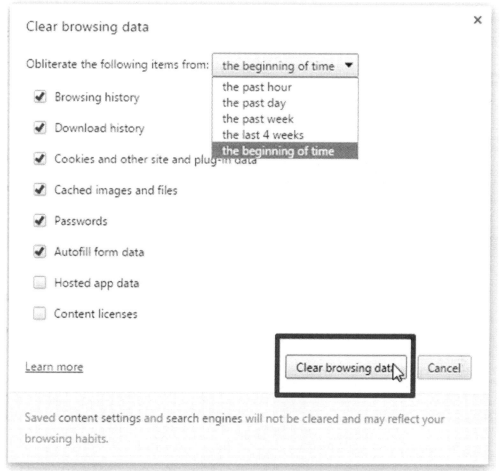

Figure: Chrome web browser's one-stop menu for clearing browser data

Web Browser Cookies

Recall that *cookies* are small text files downloaded to your device from a website to help it identify you. Cookies enable websites to remember your user preferences and settings, track your navigation of the site, log you on to the site automatically so you don't have to enter your password every time, or remind you about your past searches and display recommendations for related articles or additional products you may be interested in.

Depending on your browser settings, cookies may be stored on your device without your knowledge. Almost all websites use cookies and some use more than one.

Note that just the existence of a cookie on your device could be a privacy risk because it usually contains the website's name. For example, if you visited websites about finding a new job, researching a health problem, learning about divorce or wondering about how to declare personal bankruptcy, somebody might be able to surmise very personal things about you simply by looking at the cookies on your device.

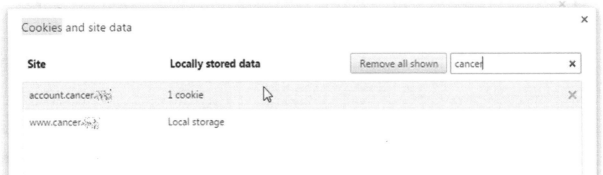

Figure: Cookie information saved in the Chrome web browser

From the figure above, you can see that I visited websites related to an illness. In the Chrome web browser, this information is accessible from the following menu choices: from Chrome's main Customize and control menu button (the three horizontal lines icon, ≡) select *Settings* and then *Show advanced settings* (near the bottom) then *Content Settings...* and finally *All cookies and site data* ..... You may be amazed to discover just how many cookies are on your device!

As with the browser history records above, you can choose to clear individual cookies or all of them. Clearing individual cookies is a lot more work, but prevents some of the inconveniences that can arise from clearing all your cookies. For example, you may want to retain the cookies for websites you visit frequently in order to avoid constantly having to reset your preferences.

To select individual cookies to clear, hover over a cookie in the listing and a small x will appear to the right. Select the x to clear the cookie. If you want to see more details about the cookie before clearing it, select the cookie and more details should be available together with a button *Remove* which will also clear the cookie.

More About: *Cookies* - A *cookie* has at least two elements: a name and a value. The *name* is simply that while the *value* can contain any number of things. It usually contains the relevant domain name that delivered the cookie, an expiration date of the cookie, and applicable user data such as usernames and sometimes even passphrases (hopefully encrypted but not always!)

You can also choose to clear all of your cookies. In Chrome, from the main menu button (≡), select *More tools* and then *Clear browsing data...* or use the keyboard shortcut *Ctrl+Shift+Delete*.

The menu that appears should be familiar from the earlier materials. To clear cookies, make sure the box is ticked *Cookies and other site and plug-in data* and remember to select from the dropdown menu the time period you want to apply. When all your selections are made, press the button *Clear browsing data*.

Web Browser Cache

While your browser history records your recent website visits, your browser *cache* saves copies of the web pages you visited. The cache uses these copies of web pages to make your browsing experience faster when you *revisit* a website. Instead of having to load the same page (and its images), the browser will take them from its cache. Clearly, the contents of the cache represent a privacy risk because it contains the actual web pages you've viewed (including their contents and images).

Clearing the web browser cache is easy and the process will be familiar to you by now. Access the clear browser data menu in Chrome by selecting from the main menu button (≡), *More tools* and then *Clear browsing data...* or by using the keyboard shortcut *Ctrl+Shift+Delete*. Make sure the box is ticked for *Cached images and files*, select the time period you want to apply from the drop down (past day, hour, week, 4 weeks or beginning of time) and then press the button *Clear browsing data*.

Web Browser Download History

Your web browser keeps tabs on the items you have downloaded to your device. This allows you to easily find and access those downloads. However, you may want to keep some of your downloaded items private. To see your web browser download history in Chrome, from its main menu select *Downloads* or use the keyboard shortcut *Ctrl+J*.

Here you will be able to see and search a list of your recent downloads. For each item listed you can select *Remove from list* or you can clear the whole list by selecting, at the upper-right, *Clear all*.

Your web browser download history can also be cleared for a selected period of time at the now familiar clear browsing data screen accessible in Chrome's main menu by selecting *More tools* and then *Clear browsing data...* or by the keyboard shortcut *Ctrl+Shift+Delete*.

Web Browser Auto Complete

Another risk to your privacy comes from your web browser's *auto complete* feature (sometimes called *prediction service*). Most web browser search bars now have an auto complete feature. If the feature has *not* been disabled, the browser retains a "memory" of past website visits and search terms. This is meant to be a convenience. As you start to type in the search bar, the web browser's auto complete feature "helpfully" displays any past matching terms searched or websites visited. Depending on your settings, the feature may even suggest websites *similar* to those you have visited in the past. While this is intended to save you time, it can also be a means for someone to detect your past searches and website visits.

To stop these predictions and the risk they represent, thankfully it is rather easy to do by simply disabling the feature. From Chrome's menu, select *Settings > Show advanced settings* (towards the bottom). Under the Privacy heading, uncheck *Use a prediction service to help complete searches and URLs typed in the address bar or the app launcher search box*. Interestingly, you *cannot* clear the auto complete predictions from Chrome's clear browser data screen as you can other types of browser data.

Top Tip - When you are web browsing in *privacy mode*, the auto complete feature will be *temporarily* disabled and the sites you visit and terms you search while browsing in this mode will not be retained or displayed as predictions for future web browsing sessions.

You can also delete specific annoying or damning entries as you encounter them. Each browser has a quick keyboard shortcut for doing so. This is handy when, despite all the earlier advice, you may have forgotten to disable auto complete or to browse in privacy mode and some sensitive website addresses or search terms are retained in your auto complete.

When such a pesky item is displayed in your browser bar, you can delete it in the Chrome web browser by using your keyboard's down arrow to highlight the specific entry and then press *Shift+Delete*. This single, specific item will now be prevented from being displayed again as a predicted search or website.

Using your Web Browser's Privacy Mode

As seen above, most web browsers keep extensive records of your activities. You also learned how to clear your web browsing data. You could clear your browsing data after visiting sensitive websites or even clear it on a regular basis. However, you can prevent much of the records from being recorded in the first place by using your web browser's *privacy mode* when visiting sites or conducting searches that you would rather not leave records of on your device.

As already covered in chapter 4, most web browsers now let you enter a kind of privacy mode, disabling all of the browser's history, cookie, autocomplete and other record-keeping features.

Contrary to popular belief, browsing in privacy mode is not used only for erotic websites. While browsing in privacy mode often has this connotation (it's sometimes called *porn mode*), it can have many uses. For example, you might want to use your web browser's cloaked mode when researching a gift online for your spouse or, for that matter, if you are researching divorce options. Or maybe you are organizing a surprise vacation for the family and want to keep this a secret from other family members that use the same device.

Whatever your reasons, browsing in private mode is handy when you want to disable your web browser's history, cache, cookies and autocomplete features. In Chrome, you can start a private browsing session (Chrome calls this going *incognito*) by accessing the main menu button (the three horizontal lines, ≡) and selecting *New incognito window*. You can also do this with the keyboard shortcut *Ctrl+Shift+N*. To open a specific link in private browsing mode, right-click on the link and select *Open link in incognito window*.

Protecting Your Bookmarks and Favorites

You also have to be careful about how you save your bookmarks and favorites, those website addresses (URLs) you wish to save in your browser for easier revisiting. These records can easily be found by anyone with access to your device and can reveal much about your preferences and perhaps even your secrets too.

I would highly recommend that you keep any sensitive bookmarks and favorites completely separate and apart from your "normal" ones. Mixing them together – even in separate folders – will only invite disclosure. Keep them private by sealing them off.

Here are some ways you can keep bookmarks and favorites private:

1) *Use a password protected profile* (also called an *identity* on some web browser apps). Your web browser app may allow you to set up different profiles (or identities) that are only accessible with a password. This way *all* your user-specific data including the bookmarks and favorites saved with your browser are somewhat protected. However, once you've logged in to the profile, anyone using your device could come across them. Maybe you are online and a family member or roommate comes up to you and says, "I want to quickly check something." In such cases, that person is but one or two selections away from finding (whether intentionally or accidentally) your stash of sensitive bookmarks and favorites.

2) *Use an <u>online</u> bookmarking app.* You can use something such as *Google Bookmarks* (free) <u>https://www.google.com/bookmarks/</u>. This way, a password (your Google password) would be needed to access your sensitive bookmarks and favorites. Having your bookmarks in the cloud this way can also be handy for accessing them from different devices and locations. Plus, many online bookmarking services have handy add-ons for your web browser that enable you to easily add or access bookmarks.

However, similar to option 1 above, once you are logged in to your online bookmarks (or if you didn't log out properly the last time you accessed it), all it takes is a quick errant selection or two for someone to find them. Plus, do you really want the online bookmark provider to be so intimately aware of your favorite websites?

In addition, if the online bookmarking tool you use has a *syncing* feature, be careful as this could undermine why you have migrated your sensitive bookmarks online in the first place. Syncing them will add them to and update them across your multiple devices, sometimes making your bookmarks more susceptible to discovery, rather than less.

3) *Organize your bookmarks with a separate standalone, <u>non</u>-cloud-based app*, perhaps installed on a separate storage device such as a USB memory stick. This method is somewhat low-tech and won't sync your linked devices, but does have its advantages.

An app such as *Compass* (premium) <u>http://www.softgauge.com/compass/</u> nicely fits the bill. Don't let the initial release date put you off as I still use this app today. Although it may seem dated and rather old fashioned, that's kind of the point as we want an *offline* app. In fact, this method can be especially handy when combined with other techniques described in this book such as encryption (see chapter 15).

Using a Separate Web Browser for Sensitive Activities

As you can see, protecting yourself from the risks posed by using your web browser app especially for sensitive activities can often mean fiddling with your settings or remembering to employ a number of tricks. That's fine except that, whenever you want the benefits that some of these features bring you have to re-enable them. This takes time and can be a hassle. And sometimes you may simply forget or be lazy to employ the various techniques.

Another option is to install and use different web browser apps for different activities. For example, if you use Chrome as your main browser app (for checking your webmail, news, social media, etc.) you can leave active any features you find useful such as cookies, auto complete, histories, favorites etc. The same goes for plugins, add-ons and extensions. This way, any links you select for example in emails will still open in your primary browser (Chrome in our example). But you could install a second browser app, such as Firefox, for your *sensitive* web browsing so it is less susceptible to discovery.

You could then adjust your Firefox settings to be tailored for your sensitive browsing. This also allows you to install different plugins for each browser, enabling you to customize and, more importantly, *segregate* your sensitive web browsing from your "normal" (non-sensitive) activities.

Each web browser app has its own advantages and so it is largely a matter of personal preference which you select, but for privacy features, *Firefox* (free) http://www.mozilla.org/ and *Chrome* (free) http://www.google.com/chrome/ are recommended. *Internet Explorer* is not recommended as it is too intertwined with the Windows operating system.

Please note that this strategy is *not* foolproof. Any second browser app you install would be visible on your device. Even if you removed any obvious traces of the browser that you use for sensitive activities from your device's menus or desktop, it would still be accessible with the most basic of searches.

Using a Separate User Account for Sensitive Activities

As discussed earlier in this chapter in the context of protecting your bookmarks and favorites, you could use and set up two (or more) separate *user accounts* in your operating system and/or in your web browser (called an identity in Chrome). You would log into and use one of the accounts (or identities) for your sensitive activities and the other one for everything else. As user accounts (and identities) can be password protected, this provides yet more protection.

However, any additional accounts on your device or identities in your browser would be plainly visible (for example, on the startup screens) and may raise questions from anyone who has access to it. "What is this account/profile for?" So if you do set up a separate account for sensitive activities, name it something innocuous such as *Test* or *Temporary*.

Moreover, whether using a second browser app or implementing multiple user accounts or browser identities, your sensitive activities will still leave traces behind that you will need to clear, as set out earlier in the chapter.

~ ~ ~

For updates and additional information about how to get rid of web browser trace information left on your devices, please visit http://www.cogipas.com/how-to-get-rid-of-web-browser-trace-information/.

* * *

Now that we have comprehensively dealt with how to clear away your web browser trace records, let's move on to avoiding *online* fingerprints.

Chapter 12: Anonymous Web Browsing – How to Throw the Online Trackers, Profilers and Snoops off your Trail (Proxies & VPNs)

Introduction

Some earlier chapters dealt with the simplest ways of keeping your personal information from getting into the wrong hands on the Internet. But now it is time to get more sophisticated and effective in throwing the online trackers and profilers (and snoops too!) off your trail.

To understand the best means of avoiding the trackers, profilers and snoops, you first need to understand how they track and profile you in the first place. This means knowing about *IP addresses*. With this knowledge in mind, you can then learn how a *web anonymizing service* can shield your IP address and keep you hidden online, such as a *web proxy*, *VPN* (short for *virtual private network*), or *Tor* (short for *The Onion Router* and discussed in the next chapter).

For example, a VPN will hide your IP address and help prevent your online presence from being detected. To the online trackers, you will look like a different person each and every time you use your VPN. This scrambling of online identities renders it difficult – but not impossible – for them to identify you. Therefore, you should really consider using a web anonymizing service, not only when engaging in any sensitive activities, but all of the time.

Using such anonymous web browsing tools may sound intimidating, but now many of them take the techno complexity out of using them. After opening an account, and downloading a small app, you will be using the Internet anonymously in no time. It really can be that simple.

But first, let's build on the topic of IP addresses which I briefly introduced in chapters 2 and 4.

What is an IP Address?

Although you may feel anonymous on the Internet, this is hardly the case. In this section you will learn about IP addresses and then use this knowledge to better understand how to stay anonymous online.

An IP address is a numerical label assigned to every device connected to the Internet at any one time. IP addresses are usually written in a set of four numbers separated by periods (this is known as *dotted quad notation*). For example, 151.196.0.0.

Each of the four numbers is in the range of 0 to 255. The further right you go in the set of numbers, the more specific the address they signify. For example, 115.169.57.01 and 115.169.57.02 might be connections right next door to each other while 115.169.57.01 and 116.169.57.01 would be completely unrelated and could be half a world apart.

IP Address = Your Online Fingerprint

Your IP address marks, like a fingerprint, all of your online activities. It attaches to your web page browsing, your email messages, your social media posts, your downloads and everything else you do online.

With a number of widely available tools, even a layperson might be able to track you down by IP address. In fact, the basic business model of trackers and profilers, often huge businesses with billions of dollars at their disposal, relies on being able to follow you by IP address. Hackers, snoops and adversaries can also exploit this targeting by launching attacks specifically aimed at your IP address looking for ways to gain access to your devices and personal information.

Top Tip - To see your IP address at any time, type "IP address" in most leading search engines or consult the resources at http://www.cogipas.com/whats-my-ip/.

The Privacy Risks

A certain amount of information is automatically sent from your web browser app to the websites you visit. This information usually includes your IP address, the type of web browser app you use, your geographic location, the web pages you previously visited, how long you stayed on a page, the site you came from (called the *referring site*), your device's operating system, perhaps the information residing in your clipboard from your last copy-and-paste, and more. Even this seemingly innocuous list of information may be enough to start building a profile on you.

Top Tip - See the resources at http://www.cogipas.com/privacy-tests/ to see the extent of information revealed from simply visiting a web page.

Once someone has your IP address, it can be cross-referenced with other data to determine the websites you visit, your email address (using *beacons* or *web bugs*), your social media habits etc. In other words, a comprehensive profile starts to be formed in no time.

Therefore, one of the most fundamental ways to protect yourself from all this potential tracking and profiling is to hide your IP address as much as possible when web browsing. Generally speaking, there are three ways to do this: with a web proxy, a virtual private network (VPN) or The Onion Router (Tor).

Web proxies are a bit old-fashioned nowadays, but are still useful, especially in some circumstances or in some parts of the world where censorship is alive and well. Plus, web proxies are usually free. In addition, first discussing web proxies and knowing how they work will help you understand and appreciate the better ways of how to browse the web anonymously, with a VPN or Tor.

How to Browse the Web Anonymously with a Proxy

By using a *web proxy*, you place a separate Internet server (with a separate IP address) between you and the websites you visit. If the proxy is functioning properly, the site receiving your web page request will detect the IP address of the proxy rather than your device's true IP address.

Think of a proxy as a middle man. The IP address of the proxy server will be reported to the sites you visit, rather than your own. This means that the earlier techniques based on IP addresses will track the proxy server's information and not yours. Instead of the IP address being traced directly back to you, the intervention of a proxy server means that anyone trying to determine your identity will need to obtain the logs from both the visited site *and* the proxy server, which is not an easy task. A proxy server makes it more difficult to pinpoint you from web browsing activities.

Note that using a proxy does *not* make you completely anonymous. Many proxy services claim that they provide comprehensive anonymity but this is not necessarily the case. Your average web proxy (especially a free one) isn't 100% anonymous. Yes, it may hide your IP address from the websites you visit and may unblock certain websites, but not much more. Your ISP will still be able to determine which websites you visit and, through your ISP, anyone else from government, adversaries or other snoops would be able to get the same information.

Further, the *administrator* of the proxy can see who you are and everything you are routing through the proxy. This administrator can even substitute websites or inject advertising or malware into your online session. In some cases, anonymous proxies are just a quick and easy fix to unblock websites, but not to keep your web browsing activities truly 100% private.

You should also remember that the proxy only protects your IP address from the web page you visit. An eavesdropper (such as your ISP or a snoop) on the communication channel between you and the proxy may remain able to see your web browsing activities. Also note that some websites, especially some webmail services, gaming sites and video streaming, may *not* work through a web proxy at all.

Given all the disadvantages inherent in using a web proxy, consider using a *virtual private network* or *VPN* for short (discussed next). A VPN lets you anonymously connect to websites without even your ISP being able to determine your activities because the VPN also establishes an *encrypted tunnel* in which your Internet traffic is protected. Your ISP or any other potential eavesdropper on your connection will only be able to see an encrypted stream of data between you and the VPN service provider. Because the VPN is also a proxy, it is the VPN's IP address and not yours that ends up being transmitted.

Web proxies can still be a good solution as they are easy to use and usually free. Sometimes the 'cheap and cheerful' option a web proxy represents is enough, but they shouldn't be used for super-sensitive activities. Generally, web proxies come in two varieties: a simple web form in which you enter the URL you wish to visit (similar to entering a website in your browser bar) or a proxy server address you enter into your web browser app's settings. Let's address each variety in turn.

Top Tip - Keep in mind that if somebody has the resources and is motivated enough to find the visitor of a web page or website hiding behind a web proxy, they probably can.

Easy-to-Use Web Form Proxies

Web form proxies are easy to use because, similar to using your web browser itself, you only need to type in the URL of the site you want to visit. The convenience also means that you usually have little or no control over the settings. In addition, as always when relying on a third party, you need to *trust* that the provider is doing what they say (not monitoring your activity or trying to exploit your connection).

- http://anonymouse.org/anonwww.html (in operation over 10 years)
- http://anype.com/
- http://www.guardster.com/free/ (allows some choice over settings)

Some web form proxies not only shield your IP address from disclosure but also hide the URLs you are visiting by scrambling the name of the destination site. This means that if your activity is being monitored, any logs being recorded (for example, by your ISP, by your employer if using the proxy from work or by a snoop) will display a different address than the site you actually visited. For example, instead of the logs recording that your browser visited www.cogipas.com, it might look like you visited www.example.com/3d3vZ2lXMuY29t.

- http://www.securetunnel.com/xpress
- http://www.work-surf.info/

But understand that even when URLs are scrambled, anyone following the link will see the destination page that you visited so don't rely on one of these proxies as a foolproof way to visit sensitive websites or to bypass censorship filters at work or elsewhere.

Top Tip - Ideally, try to use web form proxies that utilize secure SSL connections starting with HTTPS (note the 's' on the end), but these are more difficult to find, especially for free.

Finding an Open (Public) Web Proxy to Use

As you saw above, using a web-formed based proxy is easy. However, a more robust solution is to use a *public web proxy*. To use one of these proxies you will have to enter some information into the settings of your web browser app. There are many public proxies available. Some are operated by privacy enthusiasts for the benefit of the wider community and others have been made available to the public by accident. For these reasons, public web proxies tend to come and go. But they are easy to find and to enter into your web browser app's settings.

A number of websites maintain lists of available public web proxies, including those listed below. You can also perform a search in your favorite search engine for "anonymous web proxies" or "open proxies".

- http://www.checkedproxylists.com/
- http://www.publicproxyservers.com/

Once you have found a suitable web proxy, you will need to set it up in your web browser app.

Setting Up a Web Proxy in Your Browser

The steps for setting up a web proxy in your web browser app are easy and similar for most browsers. The key is to look for *proxy* settings which are usually part of your web browser's *connection* settings.

In Chrome, make the following selections: the main *Customize and control* menu button (the three horizontal lines, ≡) > *Settings* > *Show Advanced Settings* > under the *Network* heading select *Change proxy settings...* > *LAN settings* > under the *Proxy* service heading enter the required information (see screenshot). The port setting for web proxies is usually *port 8080*, but the instructions will tell you which port to use.

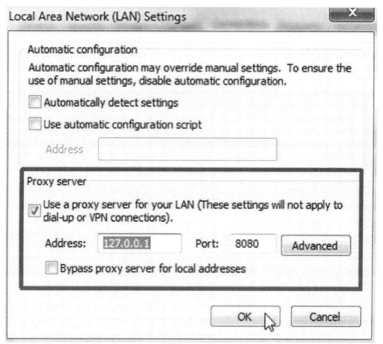

Figure: Entering the web proxy details in your browser (Chrome shown)

Top Tip - Note that a web proxy may support different *protocols*. Pay close attention to the proxy's instructions and use the proxy for as many protocols as you can. For example, most web proxies, and especially free ones, will *not* support the HTTPS protocol (note the 's' on the end) which uses *port 443*. Recall that this is the protocol used by your web browsing app to connect to secure pages (such as for credit card transactions).

Always Test the Proxy

Whatever type of proxy you use, you should always check to make sure that it is working properly. You can do this by visiting the testing sites I listed earlier in this chapter (and found at http://www.cogipas.com/whats-my-ip/). To test a web-form based proxy, type into it the address of the testing site and see what is displayed. To test an open web proxy, enable it and then visit one of the testing sites. In either case, if a test shows the proxy's location and IP address rather than yours, the proxy *is* working correctly. You should always check the proxy at the start of any web browsing activities you wish to mask as the proxy could be down, temporarily disabled or not working for a host of other reasons.

Using a Premium Web Proxy Service

The web proxies I have discussed so far have been *free* ones. There are also *premium* (paid) proxy services that are faster and more reliable. Some are similar to open proxies whereby you enter the technical details into your web browser app's settings, but may also require a username and/or a password. Other premium proxies provide you with an app which you download and install on your device to mask your web browser's activity. The end result is the same: your true IP address is hidden.

If a premium proxy appeals to you, you should choose a reliable service and this is not always easy to determine. Don't think that just because you are paying for a service it is trustworthy.

Anonymous Web Browsing Using a Virtual Private Network (VPN)

All of the advantages (and more), and none of the disadvantages of proxies are available by using a VPN. A VPN is a kind of super proxy, hiding your true IP address and encrypting your entire Internet connection. The one major drawback of using a VPN is that they are rarely, if ever, free and are usually premium in nature (requiring a subscription fee).

Unlike the web proxies just discussed, a VPN creates a tunnel of secure data between your device and the VPN provider's servers. This can mean that *all* of your Internet traffic, including web browsing, social media activities, torrent file-sharing (discussed in chapter 16) as well as chatting and messaging are channeled through a secure (encrypted) tunnel, preventing monitoring and surveillance.

Anyone snooping your Internet connection (your ISP or an adversary) while you are using a VPN will only see a stream of undecipherable encrypted data. This also makes VPN services a complete answer to the risks discussed in chapter 8 when using Wi-Fi hotspots, public wireless Internet access points.

Most VPNs nowadays are easy to install and use. Depending on the VPN you choose, you may have to set up your web browser app or Internet settings in much the same way as for a proxy by entering the VPN service's address and port. But it's usually more common that there is only a small app to download and install, which you then simply enable with a single click whenever you want to be anonymous online.

How a VPN Works

When you visit websites (or make other Internet connections supported by the VPN), the traffic is first routed to the VPN service and then to your device. Therefore, similar to a web proxy, it is the VPN's IP address that is visible at the other end of the connection. Your own IP address is kept hidden by the intermediary VPN, acting as a proxy.

Using a VPN also means that all of the subsidiary details obtainable from an IP address – such as your geographic location, the pages you previously visited, how long you stayed on a page, the site you just came from (the referring site), the operating system and web browser app you use and more - are also kept safe. When you use a VPN it keeps hidden all this information from trackers, profilers, hackers, snoops, Big Brother and adversaries alike.

As with a proxy, you should carefully choose any VPN service. The benefits described above are only as assured as the integrity of the provider you deal with. For example, how long have they been in business? Also, check whether the VPN keeps logs of your activities and whether they share your data with third parties (advertisers, partners, affiliates etc.). As tedious as it may sound, read the provider's terms of service and privacy policy (usually in the website's 'Legal' or 'Terms of Use' section).

There may also be certain advantages for choosing a VPN service based in a specific country as some jurisdictions have stronger privacy laws than others. For example, some countries are often cited by commentators as having stronger privacy protection for consumers, but always do your own homework especially as laws are subject to change.

As an added bonus, a good VPN also acts like another line of firewall-type defense for the devices you use with it. This is because your Internet traffic will first be routed through the VPN's servers which are protected by hardware, software and other resources more advanced than your own.

Many VPNs also now offer more advanced features. These can include being able to select *exit gateways* (servers) located in specific countries. Being able to select which country your Internet traffic appears to be originating from enables you to access content that would be otherwise subject to geographical restrictions such as watching online TV programs or streaming video.

Some VPN features automatically find and use the fastest exit gateway servers at any given time. Yet other features let you choose the apps whose traffic is routed through the VPN while your other apps continue to use your regular, non-VPNed Internet connection.

The features, appearance and operation of each VPN service differ, but later in the chapter I will provide some recommendations and detailed examples of how to use them.

How to Choose the Best VPN for You

Relying on any third party, including a VPN service, to act as a shield and protect your Internet activities requires a high degree of trust. For example, services purporting to offer anonymity may state that they are not keeping tabs on your activities, but how can you know for sure? You should only use reliable and time-tested services, but this is not always easy to determine.

In this section, I will outline how to choose the best VPN for *you*. A little later, I also provide some of my own recommendations for VPNs, but of course you are free and in fact are encouraged to conduct your own research and decide for yourself as everyone's circumstances and needs are different.

Emotions run high when talking about which VPN service is the "best". Everyone seems to have an opinion. But remember, the assessment depends on lots of factors and everyone's situation is different. The following are some factors for you to consider.

Cost

The price each service charges is an obvious factor in your choice and a very personal one. Some people can afford or are willing to spend more, others are not. However, as many of the services are similarly priced - on average, usually about $5-10 per month (about £3-7 or €4-8) depending on the length of the contract you choose - the decision often comes down to features and reliability. That said, these services sometimes have time-limited promotions and usually offer discounts for longer contract periods, so keep an eye out for deals.

Although different from cost, perhaps *payment options* are important to you. Some people are not comfortable paying by credit card and want to see PayPal or other payment options, such as BitCoin.

Before signing up to a longer-term plan, consider starting with a short-term one first to make sure that everything works well for you. Many services offer monthly plans. Some even offer free trials or money-back guarantees.

Exit Gateway Locations

Most VPN services will allow you to choose the location of the *exit gateways* you use. These are the countries in which the service's proxy servers are located. This gives you some control over which country the IP address your Internet traffic appears to be coming from. So, if you wanted to watch content that is only available to people based in the US and you live or are travelling outside the US, being able to choose your VPN's exit gateways would enable you to watch the content.

In addition, anyone snooping on your Internet traffic will think you are based in the location of the exit gateway, rather than your actual location. If the snoop traced back the traffic to the proxy servers where the exit gateway is located, this would lead them to the VPN service, rather than you. If you want to make sure that that's where the chain of discovery will end and cannot be further traced back to you, read the VPN service's *Privacy Policy* to learn about what information they log about customer (your) activities and for how long.

Generally speaking, you want a VPN that has exit gateways in many different locations; the more, the better.

Advanced Features

Other features offered by VPN anonymizing services might include allowing you to *automatically* select the fastest exit gateways at any given time.

A *kill switch* is a feature that disables your Internet connection should your VPN unexpectedly disconnect. This helps ensure that your true IP address is not compromised due to any technical glitches.

DNS leak protection ensures that some special connections your device makes over the Internet at a very low technical level are also routed through the VPN, ensuring the maximum level of privacy and security possible.

Yet other features will even let you "split" your connection so that the Internet traffic for some apps, such as a specific web browser or torrent file-sharing, are routed through the service and anonymized, while the traffic for your other apps continue to be routed through a regular (non-anonymized) Internet connection.

More About: *Why split?* - There may be times when you do *not* want to route your Internet traffic through foreign exit gateways, because many websites, such as search engines or online retailers, automatically redirect you to their country-specific sites or restrict the content you can stream or access.

A Word about Technical Specifications

Sometimes you will see a long list of various technical specifications included among a VPN service's features. These technical terms may include PPTP, L2TP IPSec, SSTP, OpenVPN, SSL and TLS. Don't let these confuse you. The bottom line is that they all provide a secure, encrypted connection keeping your activities safe from eavesdropping and monitoring, whether from online trackers and profilers, your ISP or from other potential snoops.

So you do not need to get wrapped up in what these are. You also don't need to worry about which one of the technical specifications is "best". Each one has its intricacies, but not enough for us to worry about for web browsing or even torrent file-sharing (discussed in chapter 16). What is important is that it provides a secure (encrypted) connection and hides your true IP address, masking it with a decoy one – all of those technical specifications listed above will do that.

Top Tip - Please keep in mind that, though these services anonymize your Internet traffic and help ensure your online privacy, they do *not* make you invincible to things such as viruses, malware and other similar threats. So keep practicing good habits on your devices, such as using anti-malware apps and being careful about the downloads, attachments and links you open.

Customer Experience

Customer experience should also be a factor that weighs on your choice of an anonymizing VPN service. While the service provider's website will tout lots of satisfied customers and testimonials (what else would you expect?), some research is in order.

You can also Google around to find information about customers' experiences. However, make sure that the advice is from a *trustworthy*, ideally independent source. For example, there are lots of websites purporting to "review" anonymizing VPN services when really these websites are not quite as unbiased as they claim. Too often, these sites are acting unethically and posing as independent reviewers without disclosing their affiliations to the services they are "reviewing", all in an attempt to lure you into signing up for services that generate commissions. Ethical practice dictates that reviewers should disclose when they are serving up potentially commission-generating affiliate links.

Recommended VPN Services

Not all VPNs are created equal. Some perform admirably and deserve a place in your privacy tool arsenal. Over the past several years, I have come to trust a handful of VPNs to help protect my privacy. In my humble opinion, here are the best VPNs on the market today at the time of publishing. Also check http://www.cogipas.com/choose-best-vpn/ for updated information.

Remember that you can often use a VPN for a number of Internet activities ranging from web browsing, social media, chat and torrent file-sharing. Carefully check the features of any VPN service as you may be able to get more bang for your buck!

I am comfortable recommending the following services to you based on my own personal satisfaction with the factors I believe are most important, including:

- Ease of use (installation, setup and day-to-day use)
- Breadth (lots of different exit gateway locations)
- Privacy (customer protections regarding logging)
- Reliability (minimal downtime and connection drops)
- Speed (fast downloading)

Best Choice for Privacy and Anonymity

Private Internet Access or PIA ¢ http://www.cogipas.com/pia gets very high marks on the five factors I listed above. After signing up and paying for the service, you will receive your user id and password credentials by email and be asked to download an app. After installing the app, you enter your credentials and off you go!

The app lets you choose an exit gateway location (see screenshot) – they offer over 2000 servers in 12 countries and growing – or you can simply rely on the app's "auto" feature to choose the fastest connection available. PIA supports advanced features such as a "kill switch" and DNS leak protection.

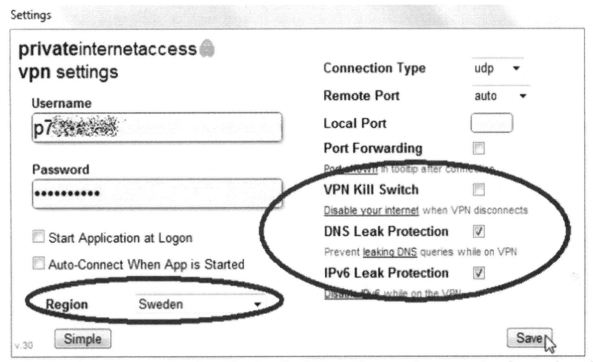

Figure: PIA's app supports region selection (letting you choose exit gateways) and a number of advanced features

PIA expressly caters to privacy conscious customers and has one of the best privacy policies in the business. PIA goes to great pains not to collect or log its user's activities in any way. You can read this for yourself in PIA's privacy policy on their website.

On my wish list for PIA would be that its app display a little more detail. Currently, only a small green icon indicates you are connected and I wish I could see more details about the connection, masked IP address and speed when the service is enabled.

Overall, PIA ¢ http://www.cogipas.com/pia is an excellent full-fledged VPN service, anonymizing all of your Internet traffic from web browsing to torrent file-sharing (discussed in chapter 16).

Best Choice for Ease of Use and Bypassing Restrictions (Accessing Streaming Content)

I have used PureVPN ¢ http://www.cogipas.com/purevpn for a number of years and have only praise for them. Established in 2006, PureVPN has earned its longevity, is very easy to use and is backed up by effective support. After opening an account on the PureVPN website you will receive a confirmation email with your user id and password for accessing the service. This same email will also contain direct links to the app you need to download. After installing the app and entering your user id and password, you will be anonymous in no time (see screenshot). That's all there is to it.

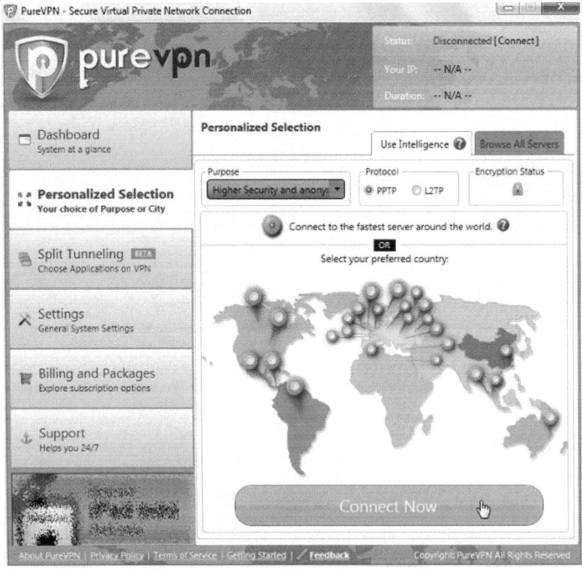

Figure: PureVPN.com's easy-to-use anonymizing app

In addition to fulfilling the five factors I listed earlier, I just really like using PureVPN's app. In one easy place, I can *Quick Connect* relying on the service to choose the best options for me or I can use *Personalized Selection* for choosing how and through which exit gateways to connect. Its *Dashboard* lets me see my connection speed at a glance.

PureVPN now offers over 450+ servers in 89 countries and counting, offering over 77,000 different IP addresses you can hide behind. PureVPN has servers that are solely dedicated for streaming content which ensures, for example, that even high-definition (HD) videos you watch with the VPN enabled will be smooth and fast. PureVPN offers great value as it lets you connect to their service with up to 5 devices simultaneously, so you can protect your desktop computers, laptops, tablets and your smartphones too with just a single account.

Importantly, PureVPN is backed up by good, responsive 24/7 online live chat support staffed by actual human beings – no endless death loops of reading generic FAQs. PureVPN's speed and reliability have been consistently excellent for me. Perhaps it's purely psychological, but I also derive some comfort from PureVPN being headquartered outside of the US and the EU. I also like PureVPN's *Split Tunneling* feature which lets me cherry-pick which app traffic to route through the anonymizing service. As PureVPN is a full-fledged VPN that protects my entire Internet connection, I use it to anonymize my web browsing and torrent file-sharing activities (see chapter 16).

Overall, PureVPN ¢ http://www.cogipas.com/purevpn is a great VPN protecting all of your Internet activities, from web browsing to torrent file-sharing. Its huge global footprint makes it especially ideal if you are new to VPNs or are focused on using Wi-Fi hotspots, accessing streaming content or bypassing content blocked from your location.

Other Popular VPN Services

If you prefer to check out different VPN services, below are some other popular ones, including as reported by *LifeHacker* and *TorrentFreak*, both reliable sources of VPN information. Of course, just because a VPN is popular doesn't mean that it's right for you, so do check features carefully against the list of factors I provided earlier in the chapter.

- *HMA* ¢ http://www.cogipas.com/HMA is a long-standing VPN with exit gateways in over 120 countries, making it one of the biggest VPNs in the industry and another good choice especially for VPN newcomers

- *TorGuard* ¢ http://www.cogipas.com/TorGuard is a popular VPN with over 1000 exit gateway servers in over 40 countries and which expressly does not log user activity. From its name you might think that it's affiliated with the free web anonymizing service, The Onion Router (discussed in chapter 13), but it's not. The "Tor" in its name is a reference more to "torrents" (discussed in chapter 16) as this VPN service caters especially to torrent file-sharing customers.

- *IronSocket* ¢ http://www.cogipas.com/IronSocket is a new VPN but looks promising with 50 servers in 36 countries and emphasizing anonymity features such as keeping no user activity logs of any kind

- If you are merely looking for solid protection when using Wi-Fi public hotspots, such as at airports and coffee shops, consider *HotSpotShield* (free) http://www.hotspotshield.com/ or its premium *Elite* version ¢ http://www.cogipas.com/hotspotshield. It is an immensely popular (200+ *million* downloads) and easy-to-use way to encrypt your web browsing activities end-to-end. The free version displays ads.

Testing Your Web Anonymizing VPN Service: What is My IP Address?

Whichever VPN you decide to use, you should always make sure that it is working properly by testing it before you start browsing the web.

The easiest way to test your VPN is at a number of websites once you've enabled (activated) your VPN. Some suggestions are listed below. Visit these sites to make sure that your web anonymizing service is working and that your true IP address is not being revealed. If it is working properly, these sites should report the IP address of your VPN rather than your true IP address.

Resources to Check Your IP Address

Depending on how detailed a check you want to perform, some of these checks are bare bones, providing a quick IP address check, while others probe more deeply, providing a more thorough check on the kind of information that can be obtained about your connection.

- in Google, or better yet https://duckduckgo.com/, simply type "IP address" and your public IP address will be displayed
- https://www.privateinternetaccess.com/pages/whats-my-ip/ (a secure https page)
- http://www.ip-adress.com/ (nice and basic with a location map)
- http://www.tracemyip.org/
- http://www.pobralem.pl/
- http://ip-check.info/ (whoa – select 'Start Test' to see comprehensive results)

Top Tip - For an updated listing of 'what is my IP address' tools, visit www.cogipas.com/whats-my-ip/. Consider adding this page to your favorites for quickly and easily verifying your IP address.

How to Use a Web Ripping App to Mass Download Items from the Web like a Vacuum Cleaner (Advanced Users)

Web ripping means downloading the content of an entire website (or parts of it) based on certain criteria you choose. These criteria could be based on item type, for example, videos, images, programs or documents. Criteria could also be based on location, for example, everything found in the subdirectory http://www.example.com/videos/.

Using a web ripping app saves you from the tedious task of having to download items from a website individually, one-at-a time. It's especially wise to use these apps with your VPN enabled.

A decent free alternative is *HTTrack Website Copier* (free) http://www.httrack.com/, a powerful, free open source web ripper. The FAQ and detailed information about filters on their website are helpful, especially if you are seeking to download particular item types from a website.

Internet Download Manager or *IDM* ¢ (premium) http://www.cogipas.com/idm is the best mass downloader around and it offers a 30-day free trial. IDM is also a great online video "grabber" enabling you to save to your device streaming video (and audio) such as those played on YouTube.

IDM's *Site Grabber* feature is what really stands out with an easy, yet powerful wizard walking you through the mass downloading process (see screenshot). You can choose to download the contents of an entire website or parts of it, whether its pages, videos, images and/or documents. If you like, the Site Grabber can immediately start downloading items or it can show you an inventory of all the items available for potential download, allowing you to select which ones to grab. It will even let you schedule your web ripping downloads and resume any interrupted downloads.

On my wish list for IDM is that it would leave behind less traces on your device about what you downloaded, so make sure that you erase trace information after using this app (see chapter 18).

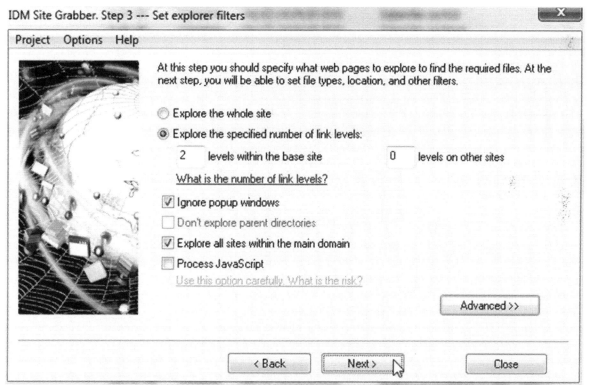

Figure: IDM's Site Grabber feature is a flexible and an easy way to "rip" website content

* * *

For updates and additional information about anonymous web browsing and how to throw the online trackers, profilers and snoops off your trial, please visit http://www.cogipas.com/anonymous-web-browsing/.

Chapter 13: Using Tor (The Onion Router) to be Anonymous on the Web

Introduction

The Onion Router, better known by its acronym *Tor*, is a special kind of web anonymizing service. Tor is similar in some ways to VPNs covered in the previous chapter but, at the same time, also nothing like them. For this reason Tor deserves its own chapter.

What is Tor?

Tor is a term used to describe a bundle of free, open source apps available for download at https://www.torproject.org/ that aim to provide users with online anonymity. Tor is cross-platform and compatible with Windows, Linux, Android, iOS, and Mac O/S. The concept behind Tor was originally developed by the US Naval research laboratory for protecting government communications. Tor helps you to achieve anonymity online and protect yourself from network surveillance by enabling anonymous connections through a worldwide network of more than 3000 *relays* (explained below).

Tor's two main functions are to allow users to browse the web *anonymously* and to *bypass censorship*. While Tor cannot 100% guarantee absolute anonymity, it makes it much more difficult for snoops to detect, trace or block your web-based Internet activity.

How Tor Works

Crucially, Tor camouflages your connection by sending data packets through a virtual path of randomly selected *relays* set up by Tor and its volunteers all around the world. Anybody can set up a relay and doing so helps support the important cause of online anonymity.

By default, data sent over the Tor network travels through at least three relays before reaching its final destination (for example, the web page you want to visit). Two relays act as *inside relays*, transmitting the data *within* the Tor network, and the last relay functions as an *exit relay* (or *exit node*) which transmits the data outside the Tor network to the final destination.

In addition, data transmitted over the Tor network is *encrypted*. This protects your data from being monitored whether by your ISP, governments, hackers or other potential snoops and adversaries.

These features mean that the *destination* of your web requests will be able to detect only the transmitted IP address of the exit node (the last contact point of your request with Tor). Your true IP address remains untraceable because your data travelled through a number of relays before reaching the exit node. The exit node remains unaware of the source of the original request, protecting your IP address. So even if a snoop could trace the IP address arriving at the exit node before the request was forwarded to the final destination, your IP address is still protected by 2 more intermediate relays. Now you start to understand why it is called the *onion* router: the protection it offers is similar to the multiple layers of an onion.

For example, with Tor enabled if you visit www.cogipas.com the route this request (data) takes looks like this:

>> you enter the URL >> *multiple inside gateway nodes* >> exit node >> destination

As you can see, Tor introduces a number of intermediary steps (the italicized ones) in what would normally be the process.

Tor May Slow You Down

All this serves to conceal the routing of transmitted data, protects your privacy and keeps you anonymous by masking your true IP address, but often slows things down. Your traffic will be traveling to different Tor relays and nodes located in different parts of the world and at varying speeds. For these reasons, your speeds when connected to Tor may be slower. But protecting your privacy at the expense of a potential small drop in your web browsing speed seems a small price to pay.

How to Get Started Using Tor

To start using Tor, visit https://www.torproject.org/ and download and install the Tor Browser for Windows. It contains a tailored version of the Mozilla Firefox web browser app which is preconfigured and requires no additional installation or settings to change.

An installation wizard will guide you. After choosing your language and the location on your device for the installation (the default locations are fine) the installation will take a few moments. At the end of the installation process you will be prompted to *Run Tor Browser*.

Now an important step: you will be prompted for 1 of 2 different connection settings. This will be determined by how you answer a question (see screenshot).

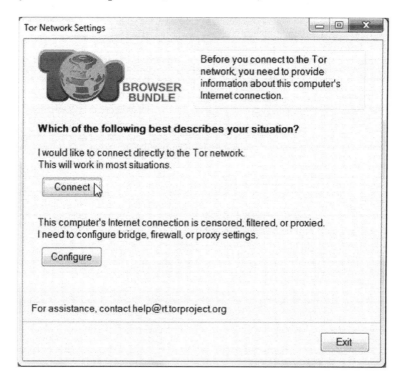

For most people, the first option 'I would like to connect directly to the Tor network' will be fine (the balance of this section assumes you have made this choice).

Top Tip - The second option applies if, for example, you are in a country that censors or restricts Internet access (in this case Tor's user interface, *Vidalia*, will also be installed allowing you to bypass censorship by connecting to Tor through something called a bridge – discussed later).

The installer will proceed to connect you to the Tor network and, once successful, to launch the Tor Browser.

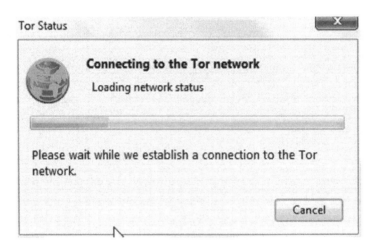

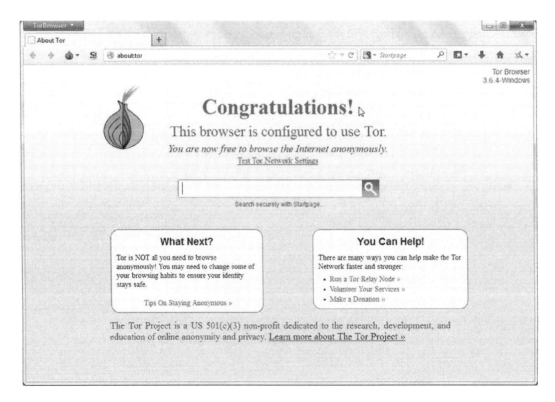

Once Tor Browser has started, you use it like you would any other web browser. You can be confident that you are anonymized when visiting websites with the Tor Browser because the associated data is being sent through the Tor network. Please note that only data sent using Tor Browser is being anonymized and sent through the Tor network. Any websites you visit using a different web browser will not be anonymized. This is important because your device may open links, for example contained in email messages, with a different web browser.

You may have noticed that the process of connecting to the Tor network is different from using a web anonymizing VPN service (see chapter 12). With a VPN you usually launch a separate app that enables the VPN and then you use your *everyday* apps, including web browser. In contrast, with the Tor Browser, all the web browsing activities you conduct with it are automatically anonymized.

Top Tip - Although it is possible to manually configure other apps supporting *SOCKS proxy* protocol to send data through the Tor network, it is highly recommended that only advanced users ever try this as doing so may still leave you open to a number of other ways that your IP address could be exposed including via cookies, JavaScript, browser plugins, etc.

If you explore Tor Browser's settings you will see that its plugins are either empty or disabled and that it comes preconfigured with a number of plugins and add-ons to enhance your online anonymity (see screenshot). For example, the *HTTPS-Everywhere* add-on ensures that you connect with a secure (HTTPS) connection to websites supporting them.

To ensure that your true IP address is indeed being shielded and kept anonymous by the Tor network, use the same methods described in chapter 12 for VPNs. That is, visit trusted 'What's my IP Address' pages on the web such as http://ip-check.info/ or those maintained at http://www.cogipas.com/whats-my-ip/ to confirm that you are connected to the Tor network and that your true IP address is not being transmitting.

Finally, when you are finished anonymously browsing the web and you close the Tor Browser, it will automatically delete your web browsing history. Because it is user-friendly and gaffe-resistant, using Tor Browser is the easiest, most popular and safest way to send data through the Tor network.

Tor's Limitations

However, Tor isn't fool-proof. If you want to reduce the risk of your web browsing activities being tracked and profiled online, and to stay hidden from snoops or overcome censorship, Tor is a great (and free!) choice. Nevertheless, if you want to rely on Tor to engage in Snowden-like whistle-blowing or other similarly super-sensitive activities, you need to know that Tor does have some limitations you need to be aware of.

For example, older versions of the Tor browser were found to be vulnerable to *JavaScript attacks*. Such attacks were used to reveal users' IP addresses. Apparently, this vulnerability was used by the FBI to track down the founder of the biggest *Darknet* hosting platform, Freedom Hosting (see box).

More About: *Darknet* - Darknet is a collection of hidden websites that can only be accessed on the Tor network, forming a sort of anonymous subset of the world wide web. The servers hosting Darknet sites are configured in such a way that inbound connections are received only through Tor. Such techniques completely hide the website's location (IP address) from the "normal" (un*Tor*ed) Internet.

Also be aware that some sites, including popular ones such as Wikipedia, Google, Yndex and Facebook, block messages sent from Tor relays in order to combat potential misuse (spam for example).

Keep in mind that your true IP address is shared with *entry relays* on the Tor network. Tor hides traffic from nodes along the way, but *not* from the exit node or the final destination, so it does not prevent traffic from being analyzed upon leaving the Tor network. In addition, Tor does not encrypt traffic that leaves the Tor network from an exit relay to the final destination server. This means that the exit node can "see" any traffic passing through it (unless end-to-end encryption was used such as the HTTPS protocol). Consequently, an exit node could in theory be able to access your transmitted data including login, password, cookie and other potentially personally identifiable information.

In addition, Tor is simply unsuitable from the get go for some activities, including torrent file-sharing (discussed in chapter 16). Tor is simply not engineered to work effectively with the huge volumes of data often associated with torrents. Trying to use Tor for torrents will not render you anonymous. Your true IP address will leak and be visible.

In addition, unless you take some complicated steps that only advanced users should consider, you cannot mask that you are using Tor. This is because the addresses of Tor exit nodes are publicly accessible and traffic coming from Tor can be detected through *sniffing* and *deep packet inspection* (DPI) techniques. These identification techniques allow website operators, governments and sophisticated adversaries to prevent connections from Tor exit relays or to limit their functionality.

Another related risk comes from *website fingerprinting*. When an adversary knows about the websites you may be interested in, they can monitor and analyze the patterns that flow between these websites and the users accessing them. These patterns can be used as a way to track you down. To minimize the risk of website fingerprinting, Tor started transmitting data in uniform sized chunks making it harder for adversaries to track patterns, but this does not completely eliminate the risk.

Generally speaking, risks to your anonymity on Tor usually result more from your own activities, such as trying to use it with unsupported, insecure or "leaky" (poorly designed) apps that reveal your IP address. Other examples of user-related actions that can breach your identity include opening unreliable documents, visiting and falling for phishing scams or, as mentioned, for torrent file-sharing.

While Tor isn't perfect, it's community is constantly working on reducing possible risks to users' anonymity and is regularly updating its technology. You needn't worry too much about these risks if you are using Tor to help thwart online tracking and profiling. The technical vulnerabilities outlined above can only be exploited by the most sophisticated of adversaries. If you are more of a typical everyday user of Tor and follow the guidelines in this chapter, you can be confident about being well protected. But many people face difficult circumstances, living under the shadow of Internet censorship, suppressed speech or oppressive regimes. So if you are an Internet campaigner and/or live in a country with an oppressive regime where Internet freedoms are curtailed, you will need to give these risks more consideration.

Best Practices for Using Tor

In order to benefit as much as possible from Tor (and to minimize the possible risks) follow these recommendations to best protect your anonymity on the web:

- Always use Tor Browser, which is configured to protect your anonymity while browsing the web.

- Don't use browser plugins, add-ons or other extensions than those already pre-configured with Tor Browser. In addition, keep turned off Flash, ActiveX, Java and JavaScript. Also avoid streaming video or audio in Tor Browser because these activities may reveal your true IP address.

- Avoid opening documents downloaded through Tor when you are online. Such documents, including DOC or PDF files, may contain hidden elements initiating a communication (for example, automatically trying to load some code or an invisible image outside of the Tor connection). This could inevitably expose your true IP address. To ensure your online anonymity, open any downloaded items *after* disconnecting from Tor or, ideally, when you have gone completely offline.

- Don't use Tor for torrent file-sharing. Instead, consider an anonymizing torrent service (see chapter 16).

- Use a different user account or profile on your device when using Tor compared to when conducting your "normal" web browsing, similar to the techniques mentioned in chapter 9.

- Use HTTPS encryption as much as possible when visiting websites. This will encrypt and protect your traffic when it is being transmitted from an exit node to the final destination. As mentioned earlier, Tor has the *HTTPS Everywhere* plugin which forces websites supporting HTTPS to connect to you with an encrypted connection. Unfortunately, not all websites support secure https connections, but *HTTPS Everywhere* helps ensure you connect as securely as possible. You should always check to make sure that URLs (website addresses) begin with *https://*. Using HTTPS encryption makes it all the more difficult for an adversary to intercept your information as they would need to break the end-to-end encrypted transmission.

Further Tor Topics (Advanced Users)

You already have the information you need to use Tor to browse the web anonymously. However, perhaps you want to delve a little deeper into Tor or its wider community. If so, I have posted additional Tor-related materials at www.cogipas.com/tor-onion-router-more/ including:

- How to Configure Relays
- How to Access Tor if you are Blocked
- How to Help a Blocked Friend Access Tor
- Accessing Tor through a Proxy

Top Tip - For ultimate protection, advanced users might consider using a *live operating system* that has Tor anonymity at the heart of its design. One such live operating system is *TAILS* https://tails.boum.org/. You can boot up a desktop or laptop computer directly into the Tails Operating System from a DVD/CD, USB memory stick or SD card. Using TAILS leaves no trace data behind on the computer and forces all Internet communications through the Tor network.

* * *

For updates and additional information about using Tor (The Onion Router) to be anonymous on the web, please visit http://www.cogipas.com/using-tor-the-onion-router-to-be-anonymous-on-the-web/.

Chapter 14: Secure, Private and Anonymous Email

Introduction

It goes without saying that is a good idea to keep your email address private. Spammers, snoops and hackers alike want to know your email address so that they can exploit it for their own gain whether by targeting your inbox with advertising or with phishing, spear phishing and spoofing attempts.

This chapter will first explain the basics of email and demonstrate how email travels over the Internet and tell you what *email headers* are all about. The materials will then address the best ways of setting up an *alternate webmail account*.

There may be times when you want to use *temporary email* (aka *disposable email*) which can be especially useful when you are reluctant to share your primary personal email address.

You will learn how it's possible to send emails (including with attachments) anonymously. The best protection available comes from using *remailers*, but these can be complicated and so are more for advanced users. Remailers empower you to send emails in such a way that the recipient (or anyone intercepting the message) will not be able to determine from where it came. You will also be shown an easier way to take advantage of remailers by using anonymizing web-based remailers.

How Private is Your Email Address?

To help give your email address a low profile, first enable any features your email app or provider supports blocking *email bugs* (also known as *beacons*). This blocking protection usually takes the form of a *block images* option in your email settings. When images are displayed in your email, this can be used to send a signal back to a third party server indicating that the message was opened.

If you don't block images Internet marketers as well as online trackers and profilers will be able to verify your email account and its active status. This will result in you receiving only more targeted advertising by email. Specific, targeted bugs or beacons can also be embedded in email messages to track your particular reaction to a promotion or other call to action.

Top Tip - If your email address becomes associated with your IP address, this becomes yet another source of information for the detailed profiles being compiled about you by those tracking and profiling online activities discussed in chapter 4.

Use the following resources to check how private your email address is. If your email address is no longer private, this may make you more widely known and therefore susceptible to spammers, snoops and hackers.

- simply type your email address in your favorite search engine (usually in double quotes is best, "name@example.com")

- *email monitoring services* (all free) such as *PwnedList* https://pwnedlist.com/, *HackNotifier* http://www.hacknotifier.com/ and *Lastpass* https://lastpass.com/adobe/ enable you to check whether your email account has been part of any password data obtained or leaked by hackers. If you want to monitor your email account for *future* hacks, most services will charge a monthly subscription fee.

- *reverse email trace* services check whether your email account shows up in *public databases* (not hacker lists). Try searching for free at *EmailTracer* ¢ http://www.cogipas.com/EmailTracer, *EmailFinder.com* ¢ http://www.cogipas.com/EmailFinder and *IP-Adress.com* http://www.ip-adress.com/trace_email/ or type "reverse email trace" in your favorite search engine to find similar services.

Top Tip - Before blindly submitting your email address to these or any other website you must be confident that the service is trustworthy and not providing your email address to third parties. If you think about it, what a great way to obtain active email addresses. That said, I'm reasonably confident that these longstanding services are legitimate, but you should always perform your own due diligence including by reading their Terms of Service and Privacy Policy.

Email Basics

Apart from keeping your email address private and undisclosed, you also may want to keep the *contents* of your emails secure and away from snoops and other prying eyes. Email remains as popular as ever but, if sent unencrypted, emails are an insecure means of communication.

For email, at a minimum, you should:

- set up and use an *alternate webmail account* that is separate from your primary personal email account, ideally accessing it while using a web anonymizing service such as a web proxy, Tor or a VPN

- *trust* the people you correspond with, especially for incoming messages containing links or attachments

Email Travels over the Internet as Plain Text

It is important to understand that your email messages pass through several systems on their journey to the intended recipient(s). The system operators (or *administrators* or *sysops*) of each of those intermediary systems, and any snoops along the way, have the opportunity to read your messages. The analogy of emails being similar to postcards, rather than letters in sealed envelopes, is often invoked and it is a good one.

Therefore, unless you take special steps or use special apps or services to encrypt your email messages, they travel as *plain text* over the Internet and are vulnerable to being saved, copied or read along their journey.

In addition, it is no secret that employers (at least in the US) routinely monitor employees' email messages. Employees should always assume that they have *no privacy* when sending email messages using their employer's equipment or facilities.

If you are engaging in any sensitive activities by email – whether for pleasure or business - you need to understand and appreciate the risks. Generally speaking, email is completely insecure and fully traceable. Just ask General Patreus. Whoops make that *former* General Patreus.

For most emails you send, this lack of security may be a reasonable trade-off for the convenience it offers. But for some of your emails you would be wise to take further measures to ensure that intercepted messages cannot be read by snoops.

You should never send any truly sensitive information by ordinary email. For sensitive messages, you should either *encrypt* your messages using something such as *OpenPGP* (free) http://www.openpgp.org/ or use a specialized encrypted webmail service (discussed in the pages ahead).

How Email Can Be Traced (Headers)

Every email consists of three elements:

1. memo-style information (Date, To, From, Subject, Cc. and Bcc.)
2. message body
3. headers

Depending on the email you use, you may never see the *headers* mentioned at item 3 above, whereas all email apps and providers display the information mentioned at items 1 and 2. In fact, most email apps and providers do *not* display detailed header information by default. To see the detailed email headers, check for options such as 'Show all headers' or in Gmail select the small down arrow icon and select 'Show original'.

Some fictional email headers are illustrated below.

```
Return-Path: <from@anydomain.org>
X-SpamCatcher-Score: 1 [X]
Received: from [176.163.40.119] (HELO anydomain.org)
    by fe3.anydomain.org (CommuniGate Pro SMTP 4.1.8)
    with ESMTP-TLS id 61258719 for to@mail.anydomain.org;
Message-ID: <4129F3CA.2020509@anydomain.org>
Date: Wed, 21 Jan 2(※※ 12:52:00 -0500 (EST)
From: Taylor Evans <from@anydomain.org>
User-Agent: Mozilla/5.0 (Windows; U; Windows NT 5.1; en-US; rv:1.0.1)
X-Accept-Language: en-us, en
MIME-Version: 1.0
To: Joe Blow <to@mail.anydomain.org>
Subject: Business Development Meeting
Content-Type: text/plain; charset=us-ascii; format=flowed
Content-Transfer-Encoding: 7bit
```

Figure: An example of some fictional email headers

- From: and Reply-To: (sometimes seen as Reply-Path: or Return-Path:)

  Though it is usually easy to change the From setting in your email preferences (putting in a fake email address), this is a low and misleading level of "anonymity" given the information contained in the headers of email messages.

  These standard memo-style fields are easily forged by modifying the Preferences or Settings. For example, in Gmail, select the gear icon in the top upper-right and then select *Settings > Accounts and Import*, and then look for the option *Send email as:*. Beside this to the right, select the small prompt *edit info*. A screen will appear letting you change the name and *reply-to* email address displayed in your messages.

- Received:

  This is the hardest header to forge and is thus the most reliable for tracking down the origins of an email. This header lists, in reverse chronological order, all the servers through which the message was relayed before reaching the recipient. Depending on the path taken by the email, some mail systems will add the IP address where the email originated.

- Message-ID:

  This is a unique value assigned to the message by the originating system that usually ends with the domain name of the server from which the message was sent.

- Comment:

  Different email apps and email providers may add additional information to the headers in the form of comments. An example of one revealing comment you sometimes see is that of Authenticated sender, the sender's supposed true identity.

- Sender: (or X-Sender:)

  This is another header you may sometimes see. Even if the From: header of an email is forged, the email app or email provider may (it's supposed to, but often doesn't) insert the sender's true identity.

Recommended Secure Email Services

The most secure email services include full encryption, not just as a secure HTTPS *connection* when signing in to them, but end-to-end encryption for message *contents* as well. Encryption helps to ensure that an email cannot be monitored, logged, analyzed and stored by your ISP, your employer, or snoops who have or gain access to the messages along their journey from you to the final recipient(s).

In the wake of Edward Snowden's revelations, there are more email services touting security features. However, you must choose wisely. Some services I recommend are found below. Please note that to fully benefit from the encryption features, often the sender *and* recipient must *both* use a compatible service or related app, such as the already mentioned *OpenPGP* (free) http://www.openpgp.org/.

When comparing any webmail services with your privacy and security in mind, it will be no surprise to hear me say that you should read the provider's Terms of Service and check their Privacy Policy, especially regarding the disclosure of your personal information to third parties.

HushMail (premium) http://www.cogipas.com/HushMail has been in business since 1999, uses strong encryption and is considered a reliable secure email provider. Free accounts are available, but must be accessed frequently to remain active.

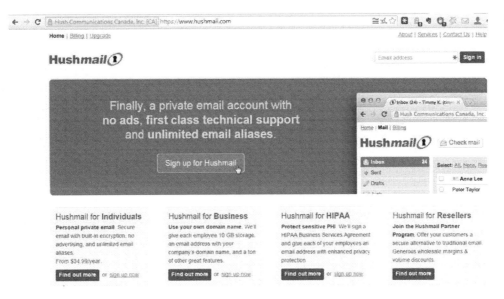

AnonymousSpeech Secure Email ¢ (premium) http://www.cogipas.com/AnonymousSpeech features offshore servers outside US and Europe, anonymity (no logging of IP addresses) and encryption. AnonymousSpeech also supports the OpenPGP Standard for email messages *without* needing to install any apps on your device; it does all the complicated work for you seamlessly in the background. A free trial account is available.

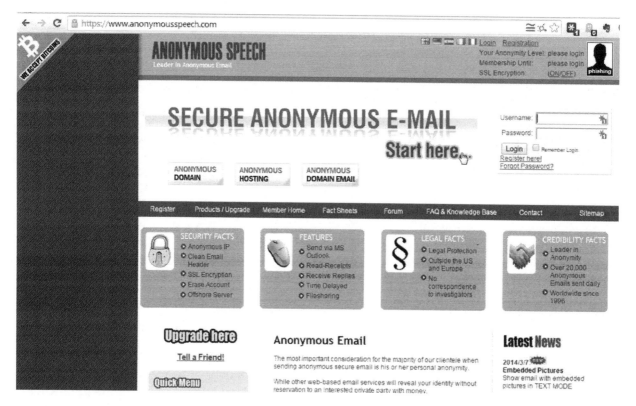

If you want to investigate other potential secure email services, type "private email accounts" or "encrypted email" into your favorite search engine, but do some due diligence to ensure the provider is reliable and trustworthy.

Using an Alternate Webmail Account for a Basic Level of Security and Privacy

A distant second best option to a fully encrypted email service is to use an alternate webmail account. This can be a quick and easy step towards some degree of protecting your email privacy. You can usually sign up providing a bare minimum of information. Accordingly, such accounts are easy to establish, including for a temporary purpose or to abandon later. There are also services offering disposable *temporary email addresses*, discussed later in the chapter.

Of course, your webmail account is only as secure as the passphrase you choose for it, so ensure that you use a strong passphrase. See chapter 3 for a refresher. However, even using strong passphrases to access your webmail account won't prevent rogue system administrators (sysops) or opportune snoops from peeking at your messages in transit over the Internet. To be clear, only encrypting the contents of your communications will protect you against this risk.

Also keep in mind that most webmail providers will log activity and track your IP address. Of course, this can be countered by accessing the site while using a web anonymizing service such as a web proxy, Tor or a VPN.

Webmail can also sometimes offer a form of enhanced *security* as webmail providers are increasingly protecting their users with an *encrypted connection*, a Secure Sockets Layer (SSL) connection, which you can see when URLs start with HTTPS (note the 's'). This enhanced connection protects your email message contents from being monitored or intercepted while in transit from your web browser to the webmail provider's servers. This is especially important if you are using a wireless Internet connection or Wi-Fi hotspot.

Another advantage of webmail is that many providers include robust *spam filters*, as well as protection against *malware* and *phishing attacks*. Coupled with virtually limitless storage, webmail is an attractive way of achieving a basic level of privacy and security.

Setting up Your Alternate Webmail Account

Follow these steps to minimize your online fingerprints when signing up for and then when using your alternate webmail account.

- If you want to conceal your true IP address when signing up for an alternate webmail account, you can enable your web anonymizing service whether a proxy, Tor or a VPN. If the webmail service uses a secure HTTPS connection, make sure that your web anonymizing service supports this, otherwise visiting these sites will by-pass the web anonymizing service and transmit your true IP address. If all is in order, you are all set to sign up for your alternate webmail account.

- When signing-up for the webmail service, avoid providing any personal information. Similarly, for your password hints do not use any information that is personally identifiable.

- If, as part of the signup for the alternate webmail account, you need to verify an already existing email address, use a disposable temporary email address (discussed next) rather than your primary personal email account.

- Once signed up and depending on how sensitive your activities, you could always use a web anonymizing service such as a proxy, Tor or a VPN when accessing the account (not only when sending messages but also when reading messages). Remember that logs of IP addresses are probably being kept by the webmail provider.

- Don't be tempted to test your alternate webmail account by sending messages to your primary personal email account. There is no point going through all the trouble above if an adversary need only check your sent items folder. Similarly, never CC or BCC messages to your primary personal email account.

- For truly sensitive messages that you need to send anonymously, understand that your alternate webmail account is *not* sufficiently secure for this and that you should instead use a *remailer* (discussed later in this chapter) to send anonymous messages.

- If you face sophisticated or well resourced adversaries and have accessed the alternate webmail without a web anonymizing service enabled, abandon the account and never access it again. In such cases it is better to start over and set up a new alternate webmail account than risk having your identity revealed.

Using Temporary Email for Private Sign-ups

Introduction

Another way to keep your primary personal email address private is to use disposable *temporary email addresses* in certain circumstances.

You should only share your primary personal email address with trusted people. This general rule also applies when signing up to unknown websites or services. Unfortunately, there is plenty of justification for being leery when signing up for online accounts.

Disreputable sites can be associated with Internet abuses such as spam, malware and phishing attempts. Even if we just take the example of spam, it only takes one unscrupulous website operator to provide your email address to anyone willing to pay for it resulting in your inbox filling up with junk mail. Before you know it, your inbox is being inundated with spam, malware-infected messages, phishing attempts or worse.

The best way to prevent this is to use a temporary email address when signing up to new accounts. This is a disposable email address that helps you to sign-up at websites and for online accounts without ever having to provide your primary personal email address, not even to the temporary email service itself.

How Temporary Email Works

When you do not want to provide your primary personal email address, you can use temporary email as follows. When signing up for, subscribing to or joining a new account, you will reach a stage where you will be asked to provide an email address. Open another web browser tab (or window) and visit the temporary email service. Follow the service's instructions to obtain a disposable email address and use it at the new account's signup page.

As usual, the signup site will send a message asking you to confirm your subscription or membership. You can access this confirmation message (and perhaps future ones) by visiting the "inbox" of your temporary email address. This inbox is usually nothing more than a webpage generated for your particular temporary email address. In this inbox you should see the signup site's confirmation email. Select it as you would for any signup confirmation.

Voila! You are signed up without ever having had to disclose your primary personal email address to *anyone*, neither the signup site nor the temporary email service. You can now login on to the site you've just joined and come and go as you please.

Features vary among temporary email services. Some provide email addresses that last only a few minutes, others provide addresses that never expire allowing you to check the inbox in the future, so choose a service that best fits with your given requirements.

A temporary email service will only need to ask for your primary personal email address if you want it to *forward* messages it receives. So, for any services asking for your primary personal email address, you will have to be confident that the service is reputable and reliable, and won't itself engage in the very spamming or other abusive practices you were trying to avoid in the first place.

But most of the services work by accessing a temporary inbox, without the need to provide it with your primary personal email address. You check the inbox for the message(s) you need, for example to confirm a signup, and then forget about it, essentially disposing of the temporary email account.

Note that these services may not be appropriate for all purposes. This technique is especially good for one-off signups such as providing an email address for a download or signing up for a website you won't have longer-term contact with. However, if you are joining a site that you may use over the longer-term, a temporary email address with a short shelf life may not be that helpful as you could miss out on future messages. For such longer-term requirements, you may prefer a temporary email service that lasts longer (sometimes you have to pay for this) or that accommodates email forwarding (but this will mean providing your primary personal email address to the temporary email service).

You can also try having the best of both worlds. If the account you want to sign up for, subscribe to or join lets you change your default email address in its settings, you can use a disposable temporary address initially as a good way to check out the account and to confirm whether you wish to remain a member. If you later decide to stay as a longer-term member, change your default email address settings from the temporary email address to your *primary* email address.

In response to the demand for temporary email, dozens of these services are now available. However, as these temporary email services grow in popularity, more sites are barring these email addresses from their signup processes. There may be times when you try signing up with a disposable email address and you receive an error such as, "Email address not valid". While the temporary email services try to stay a step ahead, it is a constant game of cat and mouse. You may have to try different temporary email services for different signup sites.

Recommended Temporary Email Services

These are some of my favorite temporary email services (all free) for disposable email needs. Of course, for ultimate privacy, visit and use these services with a web anonymizing service enabled such as a proxy, Tor or a VPN.

- *Mail Expire* http://www.mailexpire.com/ allows you to easily create an email alias and set the amount of time before it expires (from 12 hours to months). Unfortunately, the aliases it provides are not that eye pleasing (for example, tlaingeica@ farifluset.mailexpire.com) so the service may be better suited for automatic sign-ups rather than for using with real people.

- *Mailinator* http://mailinator.com/ allows you to create an on-the-spot email identity in one easy step.

- *Guerrilla Mail* https://www.guerrillamail.com/ provides you with an email address that lasts 15 minutes which you can use to receive and reply to emails within this timeframe.

- *My Trash Mail* http://mytrashmail.com/ lets you create temporary email addresses for 2 to 3 hours (and longer periods too with a premium version of the service).

- *HMA Anonymous Email* https://securemail.hidemyass.com/ (scroll down) lets you instantly create a temporary email account and supports email forwarding.

Self-destructing messages are similar to disposable temporary emails but different in that they allow you to send a message with an expiry date.

- *self-destructing email* (free trial) http://www.self-destructing-email.com/ tells you when your tracked email messages are opened and even forwarded

- *privnote* (free) https://privnote.com/ lets you send notes that self-destruct after being read

Web-based Anonymous Remailers

Remailing is a process that lets you send messages without the recipient ever knowing from whom it came. Remailing strips away all of the *email header* information from your message, such as the name and reply-to address but also the more hidden headers I described earlier, ensuring that the message cannot be linked back to its origin (you). The remailer then forwards your anonymized message to the intended recipient.

As you will see later in this chapter, traditional *remailers* can be quite complicated and technical. However, some *web-based remailers* make the process much easier. They work as follows: you enter a message into a web-based form and, when you select Send, the proper syntax is automatically applied to the message and forwarded to a remailer for relaying to your intended recipient.

Top Tip - Although web-based remailers are easier to use than traditional remailers you have less control over the process, so web-based remailers may not provide the same degree of anonymity. As with any intermediary service, you should always carefully assess the integrity of any web-based remailer you wish to use and access them with a proxy, Tor or a VPN enabled.

Recommended Web-based Remailers

Given the nature of these services, they tend to come and go. You can also type "anonymous web remailer" in your favorite search engine, but be prepared to dig and to heed the tip above about doing your homework. You can also find updated information on remailers at the newsgroup `alt.privacy` including via https://groups.google.com/d/forum/alt.privacy.

Here are my recommended web-based remailers (all free).

Anonymouse.org's *AnonEmail* http://anonymouse.org/anonemail.html has been around for over a decade in support of Internet anonymity. Messages sent from this form are randomly delayed up to 12 hours preventing *traffic analysis* and thereby increasing your protection.

AnonEmail

| AnonEmail | AnonWWW | AnonNews |

With AnonEmail it is possible to send e-mails without revealing your e-mail address or
any information about your identity. Therefore you can communicate more freely
and you do not have to worry that it might cause consequences for you.
**This service allows you to send e-mails without revealing <u>any</u> personal information.
Protect your privacy, protect your data, protect it for free.**

To:	
Subject:	
Message:	

Send Anonymously

Adverts

Members | Terms of Service | Privacy Policy | Help / FAQ | Contact Info

Copyright © 1997-2014 by Anonymouse
All Rights Reserved

Global Internet Liberty Campaign W3 Anonymous Remailer
http://gilc.org/speech/anonymous/remailer.html has a simple interface and has been around for years. However, in my experience, its reliability is not consistent (sometimes it works, sometimes it doesn't).

Paranoia Remailer Anonymous Email Web Interface
https://webmixmaster.paranoici.org/mixemail-user.cgi (you may receive a warning) is a little ugly to look at, but is a web-based remailer that supports *chaining* (sending a message through multiple remailers for enhanced anonymity).

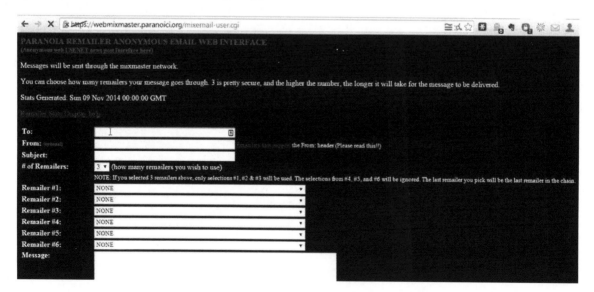

Using Remailers to Send Anonymous Email Messages (Advanced Users)

For those times when you need to send an anonymous and virtually untraceable message, use a *remailer*. The full process works as follows:

- you send your message to the remailer by regular email or webmail but using some special syntax I will show you

- the remailer strips away all of the *email header* information from your message, such as the name and reply-to address but also all the hidden headers, ensuring that it cannot be linked back to you

- the remailer then forwards your anonymized message to the intended recipient

For ultimate anonymity, it is even possible to *chain* remailers, sending a message through two or more remailers. While chaining adds layers of anonymity, the more remailers in a chain, the greater the chances your message may never reach the intended recipient. There are a variety of reasons for this:

- remailers are primarily operated for free by privacy hobbyists and thus reliability can vary

- remailers can be subject to spam and other abuses which may hamper their availability or performance

- downtimes can occur similar to any other online service, whether due to general maintenance or outages

As remailers and their availability are changing all the time you should always first check for the latest information at the remailer's relevant website or at newsgroups such as `alt.privacy` (for example, via Google at https://groups.google.com/d/forum/alt.privacy). In addition, you should always send an email to the remailer with the subject "remailer-help" to obtain its most recent help file and instructions on how to properly use the service.

At the time of publishing, here are some addresses you can try:

mixmaster@remailer.privacy.at	remailer@rip.ax.lt
remailer@kroken.dynalias.com	hsub@mixmaster.mixmin.net
remailer@reece.net.au	remailer@dizum.com

or consult the remailer statistics at http://www.noreply.org/echolot/ or http://pinger.mixmin.net/

or type "reliable remailers" in your favorite search engine

Some remailers support a delay in time (sometimes called *latency*) between receiving your email and forwarding it onwards to your intended recipient. This prevents someone from analyzing Internet traffic and implicating you as the sender by determining that you had sent the message to a remailer just before the intended recipient received a message from it. The remailer's instructions will indicate whether it supports the ability to delay the forwarding of messages.

Using the Proper Remailer 'Syntax'

You can send your message to a remailer using your primary personal email account. However, for ultimate anonymity when using remailers, send your message to the remailer from an alternate webmail account or from a temporary email account, with a web anonymizing service enabled such as a proxy, Tor or a VPN.

The instructions and syntax for using remailers can be somewhat complicated. Here's a summary:

- the *To:* field of your outgoing message should be addressed to a remailer. This makes sense as the message must be redirected through a remailer.

- the *Subject:* field of your outgoing message will be irrelevant as the remailer will delete it when stripping the headers from your message. Fill it in anyway if you like, but it will be deleted by the remailer.

- no matter which remailer you use, the *body* of your message MUST be in the format below. It is *imperative* that your first line begins with 2 colons. Follow the other directions indicated in [square brackets] below.

```
::
Request-Remailing-To: [email address of your intended recipient]
[blank line]
##
Subject: [this will appear as the Subject of your message]
[any additional header commands supported by the remailer - if not, you can omit this line]
[blank line]
[start the text of your message on this line]
```

For example, this could be a sample message sent to mixmaster@remailer.privacy.at:

```
::
Request-Remailing-To: reporter@example.com

##
Subject: Here is the Access Code to the Information They Don't Want You to See

As discussed in the park earlier today, here is the access code to the information they don't want you to see. I hope that your article stops this terrible practice. Access code: PyKDYQSPxw
```

How Safe Are Remailers?

Because you are relying on a third party to do the remailing, the privacy of your messages and the protection of your identity will depend on the integrity of the remailer operator. Remember, the message arrives at the remailer as a normal email message with your identity intact depending on how you sent it. Theoretically, risks might include:

- the remailer operator reading your messages (you don't know who they are or who they work for)

- in some circumstances it may still be possible for an adversary to compel the remailer operator to reveal your identity (through legal process or extortion)

- a hacker, snoop or government agency could be covertly monitoring the remailer

- *traffic analysis* could be used to correlate a message you sent to the remailer with a message that was sent by or received from the remailer

Advanced 'Mixmaster' Remailer Features

In response to the risks above regarding classic remailers (called *Cypherpunk* or *Type I* remailers), a newer generation of anonymous remailers emerged called *Mixmaster* or *Type II* remailers, incorporating chaining *and* encryption technology.

Somewhat similar to the process for Tor described in chapter 13, messages handled by a Mixmaster remailer make two or more stops along their journey in order that no one service knows the identity of both the sender and the recipient. Mixmaster-type remailers enhance security further by parsing all messages into equal-sized packets that are only reassembled at the final remailer before being forwarded to the intended recipient, making them less susceptible to traffic analysis.

If a remailer supports these Mixmaster features its email address will often start with mixmaster@. Regardless, if Mixmaster features are supported this will be clearly spelled out in the remailer's most recent help file.

Remailers and Attachments

Because remailers are a secure means of transmitting Internet messages, they may appeal to you for sending sensitive attachments. But use them selectively and first make sure that the remailer you want to use supports the transmission of attachments as not all of them do.

In addition, most remailers will impose a maximum file size and you may have to first *encode* the file (see box) which may further limit your ability to send attachments via remailers.

More About: *Encoding and Decoding* - Encoding and decoding refer to the conversion of binary files (for example, documents, images or videos) into plain text (ASCII characters). Most encoding occurs automatically or in the background. But sometimes for remailers (and email or Usenet) you may have to *manually* encode or decode files. The most popular encoding and decoding methods are *UU* and *yEnc*. Different utilities are available for each of these methods but are easy to find with your favorite search engine.

* * *

For updates and additional information about secure, private and anonymous email, please visit http://www.cogipas.com/secure-private-anonymous-email/.

Chapter 15: Using Encryption to Hide and Keep Safe Your Personal Digital Items, Information and Data

Introduction

If you have personal, private or sensitive information saved to your devices (and who doesn't?), it is all too easy for anyone to discover the photos, images, documents, ebooks, videos or other items saved to them that you would rather keep to yourself.

Even if you don't outright share the device with anyone, it may be that someone is actively looking for these items perhaps in an attempt to harm you. This is not to sound paranoid. There are plenty of stories where the items on someone's device have been used against them, whether by a jilted lover, private investigator, divorce attorney, co-worker, business rival, nosy neighbor, troll, hacker, or even overzealous governmental authorities.

Regardless, it's never fun having your private stuff discovered, whether accidentally by those with access to your devices (your spouse, family members, partner or roommates), or intentionally by a determined adversary such as some of those listed above.

You may think that you are clever renaming sensitive downloads and storing them on your device in a folder called 'Research', but they are easily unearthed with the most basic of searches and checks – just see *Annex B* if you don't believe me.

Or maybe you are even cleverer and keep your items and data on a separate storage device such as an external hard drive or USB memory stick. While that is safer and a better way to protect your privacy, it is hardly fool-proof. Saving your sensitive media on a portable storage device is fine as long as it remains a secret. But if someone comes across the storage media or sees you interacting with it they may naturally ask, "What's that?" Worse, if they don't believe you or you are not around, they may try finding out for themselves what's on it.

Even storing your items and data in the cloud (for example, via services such as *Dropbox* or *Google Drive*) comes with risks. If you remain logged in or have auto-login or syncing features enabled, anyone with or gaining access to your device can discover what you have stored in the cloud. Not to mention that cloud services can be hacked. The nude celebrity photo hacking scandal, *The Frappening,* received the most attention but there have been many cloud hacks.

In this chapter you will learn how to keep your files and data safe and secure using strong encryption. Think of encryption like an impenetrable safe that only you have the combination for opening.

This chapter explains why everyone should be using encryption and then shows you how to use on-the-fly encryption to protect your devices and keep your information secure. Some apps for encrypting your data are recommended as are some handy tips regarding how to use encryption with portable drives and memory cards.

The importance of good passphrases is also re-emphasized as encryption is only as good as the passphrases that you use with it. Being reminded of these guidelines will make sure your digital items stay safe from prying eyes.

Encryption Overview

Rather than storing your digital items, information and data on a portable hard drive that you hide under your bed or saving it in the cloud, a better method is to hide it *in plain sight*. Huh? You can do exactly this by using *encryption*.

Encryption is a word that often intimidates people and conjures up all sorts of complicated concepts. But these days, encryption is very easy to use, including very strong encryption that is virtually uncrackable even by the most determined, well-funded and powerful of potential adversaries. As a bonus, some of the leading encryption apps are *free*.

Encryption apps let you quickly and easily encrypt selected items or folders, entire drives, all or part of removable storage devices and even cloud-based storage. With these options, you can choose to keep your sensitive items in an encrypted location on your device, on removable storage or in the cloud. In fact, you can just as safely keep your data on your device's main storage without losing any additional space by encrypting the items.

With most of the apps once you have encrypted the relevant items, accessing them only takes a matter of seconds upon entering the correct passphrase of your choosing. To anyone that does not possess the correct passphrase you established, the encrypted data, whether on your device, separate storage media or in the cloud, will merely appear as a random jumble of data. Nothing to see here folks, just move along.

It really couldn't be easier and *everyone*, including you, should now be using encryption.

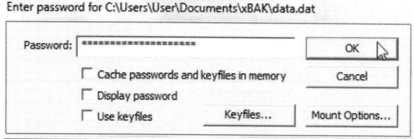

Figure: After entering your passphrase, presto, the previously invisible encrypted items will instantly appear

Encryption Keeps Your Data Ultra Secure

Everyone should use encryption for no other reason than to protect your data in the event your device is stolen, especially laptops. There are over 600,000 laptops stolen every year in the United States alone.

If you use strong and reliable encryption methods and take some other rudimentary precautions, your security measures will be virtually insurmountable regardless of the might and resources available to a potential adversary. For example, maybe you are crossing borders, whether for business or for pleasure, and do not want any foreign agents snooping your data.

Business owners and entrepreneurs should also keep in mind that they may have a legal duty to protect from unauthorized disclosure certain client or patient information. The laptop stolen from the back of your car could get you into all kinds of trouble if it contained confidential customer, client or patient information that fell into the wrong hands or was subsequently leaked.

Therefore, at a minimum, you should consider encrypting your devices to protect your data in the event of theft. Lots of adversaries, not to mention identity thieves, could have a field day with all of the unencrypted data on your devices. However, if the same data were encrypted, the adversaries will have stolen only a very expensive doorstop. The device may remain stolen (a major setback) but at least the data on it will be safe and you will be spared the worst kind of nightmare.

Most encryption apps will leave some trace of their presence on your device so the fact that you are using encryption will probably be apparent. Of course, the very fact that you are using an encryption app - or for that matter the presence of a VPN, privacy cleaning app or other tools and techniques discussed in this book - may raise questions or bring unwanted attention. That said there are enough universal concerns about privacy and security these days in our post-Snowden world to adequately answer any such potential criticism or questions. "I value my privacy" is now a reasonable and full answer when maybe 5 or even 2 years ago it wasn't.

A Quick Reminder About the Importance of Passphrases

No matter how powerful your encryption app, your protection will only be as effective as the passphrase that you use with it. It is paramount that you use strong passphrases for your encryption. Do not be lazy when it comes to passphrases and remind yourself about all the important aspects of passphrases I discussed in chapter 3.

In particular remember that your passphrases should be at least 8 characters long (but the longer the better) and use a mix of at least 3 character types (uppercase letters, lowercase letters and numbers). Ideally, you should also use symbols (! – +), if supported. And avoid using any proper names or personal information as part of your passphrases. If you follow these guidelines, a brute force dictionary attack will simply take too long to overcome your passphrase to access your encrypted data. The snoops and hackers will move on to an easier victim.

Also, don't repeat a passphrase you already used elsewhere. Develop a unique, strong passphrase *each* time. And don't repeat a simple pattern either. Hackers and snoops always try cracking the easy passwords first as many people use the same or similar passwords or password patterns for all of their passphrase needs.

Top Tip - Some encryption apps are rumored to have *back doors* built into them at the behest of governments in the interests of national security. A back door refers to a master passphrase (or other hidden means) that can be used to access the data encrypted with the app. *Reliable* information about these rumors is difficult to obtain and even more difficult to verify or refute. To be safe, I recommend that you do not use any encryption apps bundled with your operating system and that you favor *open source* apps.

How Encryption Apps Work

If you are interested in encrypting just a handful of items, the encryption process usually involves selecting these items, choosing a passphrase to apply and that's it. To access the encrypted items, you would re-select one or more of them, select the option to *decrypt* them and then enter the correct passphrase you chose earlier.

However, I would almost always recommend that you use an encryption app to set up an *encrypted virtual drive* (EVD). Using an EVD is just like using a portable storage device such as a USB memory stick. When you enter the correct passphrase a virtual drive will appear on your device (sometimes this process is called *mounting*) to which you can save, copy, view and otherwise handle items. When you are done, you re-encrypt the virtual drive at which time it disappears from your device similar to unplugging a USB memory stick (sometimes called *dismounting*). Once re-encrypted all the data inside the dismounted container is safe and sound behind strong encryption. Let's go through the process in more detail.

Encrypted Virtual Drives (EVD)

With a specific *passphrase* you create a *container file* to be saved on an existing hard drive, portable storage device or cloud-based location. Most encryption apps make setting up a container easy. You make only a few selections indicating how large the container should be and the location to where it will be saved. You will then be asked to establish a passphrase for this container. The app creates a *single* file of the size and at the location you specified, whether on your device's internal storage, a portable hard drive, a USB memory stick, an SD memory card or a cloud-based location.

It is inside this single container file that the data you wish to encrypt will be absorbed and hidden, protected by strong encryption. Once you enter your correct passphrase into the encryption app, it *mounts* the container on your system. Without the correct passphrase, everything contained on the virtual drive (in the container file) will be totally inaccessible and protected behind the encryption.

Mounting means that the container file becomes unencrypted and that you can access the data stored within it. Saving, deleting, copying and moving data from the (now unencrypted) container is easy. Once the passphrase has been entered, the container shows up, for example, as a new drive letter on your device and operates like any other storage location on it. As mentioned, once the container is mounted, the process works exactly the same as connecting a storage device such as a USB memory stick. You can manipulate data on it just as you would any other storage device.

Following our example on a desktop computer, the new drive letter 'pops up' and the data on it can be accessed. This mimicking of a portable storage device is why EVD stands for encrypted *virtual* drive.

Of course, this virtual drive will only mount with the passphrase you used to create it. Because the virtual drive acts like a normal drive, once mounted, not only can items be saved to it, but apps can also be installed to and run from it.

When you are done, you dismount (re-encrypt) the drive, usually at the click of a button. Until the passphrase is entered all your data is sealed in an encrypted mass of data that will be meaningless to any outsider who finds it and even to the most powerful forensic analysis software (see chapter 18).

One important footnote: the encryption hides your items and data, but the risk of trace information from a number of sources discussed in this book will still remain on your device. Recall that these sources of trace data include often hidden records kept and left behind by your device's operating system, web browser and apps such as movie players, image viewers, etc. So, after accessing your encrypted items, you will still need to clear sources of trace data as discussed in chapter 11 (and ahead in chapter 18). However, you can also protect against these risks by encrypting your *entire* system.

Encrypting Everything

Without any hassle, you can even encrypt your entire system, literally keeping *everything* on it safely tucked away. Until the correct passphrase is entered, the entire system including *all* data on the device (your items, apps, operating system, everything) will be inaccessible, including all those sources of trace data that could expose your activities.

You may think that's how your device works now, but that's not the case at all (see the *Top Tip* box). Being prompted to enter a password once your device's operating system loads (sometimes called a *boot* password) provides nowhere near the level of protection that full system encryption does.

Top Tip - An encryption app password is completely different from the password that, for example, Windows may ask you for. Even if a casual snoop or determined adversary doesn't know your Windows password, they can *easily* access all of the non-encrypted data on your device by using a number of methods. For example, they could startup your desktop or laptop computer using a *live CD* (sometimes called a *live operating system*) to gain complete access to everything on it. A live CD is a CD, DVD or USB memory stick containing an alternative operating system used to boot (startup) your device. Examples include *Puppy Linux* or the *Tails* live operating system. Once "inside" your system, the snoops can view and copy any data without you ever knowing about it. This is a technique commonly used by private investigators and other snoops.

Lastly, it can even be possible to set up a *hidden container* or an entire *hidden operating system* by hiding one encrypted container inside another. That's right, encryption on top of encryption. Needless to say, only advanced users should consider setting up hidden containers or a hidden operating system.

When using hidden encrypted containers or operating systems, you can set up decoy encryptions to help you explain why you are using an encryption app. Such decoys give you so-called *plausible deniability*. "Oh that, that's an app that I use to keep digital copies of my financial records. Don't believe me? Let me show you." Sure enough, you enter a passphrase - unbeknownst to the other person it is the passphrase for the decoy encrypted container, not the one with your sensitive information - and the unencrypted contents you show them will confirm your story.

Recommended Encryption Apps

I recommend the encryption apps below whether for encrypting individual items, an entire storage device or your system as a whole.

Sadly, one of the best encryption apps ever, *TrueCrypt* (free), is no longer supported. On some websites you will see scary warnings about it no longer being safe. While it's true that its development has been discontinued, the last stable version, version 7.1a, still works fine. It's what I still use today. The last stable version of TrueCrypt is available from a number of places including from links found at http://www.cogipas.com/truecrypt-resources/.

TrueCrypt is simply an awesome encryption app with amazing documentation to match and has a near cult-like following. TrueCrypt allows you to create hidden encrypted volumes and, for more advanced users, fully encrypted and even hidden operating systems.

DiskCryptor (free) https://diskcryptor.net/wiki/Main_Page is a natural replacement for TrueCrypt and is generally similar to it in terms of look and feel. DiskCryptor lets you encrypt entire drives including your system partition from where your operating system boots up. However, DiskCryptor does *not* support hidden containers or operating systems. For a decent video tutorial walk through, see https://www.youtube.com/watch?v=HaQEzA2ye4U.

VeraCrypt (free) http://sourceforge.net/projects/veracrypt/ is another TrueCrypt alternative. For former TrueCrypt users, VeraCrypt can mount TrueCrypt volumes and also convert them to VeraCrypt format.

BestCrypt (premium) http://www.jetico.com/encryption-bestcrypt/ stores your data on encrypted virtual drives (EVD) which are only accessible after entering your correct passphrase. BestCrypt uses strong encryption ciphers and is available for a free 21-day 'try before you buy' trial. The company behind BestCrypt is based outside the US in Finland.

Top Tip - Most encryption apps will present you with different encryption algorithms you can use. As a rule of thumb, use *AES* for speed (quicker decrypting) and *Serpent* for maximum security (harder to crack).

Encryption and Portable Storage Devices (Drives, USB Memory Sticks and Cards)

Portable drives are popular and practical, especially if you have lots of large downloads, such as movies. The encryption technology explained above just as easily lets you create an encrypted container on a portable hard drive, USB memory stick or SD card. Once mounted, it operates similar to any other removable drive with virtually no impact on speed. You can use an encrypted portable storage device to shuttle items from one place to another. If a snoop or adversary gets his or her hands on the portable storage device, the information on it will be completely undecipherable without the correct passphrase.

Don't be Obsessed with Capacity

These days, portable hard drives are huge and affordable. It is now quite possible to get a multi - terabyte portable hard drive for a decent price. However, one consideration to keep in mind is the actual degree of portability. Consider opting for smaller capacity portable drives that *do not* require their own power source. Products such as Western Digital's *My Passport* series ¢ http://goo.gl/rQ3lgs are large but do not require their own power source. You simply plug the drive into a USB port and that's all there is to it. No fumbling around with an extra power cord to plug in.

This is convenient especially if you are using encryption and physically transporting data between two or more places. It is easy to overlook this important factor and be obsessed with the sheer storage capacity of portable drives.

Using SD and Micro Memory Cards

SD cards ¢ http://goo.gl/RZpkjj and micro cards ¢ http://goo.gl/m1J8LP are the memory media you might associate most with digital photography. These memory cards are so small and yet of sufficient capacity that they are a great way to securely transport encrypted data. Just as it is a good idea to take the memory card out of your camera so that your pictures are not lost if your luggage (with camera) goes missing, carrying memory cards is also a handy way to physically transport data, especially sensitive data. These memory cards are smaller than USB memory sticks, are easy to keep on your person and easy to conceal (for example, tucked away hidden in your wallet).

Combined with a memory card adapter it is just a matter of slipping the memory card into the adapter, plugging the adapter into your device, launching the encryption app and entering your correct passphrase. The container then mounts and you are able to access the data on it just as if you had plugged a normal USB memory stick into your device.

In particular *micro memory cards* are about the size of your fingernail (see screenshot) making them easy to hide in transit, if necessary.

Figure: The small size of micro memory cards make them ideal for discreetly transporting data. Courtesy of James Bowe https://www.flickr.com/people/jamesrbowe/

* * *

For updates and additional information about using encryption to hide and keep safe your personal digital items, information and data, please visit http://www.cogipas.com/using-encryption/.

Chapter 16: Torrent File-Sharing and How to be Anonymous while Torrenting

Introduction

If you don't know about *BitTorrents* (I'll use the term *torrents* for short in this book), you are missing out on an amazing source of Internet downloads. Torrents and torrent file-sharing are a little different than what you may be used to if you use the Internet primarily to browse the web, chat or engage on social media.

This chapter will describe what torrents are and how they work, outline the risks of using torrents and describe how to download torrents anonymously.

What are Torrents?

Torrents were developed in 2001 (yep, that long ago) but their importance and popularity as a way of sharing files on the Internet continues to grow.

Torrents are small text files that contain just a few pieces of information on how its particular *payload* can be downloaded on the Internet. Put another way, a torrent file provides a means of where and how to download a torrent's payload.

A torrent's payload is a collection of one or more digital items ranging from full-length movies, music files, video clips, ebooks, documents, apps, software programs, images to basically any digital content that you can think of.

For example, a torrent's payload could be a single item, such as an individual music file, or it could be a set of similar items like a collection of music files, numbering upwards of dozens to hundreds. But a torrent's payload could also comprise any number of and different types of items, such as a full-length movie bundled together with a subtitles text file, soundtrack mp3 music file, a movie-themed game app and set of images from a behind-the-scenes photo shoot, all associated with a single torrent.

> **Top Tip** - If torrents are a new concept to you, don't worry. Although torrents and how to download and share them can seem a little complicated to the newcomer, once you get to understand the basic concepts, you will soon get the hang of them and be able to enjoy downloading torrents. And anonymously too! How to use a torrent app and find torrents are all explained in the pages ahead.

You download and share torrents with their own special kind of app, a *torrent app*. Even though torrents themselves are just small text files their payloads can be massive because the torrents do not actually *contain* the payload items; instead, the torrents merely *enable* your torrent app to locate and download the payload items over the Internet.

Furthermore, you can download a single torrent or have many torrents working at the same time. There is a wealth of torrents out there waiting for you to download and share, whether you are interested in movies, music, apps, video clips, games, books, erotica, images, or whole collections of these items. For example, if you find the right torrent you can download dozens or hundreds of items in one go or cherry-pick among the individual items associated with the torrent. This is one of the great things about the torrent format.

The collective group of people downloading and sharing a torrent at any one time is called a *swarm*. When you open a torrent, it informs your torrent app how to download the payload items from the torrent's swarm. Of course, a swarm is always changing as more or fewer people share a specific torrent.

Torrent files usually end in the extension *.torrent* (`download-me.torrent`). The information in the small torrent files is used by torrent apps to find pieces of the payload items shared among an entire swarm.

It's Harder to be Anonymous when Torrenting

Torrents and their payloads can be downloaded in a few easy steps, but doing so *anonymously* means taking a few extra steps in the process. However, the extra steps are not difficult and are well worth the effort.

By definition, any kind of interaction on the Internet, including file-sharing and downloading torrents, means sharing your *IP address*, your unique online digital fingerprint, as we covered earlier. As a result, the extra steps needed to download torrents anonymously include protecting your IP address from disclosure so that people cannot snoop on your torrent activities.

Downloading torrents will also leave behind certain traces of information on your device, so you may also want to take steps to clear away these traces. Thankfully, the extra steps you can take to counter these risks are also relatively easy.

How Torrents Work

In contrast to downloading from the web, torrent payloads are not downloaded from any one place. Instead they are downloaded from many other users, like you, who are online and sharing the same torrent. This is why the technology underpinning torrents is referred to as *peer-to-peer* networking or *P2P* for short.

A torrent network connects people who are downloading and sharing torrents on the Internet. As mentioned, people sharing the same torrent form a *swarm* and their torrent apps will exchange data until the torrent's payload is downloaded by all members of the swarm. Once a particular member of the swarm has downloaded a torrent's payload, the torrent continues to be shared for the benefit of the other members of the swarm.

This may sound complicated, but the matching and swarming is all done seamlessly in the background by your torrent app and with the help of some servers on the Internet known as torrent *trackers* (see the *Top Tip* box). All you need to do is find the torrents you want, download them (remember they are just small text files), open them in your torrent app, and then wait for your app to download the associated payloads. The more people that are sharing a particular torrent (the bigger the swarm), the faster you will be able to download its payload. This is why you can often download popular torrent payloads very quickly because their swarms are large.

Top Tip - The *trackers* mentioned above are servers on the Internet that coordinate the exchanges of data going on between users sharing torrents on the torrent network. Trackers can be public, sometimes called *open trackers*, which are available to all, whereas other trackers are *private trackers* often requiring registration or operating on an invitation-only basis to keep out unwanted snoops.

The transfer of data on the torrent network is actually very sophisticated because the network will match people based on the smallest chunks of information available. This means that as you *download* a torrent, you are actually simultaneously *uploading* it too, sharing your partially downloaded items with the swarm on the torrent network. As soon as they can be, even the smallest parts of an item are shared with other members of the swarm.

Each member of the swarm sharing a torrent is known as a *peer*. Peers sharing a fully downloaded torrent are called *seeders*. Peers sharing a partially downloaded (incomplete) torrent are called *leechers*. Remember, if you are downloading a torrent, this means that you are also automatically sharing it too. The more seeders a torrent has, the faster it should download. If a torrent has no seeders and too few leechers, it is possible that you may not be able to download the torrent in full. This can happen when the collective peers in the swarm do not possess a full torrent between them. Of course, at any one time seeders and leechers come and go in a swarm as its members stop sharing the torrent, go offline or close their torrent app.

This was a brief explanation of how torrents work. If you want to learn more, here is a good 3-minute video overview http://www.cogipas.com/intro-to-torrents-video. Also, this visualization is a cool way to interactively see how torrent downloading works with peers and seeds, http://www.cogipas.com/intro-to-torrents-visual.

How to Download Torrents

The technical aspects behind how torrents work are fascinating. But let's now turn to how it works in practice. Just as you use a web browsing app for browsing the web or a word processing app for opening documents, you will need a *torrent app* to open and share torrents, and to download their payloads to your device.

A good choice is *µTorrent* (free) at http://www.utorrent.com/. Please note that it is called "microtorrent", not "you torrent". Small, sleek and fast, this torrent app is as excellent as it is popular. µTorrent has tens of *millions* of active users, which helps to ensure that there are lots of people for you to share torrents with. The free version does display ads, but they are unobtrusive and can actually be used to your advantage (explained a bit later). It also has a handy *boss key* for quickly hiding the app should an unexpected visitor drop by.

Top Tip - Experience shows that, unless you are an advanced user, you should stick with the settings automatically determined by µTorrent as fiddling with them only seems to worsen download speeds. Advanced users can check my tips on the book's companion website for selecting the best privacy settings for µTorrent.

If you prefer, you can use any torrent-compatible app that you want. Another popular choice of torrent app is *Vuze* (free) at http://www.vuze.com/.

When you find a torrent file that you want to download (don't worry, I'll soon tell you everything you need to know about *finding* torrents), you click on it just as you would for downloading a document from a website.

The screenshots below show me selecting a torrent file to download (using the Chrome web browser). Upon selecting the link, your web browser will prompt you to download the torrent file. Again, this is the same process as when selecting a document online to download.

Figure: Downloading a torrent file on the web is the same as downloading any other item, just select it ...

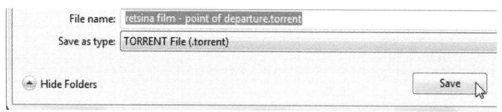

Figure: ...and save it on your device

146

As the torrent is just a tiny text file, it will download very quickly to your device. To open the torrent, you would just select it. Again, this is exactly the same process as when you successfully download a document from the web and then want to open it.

Now here is where things get a little different. When your torrent app opens the torrent that you just downloaded, you will be presented with some information and prompted to make some choices. Your torrent app will display information about the torrent you just downloaded, usually its name and the payload items associated with it. Remember, the payload could be a single item or could number in the dozens of items. Don't make the mistake of thinking that the payload items are actually *inside* the torrent file you just downloaded (in contrast to a ZIP file for example), because they aren't.

You can also make some choices before you start downloading the torrent's payload. Depending on the torrent app, you can select which of the payload items to download. This means that you can skip certain items, if you wish (see screenshot). For example, perhaps the torrent you downloaded is associated with a payload of 10 music files and you only want one of them. You can just download the one item you want and skip the rest, not wasting any time or extra bandwidth for the other items. Depending on the torrent app and the device (for example, desktop computer, tablet or smartphone) you may also be prompted for *where* on the device to save the payload items. Once you have finished making your choices, you can start the downloading process. Usually this happens when you select OK after making your choices.

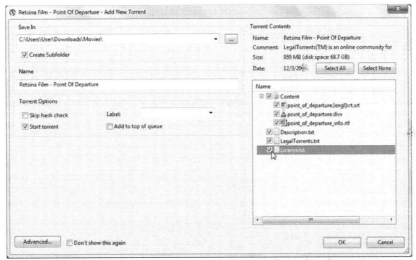

Figure: Select the payload items you want and start downloading! (µTorrent shown)

Your torrent app will now show the torrent as an *active* torrent. This means that your torrent app (with the help of the trackers I talked about earlier) is looking to join the swarm, start communicating with other peers and begin the payload downloading process. Depending on the torrent's popularity, you may quickly join a swarm and start downloading almost immediately or it might take hours or even days in the case of obscure torrents.

Your torrent app will display which torrents are active and the progress of your downloads. Once a torrent's payload is 100% downloaded (or the subset of items that you selected from the available payload) your torrent app will show that you are now *seeding* the torrent. Once a torrent's payload is completely downloaded you can stop sharing the torrent with the swarm, but good torrent etiquette dictates that you do some sharing too. After all, if no one seeded torrents, payloads would be much more difficult and slow to download.

And that's it! The payload items will now be saved to your device for you to enjoy. Later, I'll describe in detail the extra steps needed on how to download torrents *anonymously*.

The Privacy Risks of Downloading and Sharing Torrents

Downloading and sharing torrents can *feel* anonymous, but this is deceptive. Like all Internet communications, torrent activities inevitably involve the interaction of IP addresses. In order for everyone in a swarm to be able to connect to one another, this involves everyone's devices needing to share IP addresses to exchange the torrent-related data. This means your IP address is also stamped on all your torrent downloading and sharing activities.

If you do not take steps to hide your IP address, your torrent downloading activities can be easily found out. If a snoop wants to determine your IP address, they just need to share a torrent to join its swarm and then monitor the activities. To see examples of how torrent downloaders can be monitored, see http://www.cogipas.com/torrent-monitoring/.

However, if you use a *torrent anonymizing service* (discussed soon) the peers with whom you connect in the swarm will only see data transfers to and from a *masked* IP address assigned by your anonymizing service rather than your true IP address. This way, the anonymizing service acts as an intermediary standing between you and the prying eyes of any snoops, in the same way I discussed earlier regarding *web* anonymizing services such as web proxies, Tor and VPNs.

In addition, many Internet service providers (ISPs) frown on their customers torrenting because of the potentially large amounts of data involved. If your ISP detects that you are downloading torrents, they may *throttle* (slow down) your connection. There are also aggressive firms monitoring torrent activities and in some cases threatening users with payment demands or legal action (see next section).

Another factor is that some people may be downloading torrents about subjects that they would rather keep private, such as relating to health or medical conditions, financial matters, erotica or other private information that is nobody else's business. Yet other people may want to keep their online activities private purely out of principle, for example, in reaction to increasing intrusion and overreach on the part of businesses or governments (Big Brother type surveillance considerations).

As you can see, wanting to keep your torrent downloading habits private does *not* mean that you have something to hide. Not at all. You may have a number of reasons for wanting to keep your torrent activities private and anonymous.

Copyright Infringement

Speaking of risks, let me just come right out and say it. A lot of torrents are *pirated*. That's a pity. Piracy undercuts the efforts of those producing the very content we all enjoy. P2P technology is itself legal, but some or even many of the payloads being shared on the Internet are pirated copyright material. Downloading pirated copyright material, *even by accident*, can get you in trouble.

While it may not always be easy to tell which torrents are associated with pirated copyright materials, you usually know them when you see them. As with email spam and scams, the more you use torrents, the better you will be at spotting the torrents to avoid.

Torrents do not have to be synonymous with copyright infringement, so use the technology responsibly and legally. You should respect copyright and by doing so support content producers. Instead, if we all supported pirated materials – by not paying for them or otherwise failing to honor the copyright owner's terms – the materials could stop being produced.

Following this advice will also help you stay out of potential trouble with those elements that are tirelessly trying to make copyright offenders pay. Breaching copyright, whether intentionally or accidentally (hey, it can happen to anyone), can have consequences. These consequences can include your ISP cutting off your service, industry associations dragging you into lawsuits, or lawyers sending letters on behalf of copyright owners demanding monetary compensation from you.

While it is true that following the techniques in this chapter will maximize the anonymity of your torrent activities and make it difficult for anyone to discover your torrent habits, it is safest to steer clear of the pirated stuff and respect copyright. Please use torrent file-sharing for legitimate, non-copyright infringing uses.

Malware-Infected and Fake Torrents

While some torrents infringe copyright, others are infected with malware, so caution is warranted. Unfortunately, torrents are a fertile ground for the circulation of viruses, worms, Trojans, rootkits and other malware that may do damage to your devices. Some mischief-makers will circulate malware under the guise of torrents with pleasing filenames in an effort to trick you into downloading and opening them. You should use an anti-malware app to rigorously scan torrent payloads before handling them.

In addition, some torrents are fake. When you download a fake torrent, the payload does not turn out to be what you expected. Fake torrents can occur by accident (when the torrent was being created) but usually fake torrents are created intentionally as a form of mischief. While fake torrents do not pose the same kind of danger as the malware-infected ones, they result in you wasting time, effort and bandwidth.

How to Find Torrents (with Search Tips)

To find torrents, it is better to use reliable *torrent indexing sites* than general Internet search engines. This is because torrent indexing sites are essentially search engines specializing in torrents and usually only torrents, whereas search engines, especially the market leaders, are trying to cater to everyone's search needs. And, anyway, some of the major search engines seem to be increasingly censoring torrent search results, primarily due to copyright concerns.

The best torrent indexing site(s) for you to use may depend on the *type* of payload items you are looking for, whether movies, music, apps, video clips, games, books, erotica, images, etc.

Torrent indexing sites are usually searchable *and* browseable. This means that you can search for torrents by keywords (just like any search engine you are used to), but also can explore a structured set of categories which are sometimes further divided into sub-categories.

In particular, community-based torrent indexing sites offer a number of additional advantages. Members of these communities post comments and sometimes assign ratings for torrents which can help you to screen out poor quality, copyright, fake or malware-infected payloads.

Most torrent indexes will also display the number of seeders and leechers for each torrent. Usually, they just use the term "seeds" for seeders and "peers" for leechers (even if technically a seed is also a peer). Usually the greater number of seeds and peers you see, the more popular the torrent.

How to Tell which Torrents will Download Fastest

Torrents download fastest the higher the *ratio* of seeds to peers. In other words, the greater percentage of seeds in a swarm, the faster you can expect to download the torrent. For example, if torrent X has 100 seeds and 200 peers, while torrent Y has 10 seeds and 10 peers, you could expect torrent Y to download faster even though its swarm is smaller in size and has fewer total participants. That's because the percentage (ratio) of seeds to peers for torrent Y is 100% whereas for torrent X it is 50%. Size isn't everything; it's the *ratio* that is more important.

Copyright-Safe Torrent Indexes

Copyright safety is also a factor in determining which torrent indexing sites to visit because, unfortunately, too often the most popular torrent indexing sites include torrents associated with pirated materials.

Good starting points for copyright-safe torrent indexing sites include:

- *Mininova* http://www.mininova.org/ - an easy-to-use directory and search engine for all kinds of torrent files.

- *ClearBits* http://www.clearbits.net/ - a torrent directory of open licensed media, including movies, music, games and more.

- *BitTorrent's Featured Content* http://bundles.bittorrent.com/ - torrents featured by the firm that invented them (it's in their interest to offer exciting legal torrents).

- *Internet Archive* http://archive.org/details/bittorrent - movies, music, games and books that are now in the public domain (lots of "classics" from the past).

- *VODO* http://vodo.net/ - torrents of independent ("indie") film and movies.

- *Vuze Wiki* http://wiki.vuze.com/w/Legal_torrent_sites maintains a great list of legal torrent sites, organized by category.

Other copyright-friendly torrent indexes can be found using a general Internet search engine and typing terms such as "legal torrent indexing sites" or "best legal torrents".

Popular Torrent Indexes

Lists of the most popular torrent indexing sites (as measured by the number of monthly visitors) can be found here http://www.cogipas.com/popular-torrent-sites/.

If you are blocked from accessing any of these sites or other torrent indexes, whether by your government, ISP or simply by your geographic location, try accessing them with a *web* anonymizing service enabled, such as a web proxy, Tor or a VPN.

Popular torrent indexing sites can also be found using a *general* Internet search engine and typing terms such as "most popular torrent indexing sites", "torrent search engine" or even simply "torrents".

However, remember what I said earlier about copyright safety. In addition, some of the most popular torrent index sites have very cluttered pages, trying to entice you into clicking on all kinds of ads, downloads and other links, not all of which may be safe or desirable.

You could also include terms matching the category or type of payload items you are looking for, whether movies, music, apps, video clips, games, books, erotica, images, etc. For even more specific searches you could also include any subcategory of specific interest. For example,
→ torrent search engine documentary movies

General Search Engines

Although they provide less relevant results, you can also search for torrents using general Internet search engines. Searching for torrents with general search engines can occasionally unearth a hidden gem of a torrent or lead you to discover a new favorite torrent indexing site.

For general Internet search engines, you have two strategies:

You can perform a simple search for the content you seek by adding the word "torrent"
→ gorilla documentary torrent

Or, if you know what an *operator* is (it's a search parameter), you can employ the *filetype:* operator on general search engines that support it. General search engines supporting this operator include Google, Bing, DuckDuckGo and ixQuick.

Here is an example of a torrent search on a general search engine using the *filetype:* operator.
→ documentary filetype:torrent

Top Tip - Note that there is *no space* between the colon (:) and the word *torrent*. Also note that it's torrent singular, not torrents plural.

Shield Yourself with an IP Address Protection Tool

Although it is not mandatory that you use an IP address protection tool while downloading torrents, these tools help prevent "unfriendly" IP addresses from connecting with your device. For Windows, I recommend *PeerBlock* (free) http://www.peerblock.com/. PeerBlock acts similar to firewall software, but goes one step further as it filters the IP addresses trying to connect to your devices against specialized *blacklists* compiled by passionate torrent enthusiasts.

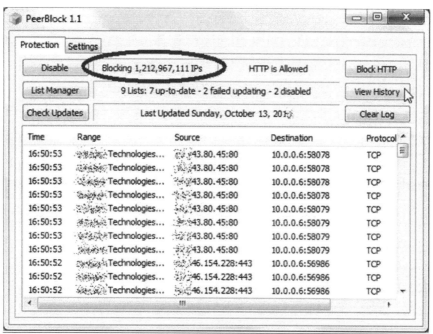

Figure: I'm being protected from over 1 billion potentially unfriendly IP addresses (PeerBlock shown)

PeerBlock lets you choose blacklists that protect you from IP addresses associated with snoopers, spammers, spyware, educational institutions, governments and, of course, anti-torrent elements (called *Anti-P2P* in the lists). The Anti-P2P lists are especially handy as they block the IP addresses of some organizations believed to be monitoring the torrents people are downloading. In addition, you can easily add even more custom blacklists (some free, some premium) from resources such as http://iblocklist.com/lists.php.

Top Tip - PeerBlock provides particularly useful protection when downloading torrents, but you can also use it for *all* your Internet activities, including web browsing.

Hide your True IP Address with a Torrent Anonymizing Service

The key to downloading torrents anonymously is to protect your true IP address from being transmitted. While an IP address protection tool (above) helps *shield* your IP address from potential torrent snoops, the best protection is to *hide* your IP address outright. This way, even if your IP address is detected while you are downloading torrents, it will not be your true IP address that is detected. After all, the IP address protection tool, though helpful, cannot be expected to block 100% of potentially unfriendly elements that may be trying to snoop on you.

The best way to hide your IP address is to use a specialized *torrent anonymizing service*. These services will hide your IP address *and* encrypt your traffic, protecting your torrent activities from being snooped on whether by your ISP wanting to throttle your bandwidth or by outside parties eavesdropping on your connection to monitor your downloads.

With a torrent anonymizing service enabled,

1) your ISP will only see encrypted (scrambled) traffic. Your ISP will still be able to see *how much* data you are downloading, but not *what* it is or even that it is torrent traffic (though it may not be that hard for them to guess if you are downloading high volumes of data).

2) outside snoops will not be able to eavesdrop on or monitor your torrent activities as they will be unable to attribute the data traffic to your true IP address. Every time you connect to the torrent anonymizing service your torrent traffic will be tunneled through, and seem to be coming from, a different IP address. Most anonymizing services will let you select the country in which the intermediary connection is made.

While nothing can 100% guarantee absolute anonymity, you maximize your privacy when using a torrent anonymizing service to hide your true IP address and scramble your torrent traffic as this makes it very difficult for snoops to monitor you.

Although using an anonymizing service may sound intimidating, many of these services are now easy to use. After opening an account with the service provider, it is usually as simple as downloading and installing a small app for your device and then entering your credentials (username and password).

Free vs. Premium Services

Unfortunately, the reality is that there is no free lunch when it comes to these services. Free options for *torrents* are few and far between. This is due to the high downloading volumes associated with torrent activities. Even when a free option emerges for torrents, it is often quick to disappear.

If you find a free service that does support torrents, be mindful about any "catches". Sometimes configuring them is difficult, especially for less knowledgeable users, increasing the chances of you getting things wrong. Or the "free" service somehow makes *you* the product, for example, by logging your activities. Plus, any free torrent anonymizing service can be expected to have a weaker *privacy policy* when compared to premium (paid) services. With any free service, you would have to be especially trusting as, remember, you will be routing your torrent activities through them.

Unfortunately, at the time of publishing I am not aware of any reliable free *torrent* anonymizing services that I can recommend. If you discover any, please share them by reaching out via the page http://www.cogipas.com/free-anonymizing-torrent-services.

Top Tip - Remember that Tor is inappropriate for torrents. Tor's own materials make this clear at https://blog.torproject.org/blog/bittorrent-over-tor-isnt-good-idea. The post is dated 2010, but the point is still valid: Tor is *not* a suitable torrent anonymizing solution.

The most convenient and fastest services supporting torrents are *premium* in nature and do cost money. Thankfully, the costs are relatively low and seem to be dropping all the time. I realize it is a personal choice, but I would say that it is worth spending a little money to get a reliable and trustworthy premium service that anonymizes your torrent activities. Most will not cost you more per month than a couple of coffees at your local cafe.

Of course, the desire to spend a little money will also depend on how much you value keeping your torrent downloading activities private. If it's not that important to you, use a free service (if you can find one) or simply rely on the IP protection tools that I described earlier. If it is important to keep your torrent downloading activities private, consider paying a little for a premium service.

* * *

Now that I've outlined *what* you'll need and in general *why*, we are ready to soon move on to the detailed steps of *how*. But first, as promised, I will provide some suggestions on the all-important topic of how to choose a torrent anonymizing service that's right for you. What service to choose is probably the most important decision you will make in achieving maximum torrent privacy and anonymity. For these reasons, I provide a number of strategies and suggestions for you to consider when making your choice. After showing you how to make the best choice, I also provide some recommendations of my own for your consideration. Then we get into the nitty-gritty steps of exactly how to *anonymously* download and share torrents.

How to Choose a Torrent Anonymizing Service

In chapter 12, I discussed at length the various factors that should go into your decision on which *web* anonymizing service to choose – cost, exit gateways locations, technical specifications and customer experience. Those same factors also directly apply to choosing a *torrent* anonymizing service, but there are a few *additional* factors you need to consider for torrent file-sharing activities, discussed below.

Supports Torrents (P2P)

The most important thing is to make sure that the service supports torrents by looking for specific statements in the service's offering and documentation. (Although you are less likely to see mention of the "peer-to-peer (P2P) protocol", this means the same thing). However, this is not always easy as many anonymizing services don't expressly advertise the fact that they support torrents as they may not want to draw unnecessary attention to this.

Your base requirements are that the service *hides* your true IP address when you are downloading and sharing torrents, and that it *encrypts* your torrent traffic.

Torrent Anonymizing and Web Anonymizing Services are Different

Remember, you need a *torrent* anonymizing service, not a *web* anonymizing service. Torrents and web browsing use different *protocols* or ways of communicating on the Internet. Web anonymizing services work with the *HTTP/HTTPS* protocol used for web browsing, but not always with the *P2P* protocol used for torrent file-sharing. You will see this illustrated in detail soon when I discuss how to make sure your torrent anonymizing service is working and hiding your true IP address. This critical difference between the two protocols and the anonymizing services associated with them is also why this book expressly distinguishes between *web* and *torrent* anonymizing services rather than, for example, just talking about VPNs generally. It's an important difference, so you may wish to keep it in mind.

Adding to the potential confusion is that sometimes the claims made by web anonymizing services are vague enough to make you think that they will also work for torrents. If you do not see "works for downloading torrents" or similar claims *expressly* listed as part of the service's offerings, it probably does *not* work for torrents. You can always directly ask the service, but be skeptical about any claims that are not backed up. Do your research. If the premium service you are considering has a "try before you buy" offer, take advantage of this and perform the verification step I describe later in the chapter before signing up on a longer-term basis.

Exit Gateway Considerations

Torrent anonymizing services may also offer some advanced features such as allowing you to choose the location of the *exit gateways* (the countries in which the service's proxy servers are located). This gives you control over which country the IP address your torrent traffic will seem to be coming from. So, if you live in the US, this kind of feature would let you pick exit gateways located in another country. Generally speaking, you want a service that has exit gateways in many different locations; the more the better. These are the same considerations I raised for web anonymizing VPNs in chapter 12.

Anyone snooping on your torrent traffic will think you are based in that other country, rather than your home country. If the snoop traced back the traffic to the proxy servers located in the other country, this would lead them to the torrent anonymizing service, rather than you. To make sure that the chain of discovery will end at the torrent anonymizing service provider and not be further traced back to you, see the *Privacy Policy* section below.

Advanced Features

Other features offered by torrent anonymizing services might include allowing you to *automatically* select the fastest exit gateways at any given time. Recall that a *kill switch* is a feature that disables your Internet connection should your torrent anonymizing service unexpectedly disconnect. This helps ensure that your true IP address is never compromised. Further recall that *leak protection* ensures that some special connections your device makes at a very low technical level are also routed through the anonymizing service, ensuring the maximum level of privacy and anonymity possible.

Download Speeds

Take any speed ratings you find with a grain of salt as a service's download speed will vary for a number of reasons, including how geographically close the service's servers and exit gateways are located to you as well as to the other peers in any torrent swarm, the amount of *load* (the number of total users at any one time), the number of servers, the quality of the connection, the ISP you use, and many more factors. For example, one person's experience with the speed of a service could be very good, while another person's experience is much less satisfactory. The best way to determine if the service's speed is good for you is to sign up for a trial or a short timeframe and test it thoroughly.

Privacy Policy

One of the most, if not *the* most, important things to confirm is that the service offers very strong privacy protections for its customers. As boring as it may sound, read the legalese on their website, whether it is called a Privacy Policy, Terms of Service or Legal Information. What you are looking for here are elements of strong privacy protections extended to customers (you).

For example, do they keep logs? Do they disclose user information? If so, under what circumstances? If these answers are not readily apparent, then write to them to find out.

Top Tip - If you want to contact the service and remain anonymous when doing so, communicate with them using a disposable temporary email address as discussed in chapter 14.

In order to ensure your maximum privacy, choose a torrent anonymizing service that does *not* keep any logs. This way, even if they are compelled to disclose information, there is nothing meaningful for the anonymizing service to actually disclose as it doesn't keep any logs of user activity.

Even after you select and sign up for a torrent anonymizing service, keep an eye on their privacy policy (by whatever name it goes by). An easy way to do this is to place an alert for the page using a service such as *ChangeDetection* (free) http://www.changedetection.com/. This way, any time the terms materially change, you will receive a notification by email alerting you about it. This is important because your torrent anonymizing service is unlikely to highlight when it *weakens* its privacy policy. When a service reduces the protections afforded by its privacy policy you can expect them instead to make the change as quietly as possible without alerting customers.

Recommended Torrent Anonymizing Service

I can recommend the following torrent anonymizing service. I have personally used it for years and am comfortable vouching for it based on my own personal satisfaction with this service.

Private Internet Access (PIA) ¢ http://www.cogipas.com/pia gets very high marks as a torrent anonymizing service.

- HQ | Exit gateway locations: US | US, Canada, UK, Switzerland, Netherlands, Sweden, France, Germany, Romania, Hong Kong, Israel, Australia, Japan
- Price: *special reader offers* ¢ via http://www.cogipas.com/pia of $5.95 monthly or $36.95 annually | normal price $6.95 monthly or $39.95 annually ($3.33/mo.)
- Privacy: PIA cannot match specific users to any activity on their service because they do *not* keep traffic logs and they use shared IP address technology. PIA's full privacy policy is in plain English and can be reviewed on their website.
- Advanced Features: Kill switch and DNS leak protection
- Payment methods: PayPal, VISA, MasterCard, AMEX, Discover, Google Checkout, Amazon Payment, BitCoin, Liberty Reserve, OK Pay, CashU. You can also pay anonymously using any number of major brand gift cards, such as Starbucks, Walmart, BestBuy, etc.

Top Tip - PIA's Android app for your smartphone or tablet is also very good and hassle-free.

Other Torrent-Friendly Anonymizing VPN Services

Below are some other VPN services I am familiar with that are reliable and support torrent file-sharing. You may want to check them out. For example, not everyone is comfortable using a torrent anonymizing service based in the US.

- *PureVPN* ¢ http://www.cogipas.com/purevpn is both a powerful yet easy-to-use torrent anonymizing service that I have also used for many years. It is headquartered in Hong Kong, has been around for a long time, and maintains *torrent-friendly* exit gateways in many countries including Brunei, Germany, Luxembourg, Netherlands, Romania, Russia, Sweden and Turkey. In addition, it supports advanced features such as a *kill switch, DNS leak protection* and *split tunneling*. Finally, PureVPN's 3-day money back guarantee ensures you can properly test and verify it as an appropriate torrent anonymizing service.

- *TorGuard* ¢ http://www.cogipas.com/TorGuard, as its name suggests, caters to torrent file-sharing activities. It is US-based and expressly does *not* log user activity. TorGuard offers a 7-day money back guarantee. As mentioned in chapter 12, it is *not* affiliated with The Onion Router as its name may suggest.

- *IronSocket* ¢ http://www.cogipas.com/IronSocket is a new VPN based in Hong Kong, but looks promising especially for torrent file-sharing as it has 50 exit gateways in 36 countries and places special emphasis on anonymity including by keeping no user activity logs of any kind. IronSocket offers a 7-day money back guarantee.

Top Tip - In addition to torrent-supporting VPNs, another variant of torrent anonymizing service is something called a *SOCKS proxy*. If you want to learn more, search for "SOCKS" at www.cogipas.com.

* * *

Whether you choose one of my recommended torrent anonymizing services or find one on your own, you now have everything you need to start downloading and sharing torrents anonymously. The remainder of this chapter will provide you with these detailed steps.

How to Download Torrents Anonymously (in Step-By-Step Details)

Introduction

The sections below explain in detail the steps you need to take to download torrents anonymously. I highly recommend that you use *both* an IP address protection tool (step 1) *and* a torrent anonymizing service (step 2) when downloading and sharing torrents. However, if you make the informed choice *not* to use one or both of them, you can skip the relevant step(s) and still enjoy torrents. But please understand that you will be compromising your privacy and will *not* be anonymous (your IP address will be easily ascertained by snoops). That may be fine for some people provided that they understand the trade-offs they are making.

The screenshots below show the Windows torrent app, µTorrent http://www.utorrent.com/ and torrent anonymizing service, *Private Internet Access* (PIA) ¢ http://www.cogipas.com/pia. If you use a different torrent app, anonymizing service or device, your screens may look different, perhaps substantially different, but the same general concepts will apply almost universally.

Step 1: Start your IP Address Protection Tool

If using an IP address protection tool, start it up. Recall earlier in this chapter my recommendation to use a tool such as *PeerBlock* (free) http://www.peerblock.com/ to block undesirable or otherwise "unfriendly" IP addresses from connecting to your device.

The first time you run PeerBlock you will be taken through a setup wizard. In addition to the Anti-P2P list, select any other lists of interest to you. An IP protection tool is only the *first* (and optional) layer of armor in protecting your privacy, whether or not you use a torrent anonymizing service.

Step 2: Start your Torrent Anonymizing Service

Whichever torrent anonymizing service you decide to use, launch it before you start downloading or sharing any torrents.

With Private Internet Access (PIA), launch its app, make the selection you want for the appropriate *exit gateway* (or simply rely on PIA's auto feature to use the fastest gateway available), further select any advanced features you may want to employ, save them and then connect.

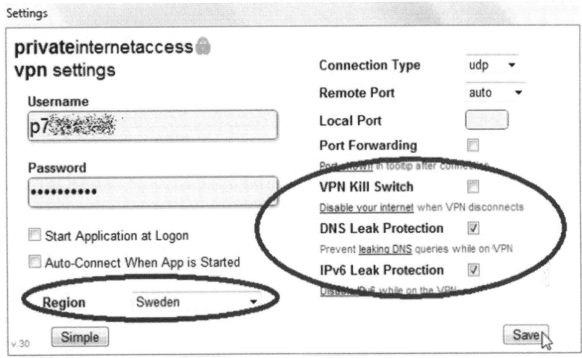

Figure: Make the selections you want, save them and then connect (all via the PIA icon in your system tray)

Step 3: Confirm what IP Address your Torrent App is Transmitting

Now you can start your torrent app. But before you start enthusiastically downloading and sharing torrents, you should first check what IP address your torrent app is transmitting. Make sure that your torrent anonymizing service from step 2 is functioning and masking your true IP address. This way you can be assured that snoops will not be able to determine your true IP address.

If you last closed your torrent app while it was in the midst of downloading or sharing torrents, select all of the active torrents in your torrent app and pause them for now until you finish this confirmation step. If you don't pause your active torrents and something is wrong (for example, you forgot to activate your torrent anonymizing service or it is temporarily down), your true IP address could be transmitted, risking its disclosure.

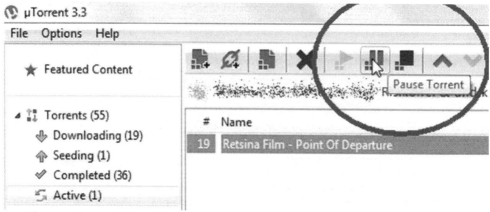

Figure: Pause any active torrents in your torrent app (µTorrent shown)

Top Tip - It is good to get in the habit of pausing your active torrents every time *before* shutting down your torrent app. That way, the next time you start your torrent app, no torrents will be active and this allows you to perform this confirmation step before activating them.

To check what IP address your torrent app is transmitting, you will need to perform a *special* method of verification. It is *not* sufficient to visit plain old "what's my IP address" websites for checking whether your torrent anonymizing service is working. In fact, this can be a dangerous practice because it can give you a completely false sense of anonymity. Let me explain.

As mentioned, it can be the case that a VPN hides your IP address when browsing the web, but not for downloading torrents. So, if you visited a "what's my IP address" website it would display your masked IP address for web browsing, giving you the impression that your online presence is anonymous and encouraging you to download torrents thinking that you are protected. Unknown to you, it's "only" your web browsing that's being anonymized and *not* your torrent activities. Therefore, a different way of checking your transmitted IP address is needed for confirming that your torrent activities are being protected.

Checking Your Torrent IP Address

The best way to check what IP address your torrent app is transmitting (in other words, the IP address any torrent monitoring snoops could detect) is to undergo a check especially developed for torrent file-sharing. There are a number of sites where you can perform such a test, an up-to-date list of which you can always find at http://www.cogipas.com/check-your-torrent-ip/. At the time of publishing, my favorite torrent IP check sites were those at:

- IPLeak.net http://ipleak.net/
- TorGuard http://torguard.net/checkmytorrentipaddress.php

- ipMagnet http://ipmagnet.services.cbcdn.com/

The instructions are usually fairly similar. You download a small torrent, open it in your torrent app and then monitor the IP address your torrent file-sharing is transmitting. The IP address you are transmitting can be found displayed on the same page from where you downloaded the test torrent and/or under the 'Trackers' tab in your torrent app for that torrent. Let's walk through the process in a bit more detail.

At each site, you will be prompted to download a torrent file. Once the torrent file is downloaded, open it with your torrent app just as you normally would for any other torrent. You will see that the torrent's payload is usually a small image file (see screenshot). Select OK to start downloading the payload image.

Figure: Your torrent app will attempt to download the test torrent's payload

Your torrent app will dutifully attempt to download the small payload image file, but it will never actually succeed. But that's exactly the point. This keeps the torrent in a continually active downloading mode so that the IP torrent checking service can detect and regularly report the IP address that your torrent app is transmitting.

To verify the IP address being transmitted by your torrent app, *some* of these checking services (including IPLeak and ipMagnet) will display your torrent IP address right on the same webpage from where you downloaded the test torrent (see screenshot).

In addition, all of the services (including all those listed above) will let you check your torrent IP address by going to your torrent app's list of torrents, selecting the torrent you just downloaded and checking its *Trackers*. In µTorrent, trackers can be found displayed under the *Trackers tab* (at box 2 in the screenshot below).

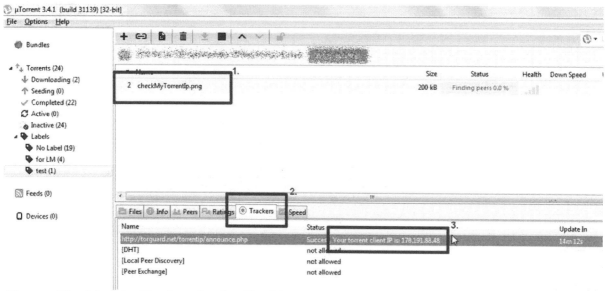

Figure: Checking the Trackers for the CheckMyTorrentIP torrent in your app (µTorrent shown)

You will see (in the lower right-hand highlighted area of the screenshot above at box 3) that a short message is displayed reporting on the IP address that your torrent app is transmitting. Check it carefully. This IP address should *not* be your true IP address, but instead be the IP address assigned by your torrent anonymizing service.

If the IP address information displayed under the Tracking tab displays your *true* IP address rather than your masked one, something is wrong. Either the torrent anonymizing service is not functioning (double-check that you did actually activate it in Step 2) above or it *does not support torrents*. If the Trackers for the torrent IP check report your masked IP address, you know that your torrent anonymizing service is working.

Keep the IP check torrent active in your app even though the payload will never download. This way, every time you open your torrent app you can check the Trackers for this torrent and confirm that your anonymizing service is working and that your true IP address remains hidden from snoops.

Top Tip - If you are using a torrent app that displays ads, such as the free version of µTorrent, you can actually use these ads to your advantage. The ads can serve as an *indication* that your torrent anonymizing service is working. If your torrent app is displaying ads from a foreign country (matching the location of your torrent anonymizing service's exit gateways) rather than the location of your true IP address, this gives you further comfort that the service is working. However, this is an *additional* tip; always verify your torrent IP address as described above.

Checking your Torrent IP Address by Monitoring Your Ports (Advanced Users)

More advanced users may wish to monitor their active ports to ensure that their torrent traffic is actually being routed through their torrent anonymizing service. Ports were introduced in chapter 9.

A port monitoring utility allows you to monitor the connections made to and from your device. This is also how a firewall works in the background. Port monitoring utilities let you see which *process* (generally apps) has opened which port, shows each connection's local and remote IP address. The app may even let you terminate a process.

I recommend *CurrPorts* (free) short for current ports http://www.nirsoft.net/utils/cports.html. If you see your torrent anonymizing service's masked IP address in the 'Remote Address' column of CurrPort's display for your torrent app process, you can be confident that you are making connections through the service and that your true IP address is safe.

Process Name	Process ID	Protocol	Local Port	Local Port Name	Local Address	Remote ...	Remote Port Name	Remote Address	Remote Host Name	State
firefox.exe	5144	TCP	62444		127.0.0.1	62445		127.0.0.1	AcerLaptop	Established
firefox.exe	5144	TCP	62445		127.0.0.1	62444		127.0.0.1	AcerLaptop	Established
firefox.exe	5144	TCP	62453		127.0.0.1	62454		127.0.0.1	AcerLaptop	Established
firefox.exe	5144	TCP	62454		127.0.0.1	62453		127.0.0.1	AcerLaptop	Established
iexplore.exe	2748	UDP	58877		127.0.0.1					
iexplore.exe	4692	UDP	62445		127.0.0.1					
RIMAutoUpdate.exe	2752	UDP	54200		127.0.0.1					
Skype.exe	3268	TCP	64080		10.0.0.99	10490		189.69.114.75	189-69-114-75.dsl.tel...	Sent

Figure: A screenshot of CurrPorts a free port monitoring utility

* * *

Whichever test you performed (or maybe you performed all of them), once you confirm your torrent anonymizing service is working and transmitting a *masked* IP address and not your true one, you can confidently go about downloading and sharing torrents (you can also now safely un-pause any torrents that were already loaded).

Step 4: Make Sure to Use a *Web* Anonymizing Service When Visiting Torrent Indexes and Other Websites related to your Torrent Activities

I know you are keen to start finding and downloading torrents, but there is an often overlooked step that I need to tell you about. As a further precaution, you should visit any websites related to your torrent activities with a *web* anonymizing service enabled. This means enabling your web anonymizing service (whether a web proxy, Tor or a VPN) when visiting websites such as torrent indexing sites, torrent-related forums, movie subtitle archives, and perhaps even the torrent IP address checker websites at step 3 above.

There may be little sense taking the precautions outlined in this chapter for downloading torrents anonymously only to inadvertently reveal your true IP address while searching for torrents or torrent-related information.

Take a simple example. You search for torrents about a private or delicate personal matter. Maybe you are looking for documents or videos about how to declare personal bankruptcy or deal with a serious illness or medical condition. Unfortunately, you conducted these searches on the web (perhaps using a major search engine) *without* taking the precaution of enabling a *web* anonymizing service (shame on you as I told you earlier about some free ones!). Those web searches are now "stamped" with your true IP address for any snoops to discover and use. Maybe the snoops are monitoring and logging the IP address information to eavesdrop on you in real-time or maybe they are collecting this information to use it later, maybe even much later.

Thirty seconds after you performed those web searches, someone with a different IP address and who seemingly lives half-way across the globe starts downloading one or more of these torrents. Of course, that person is you but you are downloading the torrents with your torrent anonymizing service enabled which transmits an entirely different IP address. But, depending on how popular those torrents are, snoops can cross-reference these two separate activities - the web searches and the torrent downloads - and still pinpoint or deduce that you are the same person.

It is very simple: X searched for Y, then Z started downloading Y, therefore X must be Z.

Even for popular torrents that are being searched for and downloaded by thousands of people, don't think that you can hide in the swarms and avoid these cross-referencing techniques (called *traffic analysis*). In these more complicated cases, the conclusion to the formula above simply becomes: therefore X is more likely to be Z. But with enough cross-references, this can be determined very accurately and the *probability* that X is Z can become almost a certainty.

Back to our simple examples and tying them to earlier materials in the book, the snoops now know that you are facing personal bankruptcy or have a life-threatening medical condition. Who knows how the snoops will use this information. Perhaps you will "only" start seeing more online ads on these topics. Or maybe this information is quietly added to your profile in secret databases and later used (unknown to you) to deny you medical or insurance coverage, fail a job screening, reject a loan application, etc. Or maybe the snoops are of a criminal variety and use this sensitive personal information against you in ways ranging from harassment to extortion (don't roll your eyes, this happens, and is on the rise).

Hopefully I have convinced you that you should, when engaging in any web browsing that is related to your torrent downloading activities, use a web anonymizing service. You don't want to make it any easier for the snoops by taking steps to download torrents anonymously only to then give yourself away when web browsing unprotected. Of course, many torrent anonymizing services – including the ones I recommend – also anonymize web browsing so you will already have this capability on hand.

Step 5: Start Downloading and Sharing Torrents!

Of all the steps, this is the easiest and most fun. Now you can find torrents using the techniques I explained earlier in the chapter. Of course, the difference now being that your IP address protection tool will be shielding you from unfriendly elements and your torrent anonymizing service will be encrypting your connection and the torrent traffic within it, and masking your true IP address.

Optional Steps: Encrypt Your Torrent Downloads and Clear Trace Information from Your Device

These next two steps are optional but for the small investment of time and effort (and no or little cost), I take these extra steps to further safeguard my torrent downloading habits from being discovered by anyone with, or gaining access to, my device.

As you have gone to some trouble to protect yourself from *online* snoops, you should also strive to keep your torrents and downloads safe from the prying eyes of *offline* snoops. Not to sound alarmist, but it may be counterproductive to take precautions downloading torrents anonymously only to inadvertently leave obvious traces of your activities on your device. Preventing this means taking one or two additional (but easy) steps to minimize your *offline* fingerprints.

To best protect yourself, encrypt your torrent downloads and further cleanse your device of the traces of your torrent activities. These important techniques can apply, not only to torrents, but to *all* of your activities (see chapters 11, 15 and 18).

* * *

For updates and additional information about torrent file-sharing and how to be anonymous while torrenting, please visit http://www.cogipas.com/how-to-download-and-share-torrents/.

Chapter 17: Secure, Private and Anonymous Usenet

Introduction

Usenet is not well-known, but once you get the hang of it, it is an easy and abundant source of information and especially downloads, including audio, documents, images, videos and movies. Usenet is one of the first Internet-based bulletin board discussion systems, but it is still much in use, despite the rise of social media and torrent file-sharing.

You may not have heard of Usenet and your Internet access package probably does not come with any Usenet access or even any mention of it. In some circles, Usenet is thought to be a bit archaic, but it isn't. In fact, it's as popular as ever and its popularity may even be increasing, particularly because of the privacy advantages it offers.

Practically speaking, gaining full, uncensored access to Usenet newsgroups means you will need to access open (public) services or subscribe to a premium (paid) service. But let's first learn about the basics of Usenet.

About Usenet, its Newsgroups and its many Downloads

Usenet is a collection of *newsgroups* and can be understood as another standalone element of the Internet with its own protocol, as with the web, email or torrents. Usenet still represents somewhat of an untamed frontier as it has a completely decentralized structure. It is akin to a huge database that is continually on the move between the thousands of servers hosting its contents (a mass of newsgroup messages). If your ISP offers you Usenet access, your ISP either hosts the Usenet database on their own servers or, more likely these days, subcontracts the access through a specialized third-party Usenet provider.

Like other elements of the Internet, Usenet requires its own primary app (called a *newsreader*) and has its own terminology. Your newsreader app accesses a *news server* which contains *newgroups* which further contain messages (called *newsposts, posts* or *articles*).

Accessing Usenet is somewhat analogous to email except that each Usenet "inbox" and its messages are available to everyone for both reading (downloading) and sending (uploading or posting). There are many thousands of these Usenet "inboxes" (newsgroups) in total, one for every conceivable topic of interest. The email analogy also generally applies to how you go about reading and sending messages except that Usenet messages are received from and sent to a newsgroup's address rather than to a specific user or email address.

In addition, you can send and receive messages to and from newsgroups that include attachments, called *binaries* in Usenet speak. Many newsgroups specialize in binaries, especially movies, videos, images, audio and other media items. Like Usenet as a whole, there is a binary group for almost any subject you can think of.

However, the number and type of newsgroups available to you can vary, especially the binary newsgroups. Many providers *censor* the number and type of newsgroups you can access.

How Usenet is Organized

Newsgroups are organized in a hierarchy. Similar to domain names for websites, the components of a newsgroup name are separated by dots (.). The first segment of the name is how newsgroups are categorized.

The *traditional* categories of the Usenet hierarchy (the normal, more news-like and non-binary newsgroups) are categorized as follows:

> `comp.*` = computers
> `rec.*` = recreation
> `humanities.*` = humanities
> `sci.*` = science
> `misc.*` = miscellaneous
> `soc.*` = society
> `news.*` = news
> `talk.*` = talk

However, you may not be as interested in these categories as you are in the *alt.* hierarchy which stands for <u>alt</u>ernative. The alternative genre of Usenet is often where lots of interesting, different and off the beaten track things can be found. Many people are specifically interested in the `alt.binaries.*` newsgroups, the newsgroups that contain the most media items.

Even when an ISP provides Usenet access, they usually don't offer all, most or even many of these *binary newsgroups*. Depending on your ISP, you may have access to none or hundreds of these binary newsgroups. Because some of these newsgroups can be controversial, including for copyright issues, many ISPs will carry only a subset of what is fully available, essentially censoring the rest.

For example, though some Usenet newsgroups are accessible via Google (see https://groups.google.com/) and other free online portals, they usually only cover the traditional categories mentioned above. If they include alt newsgroups, the access will usually be limited to 'text only' alt newsgroups and not any of those carrying binaries.

What Are You Missing? (Censored Newsgroups)

To compare your current level, if any, of Usenet newsgroups to what is potentially available try the full newsgroup listings and newsgroup searches at:

- http://www.cogipas.com/usenet-search-newsgroups/

- or type "full newsgroup listing" or similar terms in your favorite search engine such as https://duckduckgo.com/

If you do not have access to any newsgroups or to as many as you would like, there are 2 ways you can gain greater access.

The first (and free) option is to try accessing so-called *open servers* (these are news servers made available for the general public's use). The second option is to pay for separate access to Usenet newsgroups through a specialized premium service. Both of these options - open servers and premium Usenet providers - are covered in the pages ahead.

In either case, you will first need to know about the kind of app used to access Usenet newsgroups, a *newsreader* app.

What is a Newsreader App?

Just as you need a browser app for accessing the web, an email app (or service) for accessing emails and a torrent app for accessing torrents, you will require a *newsreader* app for accessing Usenet, its servers, newsgroups and posts.

Like most apps, you will need to enter some basic setup information into your newsreader app. This information includes a special Internet address for a *news server* (often in the form, `news.example.com`).

Furthermore, just as web browsing, email and torrent activities each use a specific Internet *protocol*, HTTP, SMTP and P2P respectively, Usenet also uses its own protocol, *NNTP* which is short for *Network News Transfer Protocol*.

Similar to setting up an email account, most newsreader apps will prompt you to enter personal information such as your name and email address. To protect your privacy, do *not* use your real name, email address or any other personal information when setting up your newsreader app. Either leave these fields blank or enter aliases.

! Warning ! - Please read this entire chapter before attempting to *post* messages to Usenet newsgroups.

When you first connect to a news server, your newsreader app will download all of the newsgroups that are available from the selected news server. From this list of what's available you then choose the newsgroups to which you want to *subscribe*.

Most newsreader apps will also let you search through the list of available newsgroups by keyword. This lets you quickly find and subscribe to groups that you are most interested in, such as the alt.binaries newsgroups.

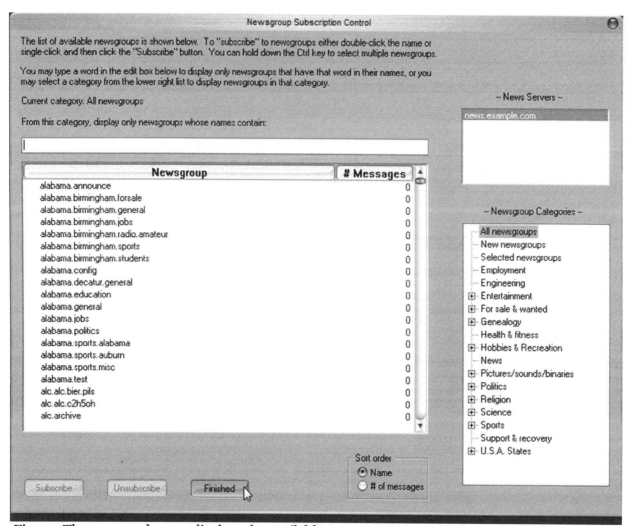

Figure: The newsreader app displays the available groups you can subscribe to and often lets you search the names of newsgroups

Recommended Usenet Newsreader Apps

Below are the Usenet newsreader apps I recommend.

- *Agent* (30-day free trial) http://www.forteinc.com/agent/ is a solid overall Usenet newsreader. It is equally effective and easy-to-use for both text-based and binaries newsgroups, making it a great choice for newcomers to Usenet. Unfortunately, it is only free for the first 30 days.

- *GrabIt* (free) http://www.shemes.com/ may take some time to get used to, but after an hour you should understand it well. If you want a newsreader primarily for downloading binaries, GrabIt allows you to preview articles and informs you about which messages and binaries are *complete* or not. This saves you from wasting time and bandwidth downloading incomplete items. GrabIt also displays downloads in batches letting you increase or decrease the priority of a specific download, pause all your downloads, or have your device automatically shut down after the batch download is complete.

Privacy Risks (How Safe is Usenet?)

There are a number of privacy risks by *posting* to Usenet newsgroups and even by merely *retrieving* messages. However, before discussing the risks, it is good to know that Usenet also offers a number of privacy *advantages*.

Similar to web browsing and email, you can be safe from eavesdroppers while accessing Usenet *provided* you are using a secure (SSL) connection. Most premium Usenet providers use these encrypted connections.

You are also safe from third party monitoring while downloading from Usenet because, in contrast to torrent file-sharing, you are *not* downloading the content from other users. With Usenet, you are downloading directly from your Usenet provider's news server. This means you also don't have to rely on the availability of seeders or peers as you do with torrents. Obviously, you have to trust your Usenet provider. But that's more manageable than trying to trust hundreds or thousands of fellow torrent users. However, like torrents, your ISP may be able to detect if you are using Usenet, so make sure to always mask your Usenet connection by using services with secure (SSL) connections.

Please note that the technology employed by Usenet also means that using a VPN offers you no additional protection for Usenet activities *unless* you are using a web-based Usenet service (discussed in the pages ahead).

Even Only "Lurking" Leaves a Trail (How Safe is it to Download from Usenet?)

Lurking refers to when you only download and read messages and binaries, but never post them. Even merely lurking might be logged by your Usenet provider. Conventional wisdom is that your provider simply does not have the inclination, time or resources to scan through the logs to discover which newsgroups and individual messages (and binaries) you are accessing. This is more of a concern if you have Usenet access through your ISP. However, you still need to be aware of this possible risk.

You should check your provider's *privacy policy* to determine whether they are logging, what they log, how long they keep logs and under what conditions they disclose customer activities reflected in the logs.

Posting is Traceable

From its inception, the entire Usenet has been and continues to be archived. Searchable archives exist of more than 700 million Usenet posts covering a period of decades (see screenshot or http://www.cogipas.com/UsenetGoogle)! This means that unless you have given anonymity some thought, any and all articles you post to Usenet (attaching binaries or otherwise) will be recorded. Such posts could come back to haunt you.

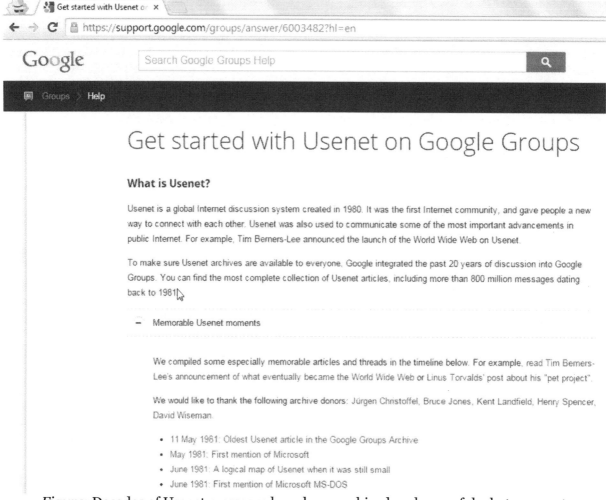

Figure: Decades of Usenet messages have been archived, so be careful what you post

To illustrate the privacy risks of posting to Usenet, browse or search Google Groups https://groups.google.com/ to find a message of interest. Once you have opened a message, click on *More message actions* (the small down arrow) and then *Show original*. Notice how some of the fields contain potentially revealing information (such as the message ID or even an IP address). Posting to Usenet newsgroups without taking measures to protect your privacy means revealing details that, once posted, are impossible to undo.

This is why, at an absolute minimum, you should *not* enter your name or email address in the settings of your newsreader app. Although this makes your posts untraceable for simple Google-type searches, there are still more precautions you should take.

Posting Under an Alias is Still Traceable

Even if you post to Usenet under an alias using a fake name and email address, the post is still traceable back to you. Just as your Internet browsing, email messages and torrent file-sharing activities are stamped with an IP address that can be traced back to you, Usenet posts are too. Similar to email messages, Usenet posts contain a number of *headers*. One or more of these headers will contain information that can be traced back to the poster.

For example, the following headers are taken from an actual Usenet post I made in 1996 using my name and then email address. The post is clearly traceable from a number of the headers.

```
From: mtbai...@sonetis.com (Matthew Bailey)
Subject: !NAMTAR!.WAD Homepage is on-line.  Screenshots,
demos and the WAD itself all available now.
Date: 1996/05/28
Message-ID: <4o2dq8$hs4@lisa.iosphere.net>#1/1
X-Deja-AN: 157150554
sender: t...@mantis.co.uk
content-type: text/plain; charset=iso-8859-1
organization: Channel One
mime-version: 1.0
reply-to: mtbai...@sonetis.com
newsgroups: rec.games.computer.doom.announce
```

Figure: Headers in Usenet posts contain information that can be traced back to you

The vast majority of Usenet providers *log* the activities on their news servers, including for technical reasons, legal requirements and to deal with abuse or complaints (for example, spam). By comparing the headers of a post to these logs, a message you posted can be traced back to you even if you posted it under an alias using a fake name and email address.

To post *anonymously*, you need to use a news server that omits any traceable path back to you. Even when you think you have found a news server that eliminates traceable headers, *always* do a test post to the *alt.test* newsgroup to ensure no identifying information appears in the headers of the post.

Bypassing Usenet Censorship

If you don't have any access to Usenet newsgroups or you do but your ISP is censoring some of them, especially in the `alt.binaries.*` hierarchy, there are two things you can do to access the newsgroups you want:

1. Use a premium (paid) Usenet service. Most of these services offer NNTP news server access but some also offer web-based Usenet access.

More About: *Web Usenet* - Web-based Usenet allows you to access Usenet newsgroups through a web browser interface rather than with a newsreader app. You will normally *not* need to enter an NNTP news server address, but instead access the newsgroups and posts with your web browser after entering a username and password at the provider's site.

2. Use an *open news servers*. Open news servers are accessible to the general public. This is a more complicated way to access censored newsgroups, but is free.

Each of these methods is discussed in detail below.

Using Premium Usenet Services to Access Censored Newsgroups

The easiest way to bypass censorship and access newsgroups you are prevented from accessing is to pay for it. The services listed below are not free, but the quality is excellent featuring fast download speeds, the largest number of available newsgroups, including the binaries groups, long *retention periods* (meaning older posts stay available for longer) and privacy considerations such as keeping no user activity logs.

What to Look for in a Usenet Provider

When trying to determine which Usenet provider is right for you, look at the following factors:

Price: depending on how cost conscious you are, you can expect to pay about $10-$20 per month (€8-16 or £6-12) for a premium Usenet provider's services.

Newsgroup coverage: the breadth of newsgroup coverage can vary between providers and some providers may emphasize certain binary newsgroups over others. Make sure to check that they have the newsgroups you are interested in by first searching or browsing the newsgroups they carry.

Secure Connections: a service that provides secure encrypted (SSL) connections helps ensure that your Usenet activities cannot be snooped on or monitored by third parties.

Anonymity: choose a Usenet provider that has a no logging policy. Some providers even facilitate your ability to post (upload) anonymously to Usenet newsgroups.

Data Retention: this will usually be expressed in number of days and describes how long in time the provider's Usenet archive goes back. Data retention periods can vary considerably, usually about 1200 days on average, but can be as high as 2000 days.

Monthly Transfer Limits: this is the amount of data the provider will let you download each month for the package you buy. This too varies, usually from 5 GB per month to unlimited amounts.

In the end, it's all about trial and error. It's not just the provider you pick that's a factor in how good is your Usenet access, but a multitude of things such as your location, your ISP and even the time of day you use it. All the various elements at play mean that everyone's experience with a certain Usenet provider can vary. This is why, in the comments section of an online review for a Usenet provider, you may see some people praising the service and others lambasting it.

Recommended Usenet Providers

Below are some premium Usenet services I recommend. Of course, you are free and are encouraged to research and choose your own. Each provider will have its own set-up instructions and will provide you with the NNTP news server address to enter into your newsreader app.

- *Newshosting* ¢ http://www.cogipas.com/newshosting gives you full uncensored access to over 100,000 newsgroups and respects your privacy with a no logging policy. Newshosting boasts massive retention periods of over 2000 days, uses secure (SSL) connections, and allows both unlimited speeds and unlimited data transfers. Its customer packages come bundled with classic NNTP news server access as well as with an easy-to-use web browser access, EasyNews, which is especially great for beginners. A free trial is available.

- *UsenetServer* ¢ http://www.cogipas.com/UsenetServer carries over 80,000 newsgroups including a massive number of the binaries newsgroups. You can check for yourself by consulting UsenetServer's newsgroup search http://www.usenetserver.com/en/searchgroups.php and its current group list http://www.usenetserver.com/groups.txt. You can also take advantage of UsenetServer's free 14-day trial. UsenetServer has one of the industry's highest retention periods at over 2300 days and allows unlimited data access with up to 20 concurrent secure (SSL) connections. Lastly, its custom global search tool makes searching newsgroups a snap.

Other Tips for Effective Usenet Downloading

Overall, the most important factor for fast Usenet downloading is your choice of provider.

Regarding your newsreader app settings, the sweet spot for the number of *simultaneous connections* for Usenet downloading is usually 8 to 15. Counterintuitively, using more connections may actually *decrease* your downloading speeds unless you benefit from a super-fast connection such as 100+ Mbps connection in which case you could go up to as many as 50 simultaneous connections.

Sometimes *incomplete binaries* can be a nuisance on Usenet. Large Usenet binaries, such as movies, must be split up over many, sometimes dozens of, Usenet posts. If the Usenet server you are using is missing even one of those posts, the file will be incomplete and, after taking precious time to download it, you may not be able to properly open it.

If incomplete Usenet binaries are starting to become a problem for you, try using *NZB files*. The NZB format tries to fill in these gaps by locating all the different possible locations of these sometimes elusive posts. The Usenet newsreader apps and Usenet providers I recommended earlier support NZB files.

More About: *NZB Files* - NZB files are to Usenet what torrent files are to peer-to-peer file-sharing. More than 10 years ago, the Usenet website Newzbin started to index Usenet downloads and created the NZB file format. Like a torrent file, a NZB file acts merely as a pointer to where certain downloads are available on Usenet.

Bypassing Censorship Using Open News Servers

Another way to access censored Usenet newsgroups is by accessing *open news servers*. Open news servers are freely accessible (sometimes by accident) at no cost but usually have a very limited number of newsgroups available. Open news servers may be operated by educational institutions or Usenet enthusiasts. Using an open news server is usually slow but can provide you with access to newsgroups and *may* increase your privacy.

You can find lists of open news servers on the web or, if you are an advanced user, you can find open news servers on your own by using a *NNTP sniffer* app to find them.

Below are some listings of open news servers. Many links of this nature may be temporary or come and go. If you are getting dead links when clicking on them, keep drilling down the list or type "open news servers" in your favorite search engine.

- *newzbot Public News Servers* http://www.newzbot.com/ maintains a list of open servers ranked (and sortable by) the number of newsgroups carried, server speed, message count and the length of time it has been open to the public. The service also allows you to search for a particular newsgroup at http://www.newzbot.com/search.php.

- *Publicly Accessible Free Usenet News Servers* http://freenews.maxbaud.net/ is a comprehensive and up-to-date site packed full of information that lets you search for specific newsgroups.

- *Open Directory Project (dmoz) List of Open Public News Servers* http://www.dmoz.org/Computers/Usenet/Public_News_Servers/ is a good list of open news server sites.

Please note that your ability to access open news servers may vary. This happens for a number of technical reasons and means that, although your friend may be able to access a particular open news server, you may not be able to.

How to Use an Open News Server

To use an open news server, change your newsreader app's *News Server* or *NNTP* setting (look under menu items such as Settings, Options or Preferences). In that box, type in the NNTP address of the specific open news server you want to use. If you want to try one of the open news servers listed in the sites above, you would enter the corresponding NNTP address (see screenshot).

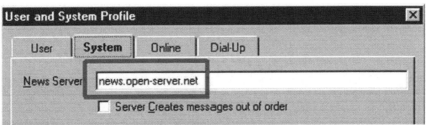

Figure: Look for a place to enter the NNTP address in your newsreader app's Settings, Options or Preferences

Using this open news server, you can obtain its full newsgroup listing, subscribe to newsgroups and retrieve (read) messages, sometimes supporting binaries. You may even be able to *post* Usenet messages through some open news servers.

Top Tip - Never post through an open news server unless you are certain that no traceable information will appear in any of the message headers. The only way to be sure about this is to post a test message, retrieve it and carefully look at its full headers. The appropriate newsgroup for this is *alt.test*. Please follow proper Usenet etiquette and insert the word *ignore* in the post's subject line.

Furthermore, even if you are posting through an open news server which is not passing traceable information in the message headers, this can change at any time due, for example, to technical changes made by the system operator. This is another reason why you should always first check what information is appearing in the headers before posting messages.

Finding Open News Servers with an NNTP Sniffer (Advanced Users)

Another way to gain access to uncensored newsgroups is to find *open news servers* yourself. You can do this using an NNTP *sniffer* app. In fact, the people maintaining the listings above of open news servers are using similar apps and tools to generate their listings.

Using an NNTP Sniffer App

An NNTP sniffer app helps you track down open news servers. Because you perform the search, this method has the advantage of finding open news servers that are accessible for your particular setup and circumstances. Recall from earlier that access to open news servers may vary from user to user for technical reasons.

An NNTP sniffer app uses your own connection as a starting point and tries to find as many news servers as it can. Then, the app tests each one to see which are open to you.

Depending on the app, usually you will need to enter a starting NNTP news server address and a newsgroup that the news server carries. If you have Usenet access through your ISP, you can enter your news server (*news*.example.com) and use the `alt.test` newsgroup, or some other newsgroup that you know your starting news server carries. If you do not have Usenet access, find an open news server on one of the listings I mentioned earlier and enter its NNTP address as the starting news server in the sniffer app.

From there, the app will do the rest of the hard work, presenting you with a list of available open news servers and the newsgroups they carry. Depending on the functionality of the app, it may also tell you which servers allow *posting* as well as the estimated download speeds and retention periods.

! Warning ! - Some ISPs consider the use of NNTP sniffer apps as an undesirable activity (some may even liken it to "hacking") so please first *carefully* read your ISP's Terms of Service to make sure that you are not prohibited from using sniffer apps. Do *not* try using a NNTP sniffer app if you have any doubts.

The screenshots below (with the server name results blurred out) are from the *NewsHunter* app and appearances will vary for different NNTP sniffer apps.

News Hunter 4 (free) http://news-hunter.software.informer.com/4.0/ is an NNTP sniffer app. If this link doesn't work, try typing "News Hunter 4 NNTP" in your favorite search engine or torrent index search to find the app.

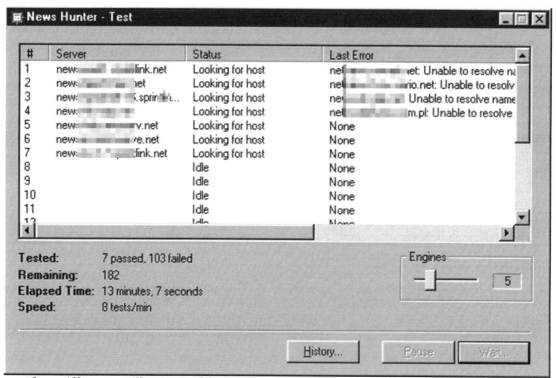

Figure: The sniffer app will start probing news servers to determine whether they are open to you

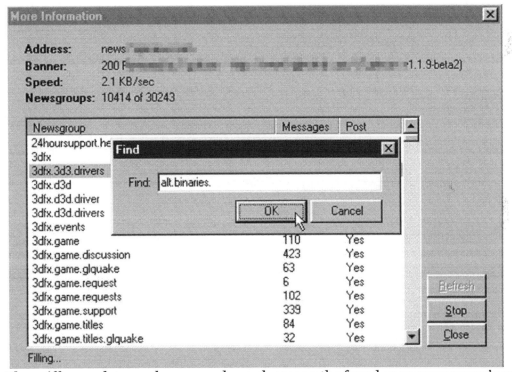

Figure: When the sniffer app is finished, you will be presented with a list of available open news servers and some of their features

Figure: The sniffer app lets you browse and search among the found open news server's available newsgroups

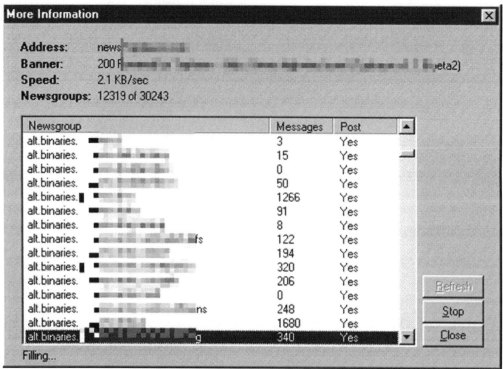

Figure: This open news server carries many binaries newsgroups and even allows posting

Remember, you should only post to Usenet if you know what you are doing. The rest of this chapter is dedicated to that subject.

How to Anonymously Post to Usenet (Advanced Users)

Introduction

Your reasons for wanting to post anonymously to a Usenet newsgroup may include simply wanting to prevent spammers from obtaining your email address, having general privacy concerns, or wishing to protect your identity for a controversial post (for example, if you are a political activist or a whistleblower).

There are a number of ways you can post *anonymously* to Usenet newsgroups. As we have seen, it is insufficient and you are *not* anonymous posting under an alias by entering a fake name and email address in your newsreader app's configuration settings. Most news servers will pass on enough information that posts made through them will be traceable back to you.

Usenet Headers Can be Traced Back to You

As mentioned at the beginning of the chapter, Usenet is decentralized and its newsgroup posts scattered all over a constantly changing group of servers that store and forward messages to each other. By its nature, Usenet is beyond any central control.

Nonetheless, messages posted to Usenet contain information that could be used to identify the poster, such as a message ID or even an IP addresses buried in the technical (and usually hidden) *headers* that are part of the post. The headers in any given post may vary depending on a number of things.

Below is a fictional sample of a Usenet post's headers. The bolded lines indicate those that contain information that could potentially identify the person posting the message.

```
Newsgroups: soc.support.acceptance,alt.general,mindspring.local.atlanta
Path: mindspring!firehose.mindspring.com!newsfeed1-
hme1!newsfeed.internetmci.com!128.174.5.49!vixen.cso.uiuc.edu!uchinews!news
From: Suzy Smith user@example.com
Subject: Re: Help with headers?
Nntp-Posting-Host: ip14.an4-atlanta2.ga.pub-ip.psi.net
Message-ID: <32146bef.10426023@news.interamp.com>
Reply-To: suzy@other.place
Organization: Anything You Like
References: <20110901140100.KAA29407@ladder02.news.aol.com>
<EFy5Ar.3pq@world.std.com> <340DC46C.3A62@wco.com> <5umekl$44m@dfw-
ixnews9.ix.netcom.com> <5v3g50$hsl$1@news.smart.net>
Date: Tue, 5 Jan 2015 21:17:39 GMT
X-Newsreader: Offline Reader
X-No-Archive: yes
Lines: 24
```

For an in-depth list of Usenet headers, from the common to the rare, see https://www.cotse.net/privacy/newsgroup_header.htm

You Can't Achieve Usenet Anonymity using a Web Proxy, Tor or a VPN

Recall that Usenet newsreader apps use the *NNTP protocol*, just as web browsing apps use the HTTP protocol, email apps use the SMTP protocol, and torrent file-sharing apps use the P2P protocol. Because a different protocol is used for Usenet, the techniques for remaining anonymous on the web (see chapter 12), email (see chapter 14), or torrent file-sharing (see chapter 16) will *not* make you anonymous on Usenet.

In particular, it is worth repeating that using a web proxy, Tor or a VPN to mask your IP address on the web will *not* work for Usenet. These tools will mask your HTTP protocol-based activities, but will *not* protect your Usenet activities because your newsreader app uses a different protocol, NNTP.

Top Tip - You might think that a web proxy, Tor or a VPN can make you anonymous when using a *web-based* Usenet service. While this is partly true, it still carries risks. Normally web-based Usenet services will require you to provide sign up and payment information. This can defeat the purpose of trying to post anonymously in the first place because posts could be traced back to the service and then to you as they will have your personal details on file. This is why you have to pay close attention to a premium Usenet provider's Privacy Policy, especially if you intend to make sensitive posts.

How You Can Post Anonymously to Usenet

! Warning ! - Trying to post anonymously to Usenet using the methods below is for *advanced users* only. It is not an easy process. If you make a mistake you could leave behind information that makes posts traceable back to you.

Achieving anonymity posting to Usenet newsgroups means doing so without leaving your fingerprints on posts. There are a few ways that you can do this and they are presented below in order from least to most difficult. Generally speaking, the more difficult the method, the more protections it offers.

<u>Using a Web-based Form to Post Anonymously to Usenet</u>

You can use a web-based form to post anonymously to Usenet. The process for most of these forms is the same: you enter the name of the newsgroup, the subject of the message and the contents of the message you wish to send. When you select OK, the form takes care of the posting on your behalf. However, often these forms do not indicate which newsgroups or message sizes are supported (important if you were hoping to post to binary newsgroups).

For example, try the *Anonymouse.org* AnonNews form http://anonymouse.org/anonnews.html (see screenshot). This is a free, web-based form which allows you to post anonymously to Usenet newsgroups.

Figure: AnonNews is Anonymouse.org's web-based Usenet posting form

Similar forms can also be found by typing "anonymous Usenet post web form" (or similar searches) in your favorite search engine, but be prepared to dig through lots of links, including defunct ones. Over the course of time, web-based newspost forms tend to come and go.

One risk with this method is that you may not be anonymous if your IP address (transmitted to the site hosting the web form) is being passed along with the post. In addition, your IP address could be logged by the website.

Therefore, always access anonymous web-based Usenet posting forms with a web proxy, Tor or a VPN enabled, though this may have an impact on the web-based form's functionality.

As always, only use a web-form service you trust. To establish this trust, search, read reviews and make an informed decision about which operators are trustworthy before you use them. Ideally, the web-based form should support an encrypted SSL connection (HTTP_S_://), but these are difficult to find.

More About: *Encoding* - If trying to post binaries to Usenet through a web-based form (or a mail2news gateway – discussed next), you may first need to translate the media file into plain text, a process called *encoding*. Usenet can only handle plain text, so encoding is the process whereby binary files (such as images or videos) are translated into plain text. When you use a newsreader app, all the encoding (and decoding) is done automatically in the background and so you never become aware of it. But when you want to *manually* post a binary file to Usenet using a web-based form (or mail2news gateway), it may be necessary for you to first translate it into plain text (encoding it). The most popular encoding and decoding methods are *UU* and *yEnc*. Different tools are available for each of these methods and can be found with your favorite Internet search engine.

Post Anonymously to Usenet with a Mail2News Remailer Gateway (Advanced Users)

The second way to post anonymously to Usenet is to use an anonymous remailer (see chapter 14) *together* with something called a *mail2news gateway*. This is a two-step process.

Recall that a remailer will take your email message, strip out the original headers (including those containing any traceable information), and then re-send the message to its final destination, attaching its own new headers. This ensures that you are not identified as the original source of the message.

The major drawback with this method is that you must have absolute faith in the remailer - that the service is indeed doing what it claims to do - because you will be sharing your email address with it. In addition, the remailer must not keep any logs or visitor information that could potentially fall into unsafe hands and be used to identify you.

Further recall that you can chain remailers, sending your email from one anonymous remailer to another, thus reducing the chances of detection. You can also use a web-based remailer form to make the process a little easier.

However, an additional step is needed to have your email message transformed into and sent as a Usenet post. This step involves addressing your email message to a *mail2news gateway*.

You can try the mail2news gateways listed below. You need to read the specific instructions for each mail2news gateway about how to specify the newsgroup to which you wish to post. You can usually receive this information by sending a blank message to the mail2news gateway address with the subject "help".

To: Address (mail2news gateways)

- mail2news@reece.net.au
- mail2news@dizum.com
- mail2news@mixmin.net
- mail2news@m2n.mixmin.net
- mail2news@tioat.net
- mail2news@m2n.tophat.at
- or type "mail2news gateway" in your favorite search engine and be prepared to do some digging

If trying to post binaries, make sure the mail2news gateway supports binaries. This is a big if as most don't. If not, you will have to first encode your files (convert them into plain text) as discussed in the *More About: Encoding* box above.

Lastly, if you are *chaining* remailers, the mail2news gateway must be the final recipient in the chain.

Using Specialized Apps to Post Anonymously to Usenet (Advanced Users)

Apps are available that can post anonymously to Usenet newsgroups. These apps essentially do all the hard work described above, but seamlessly and in the background. This includes applying the proper remailer syntax, encoding the message, sending it through a remailer addressed to a mail2news gateway and (in some cases) encrypting the message to prevent it from being intercepted in transit.

These apps include *Quicksilver* (http://quicksilvermail.net/) which is free and uses the higher security protocol Mixmaster so that your message is encrypted, sent through a chain of remailers and then to a mail2news gateway. Each remailer strips from the message the information of the previous sender before forwarding it further onwards, ensuring that your message is virtually untraceable. The app may seem a bit dated but is still a popular choice.

Other apps include *Jack B. Nymble* and *Private Idaho*, both free apps that use a series of remailers and a mail2news gateway to post anonymously to Usenet.

However, please be aware that all of the apps above are complicated. They will require a certain amount of configuring and tinkering to work properly and are suitable for advanced users only.

* * *

For updates and additional information about secure, private and anonymous Usenet, please visit http://www.cogipas.com/secure-private-anonymous-usenet/.

Chapter 18: Getting Rid of Other Kinds of Trace Information Left Behind on Your Devices

Introduction

As we saw in chapters 4 and 11, your web browser retains records of your website visits, your searches and your downloads. However, your web browser is not the only source of trace information being left behind on your device that can give away your activities and habits. You may not even realize it, but your device's operating system and apps also keep detailed records of your activities.

You trust your devices with your most private activities and items. Sometimes you might not even realize you're storing sensitive information on your device. Anyone with access to your device could quickly find out all manner of things about you and perhaps use that information against you.

You might be surprised how easy it is to uncover this kind of information. This chapter starts by highlighting the extent to which information is left behind on your devices. You'll learn how easy it is for anyone with access to your devices to access this kind of information. Then I'll jump right to the *solution* for getting rid of trace data on your device.

You'll also learn about forensic software that can be used to reveal *hidden* information on your device. Finally, we'll look at how you can manually clean sensitive information from the guts of your operating system (in the Windows Registry and some other special files).

Why You Need to Remove Trace Data from Your Devices

Once information is accessed or stored on your device, that information could be recovered even after being deleted (and emptying the Recycle Bin). Hard drive capacities are now so large that data and information from many years ago (including deleted items) can still be recovered in perfect condition.

Imagine what somebody might learn about you if they snooped on your most recently accessed documents or media files or items you've deleted. By digging a bit deeper, they could discover data that is even harder to get rid of on your devices such as the names of documents, pictures, video clips or web pages that you searched for, downloaded, saved, opened, renamed or deleted.

These risks are particularly important if you ever sell, donate or dispose of your device or storage media, whether hard drives or removable memory. If you do not properly go about removing the data, it could be easily recovered and used against you by adversaries.

There are a number of things you can do to ensure that this kind of information cannot be recovered. Some techniques can be accomplished manually, but apps are a big help, as you'll see.

The Kinds of Trace Information Left Behind on Your Devices

Aside from the trace information left behind by your web browser app which we covered in detail in chapter 11 (and will cover in further detail later in this chapter), your device's operating system also keeps lots of records of your activities. This includes records of the items you most recently accessed on your device, whether images, videos, movies, ebooks or documents. In Windows, these are called *Recent Items*.

In addition to your operating system, *each* app you use will also usually keep a history of items you most recently accessed with that app. These history lists are found in apps ranging from word processors to image viewers to ebook readers to video and movie players.

The recent items feature is to help you quickly open items accessed most recently or most often. This is fine most of the time, but of course can also disclose activity that you would rather keep private. In other words, after accessing, viewing or downloading anything you consider sensitive, all kinds of traces of your activities are left behind on your device, much of it not so easy to find let alone get rid of.

You could manually delete all this trace information, but that is time-consuming and you are prone to miss something.

How to Use a Privacy Cleaning App

Normally I would present the risks first and then the solution to preventing them. However, because the risks discussed in this chapter are somewhat complicated, I will first describe the solution and then present the risks in detail.

The best and easiest way to eliminate the traces of your activities from devices is to use tools specifically built for this purpose. *Privacy cleaning apps* (sometimes called eraser, washing or scrubbing apps) are tools that eliminate all of this trace information left behind on your device, helping keep your privacy intact. Many of these apps do the job at a single click. There are dozens of such apps to choose from for all devices, some of which are free.

If you don't think you need a tool to eliminate trace data, think again! Perform the checks described in this chapter and especially in the book's *Annex B: Device Privacy Checks You Should Do Right Now* to see what trace information may be on your device for others to discover. Ask yourself, if someone used those simple techniques what would they find? With many free apps available for just about every device on the market there really is no excuse for not using a privacy cleaning app.

Whichever app you choose, free or premium, make sure that it is adequately supported and frequently updated. After installing the app, spend a minute to set it up, selecting the sources of trace data you would like it to cleanse including from Windows, your web browser and other apps. Good choices are the apps you use most frequently for your sensitive activities and might include your video player and image viewer apps.

Perform an occasional privacy audit on your device (including those steps found in Annex B) to see if any new sources of trace data are showing up. If so, update your settings accordingly. You can clean up after each sensitive session on your device or, if you like, schedule regular cleanings or have the app clean up automatically at every start-up and/or shut down.

Recommended Privacy Cleaning Apps for Clearing Unwanted Trace Data

The easiest way to clear unwanted trace data from your devices is to use a specially-designed app. Most privacy cleaning apps provide lots of choice about what you can cleanse from your device. I recommended the following apps.

BleachBit (free) http://bleachbit.sourceforge.net/ is a powerful yet simple app, appealing to novices and advanced users alike. BleachBit enables you to delete unwanted trace data from the sources you would expect and from a wide range of apps. It is also available as a *portable* distribution, meaning a version you can run from a USB memory stick.

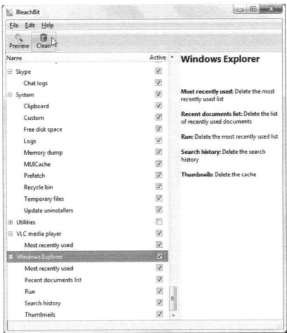

Figure: Selecting options in BleachBit for cleaning sources of trace data

Privacy Eraser Free http://www.cogipas.com/pef and its premium counterpart *Privacy Eraser Pro ¢* http://www.cogipas.com/pep are some of the best privacy protection apps around. Each has a clean and intuitive interface and has features to remove the trace data left behind by your web browser, operating system and hundreds of apps by virtue of dozens of plugins available. Privacy Eraser also allows you to build and add your own custom items for cleaning, if needed. As a bonus, it has built-in file shredding and drive wiping capabilities (see chapter 19), and other handy tools. It also comes in a portable version that you can run from a USB memory stick

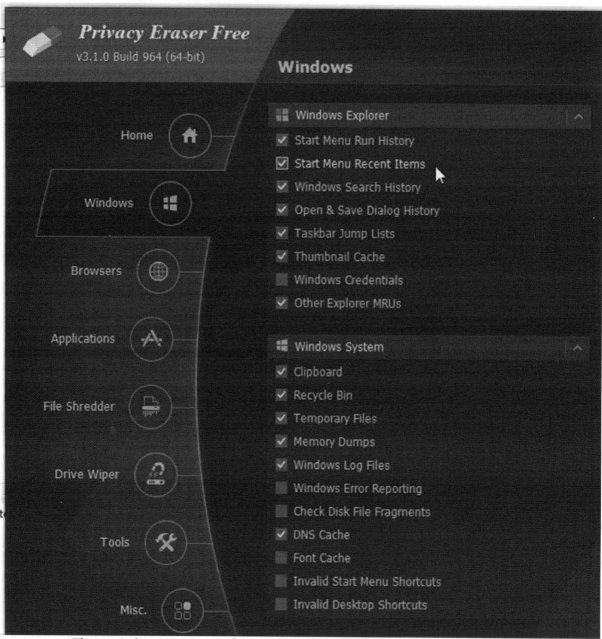

Figure: Privacy Eraser makes it easy to get rid of trace data on your device

~ ~ ~

With the solution now presented, let's get into the details of the risks these apps protect you from.

Clearing Your Most Recently Used (MRU) Records

Depending on your settings, Windows keeps records of the most recently used (MRU) items you have accessed, including documents, images, and videos. Windows also keeps records of the most recent searches you performed. These MRU records are easily accessible from the Windows Start menu under the fly-out menu item *Recent Items* and in *Jump Lists* (when you right-click on an app icon on the task bar).

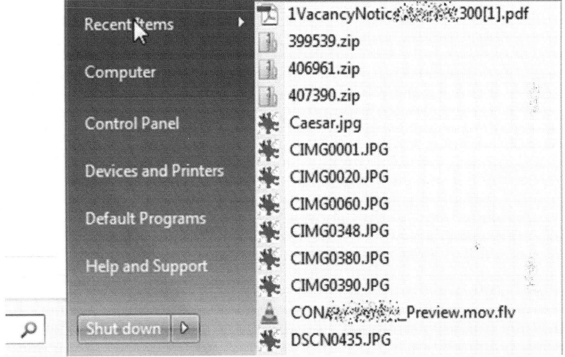

Figure: Window's Recent Items, accessible from the Start menu, are an example of MRU records

Windows MRU records are easy to disable: in the Start menu type *Taskbar* and you should see the *Taskbar and Start Menu* Control Panel item displayed in the menu (or *Jump Lists* in Windows 8.1). Select it and *uncheck* the 'Privacy' selections (see screenshot).

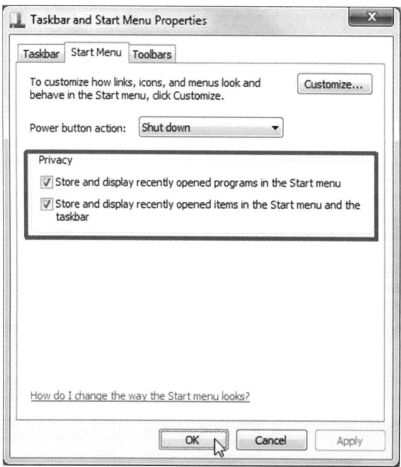

Figure: To disable Windows most recently used settings you need to *uncheck* these items

In addition, many individual apps also have their own MRU features. Although they are meant to save you time when searching for recently or often used items, they enable anyone with access to your device to open your apps and quickly see what files you have been accessing with them.

If the referenced item remains saved in the same place on your device, selecting the item in the list of MRU records will actually open it. You should check the Preferences, Setup or Options for each app to see if it is possible to disable its MRU features. An example is shown below for the popular image viewer app IrfanView.

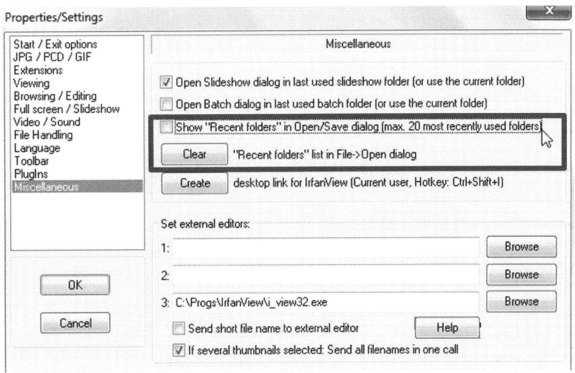

Figure: Disabling the MRU features in the popular image viewer app IrfanView

The Records Windows Registry Keeps

As we have seen, Windows and most apps store the names of your most recently used (MRU) items. But MRUs are just the tip of the iceberg.

Windows consolidates and centralizes many settings and configurations into a complex database, called the *Registry*. The Registry tracks and records a great deal of what is done on your device. Therefore, it is a gold mine of sensitive information for snoops. For example, the Registry can be analyzed to reveal:

- records of websites you visited and searches you performed (*independent* from your web browser's records)
- the names of downloaded items
- the sites from where you downloaded items and where they were saved on your device
- possibly passphrases stored by apps for the accounts you use (although well designed apps *should* store passphrases securely)
- lists of previously connected storage devices
- the names of Usenet newsgroups to which you subscribe (see chapter 17)

- records of wireless networks to which the device connected (revealing clues about where you have been)

- and much more

You can see how some of this information could come back to haunt you. To make matters worse, sophisticated forensic analysis software (discussed in the pages ahead) quickly examines and easily extracts information from the Registry.

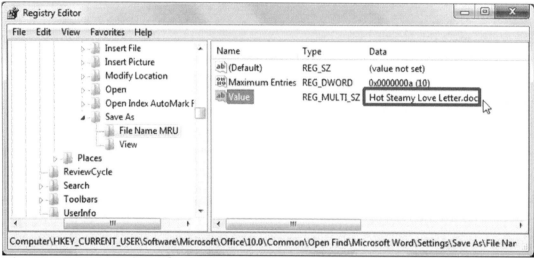

Figure: Oops. Sometimes the Registry can reveal information that you rather it didn't

Because the potentially sensitive information mentioned above is tucked away in the Registry, it can be difficult to find and purge from your device. While you can sift through the information manually by browsing through your Registry (see the next section) it is better to use the specialized privacy cleaning apps I recommended earlier in this chapter.

Cleaning the Windows Registry of Trace Data (Advanced Users)

Introduction

One of the trickiest device privacy problems is how to remove the item names, folder names, search terms, and MRU histories that get embedded in the Windows Registry. Even if your items are safeguarded by the world's strongest encryption apps (see chapter 15), the Registry can still pose a significant risk as a source of personal or sensitive information.

In this section, you will learn how to clean trace data from your Registry. Because the Registry contains information that Windows requires to work correctly, please take particular care when accessing it.

Accessing the Registry

! Warning ! - When following the instructions below, be careful only to view entries and not to delete or change any entries because this could cause serious problems in Windows, including stopping your device from starting up.

Part 1: Finding the Sensitive Information

In the Windows Start menu type "regedit". When you see *regedit.exe*, select it.

Registry Editor's interface (see screenshot) is somewhat similar to Windows Explorer, which is used for browsing items and folder on your hard drive. They both show roots and branches

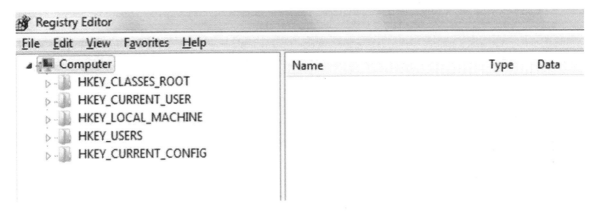

Once Registry Editor opens, go to Registry Editor's menu and choose *Edit > Find* (or use the keyboard shortcut *Ctrl+F*). Type a search term in the dialogue box and select *OK*. In the example below, "\downloads\" is used, but you can enter whatever term you like relating to the private activities you wish to check. The searches are *not* case sensitive. You can repeat the same search throughout your Registry by choosing from the menu *Edit > Find Again* (or by pressing the *F3* key on your keyboard). Keep going until you are told that you have reached the end of the Registry.

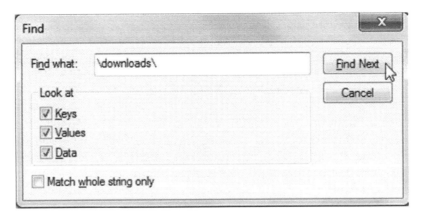

Good terms to search for are:

- item and folder names related to your private activities

- some other terms that reflect your private activities (for example, terms or items you recently searched)

- the downloads folder path ("\downloads\" *without* the quotes)

- "recent", "history" or "log" (*without* the quotes)

- the *extensions* of items (the letters after the dot in filenames) related to your private activities (you will turn up lots of innocuous hits, but this is a thorough method)

    • documents and texts (.DOC, .PDF, .TXT files)
    • videos, movies and films (.MPG, .AVI, .WMV files)
    • pictures and images (.JPG, .PNG files)
    • torrents (.TORRENT files)
    • sounds and recordings (.MP3, .WAV files)

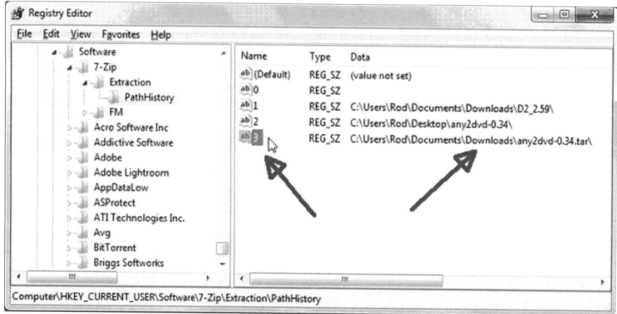

Figure: Registry Editor finds a search hit for the term "\downloads\" which provides information about what you have been downloading to your device

Part 2: Removing Sensitive Information from the Registry

You can delete entries manually (be careful!) by clearing out the actual *Value data*. To do this, double-click on the entry that your search has just highlighted. A small window will open showing you the *Value name:* and *Value data:* of the registry entry that you just selected. Make sure you only delete the Value Data entry and nothing else, especially the Value Name or anything in the left-hand display of branches.

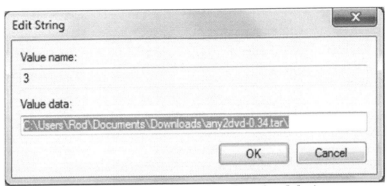

Figure: Selecting the *value data* for deleting

Highlight the sensitive information you wish to delete in the Value data: box, whether some or all of the entry, and simply press delete on your keyboard (or right-click and select Delete) and then select OK. This instance of the data is now removed from your Registry. You will have to perform similar manual deletes for all of the sensitive hits that you find.

Of course, this can be a major hassle because you would have to do this every time after engaging in sensitive activities.

Top Tip - You can also later use this Registry information to clean the entries manually. As you find sensitive information in your Registry, add its location to Registry Editor's *Favorites* for your future reference and for the next steps described below. To do this, go to the menu and choose *Favorites > Add to Favorites*.

It is possible to create and run a Registry *batch file* (a sort of mini-program) that can clear these sensitive entries. However, given the number of good apps that can accomplish (safely) the same thing, it is recommended that you keep life simple and use a privacy cleaning app instead. This is the easiest, safest and recommended approach. In addition, most good privacy cleaning apps will also let you add custom Registry entries to its list of items to wash should its default settings not cover all your needs.

Even if you use a privacy cleaning app it is still good to know how to search the Registry as you may still wish to manually search it to find the locations of sensitive data in the first place and/or to confirm that the privacy cleaning app is doing a good job of properly clearing trace data from your device.

Cleaning Difficult Trace Data from Your Windows Device (Advanced Users)

Log files, metadata and temporary files created by your apps can remain on your devices too, sometimes for years. It's even possible to recover information from your device's memory (RAM) for a short period of time after you have shut it down. So, in addition to worrying about protecting the privacy of items and materials you *actively* download or access yourself, you also have to worry about *passive* activities on your devices; what your operating system and apps are doing and saving in the background, hidden from your sight.

Removing Temporary Files

Windows and a number of apps save data *temporarily*. If a process is interrupted, an app quits unexpectedly or it is poorly designed and does not bother cleaning up after itself, trace data may remain on your device.

For example, the Windows `C:\WINDOWS\TEMP\` folder is a common location for these purposes. Explore this folder to see what it contains.

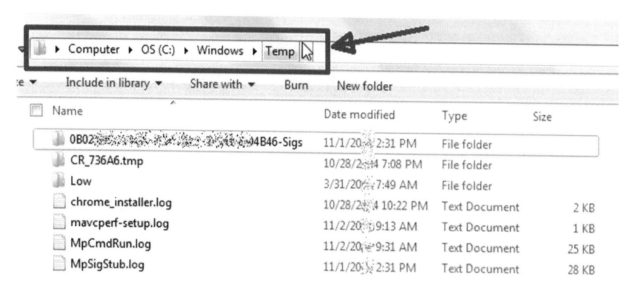

Figure: Check what's in your Windows Temporary folder

You can usually manually delete these temporary contents, or most of them, but any good privacy cleaning app will also take care of this automatically.

Finding and Deleting 'Flash' Cookies

Flash cookies are used by websites that use the Adobe Flash Player for certain features such as animation, audio or video. Similar to customary browser cookies, flash cookies store a small amount of data on your device so that websites can recognize you when you return.

Flash cookies are rather insidious because you would reasonably expect that they are deleted along with browser cookies when you clear data from your web browser app, but they are not.

To see the Flash cookies on your device, go to the Windows Start menu and type (or copy paste the text from here) `%APPDATA%\MACROMEDIA\FLASH PLAYER\#SHAREDOBJECTS`. You can also type (or copy paste) this same string into the Windows Explorer bar.

The `%APPDATA%` part is simply a generic reference to where your application data is stored on your device because the location will vary for each user. For example, `C:\Users\Matthew\AppData\Roaming\Macromedia\Flash Player\#SharedObjects\` is one location, but yours will be different. The folder's name refers to Macromedia as opposed to Adobe as the Flash Player was originally developed by the former and acquired by the latter.

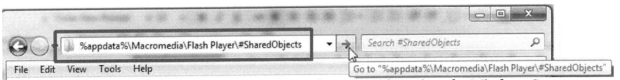

Figure: Navigate to your Flash cookies in the Explorer bar (shown) or the Windows Start menu

You should now be at the folder(s) containing your Flash cookies. Thankfully, they can be deleted like any other items (see screenshot) or better yet permanently deleted (as I'll explain in chapter 19).

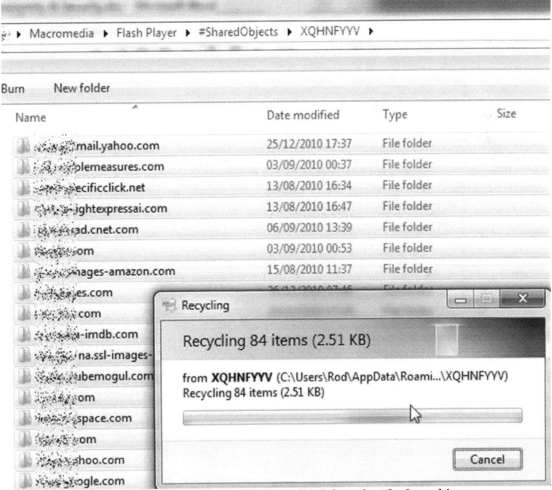

Figure: Once at the folder listing, you can manually delete the Flash cookies on your system

Flushing Cached DNS Entries

Like your devices, websites also use and are identifiable by IP addresses. Domain names are used to point your web browser at the right IP address for a particular website, because domain names are much easier to remember than IP addresses. When you enter a domain name to visit a website, your operating system fetches the underlying IP address from something called a *domain name system* (or DNS) server. This action is *independent* from your web browser and so records of *cached DNS entries* will remain on your device even after running your browser's clear privacy data feature.

In addition, the records of cached DNS entries will remain on your device even if you visited the sites in a private browsing session such as Chrome's incognito mode, Firefox's Private Browsing mode or Internet Explorer's InPrivate mode.

You can verify this for yourself. Access the *command* feature in Windows by typing "command" in the Start menu and selecting the Command Prompt (or CMD.EXE) program to open a command prompt window (sometimes called a DOS prompt).

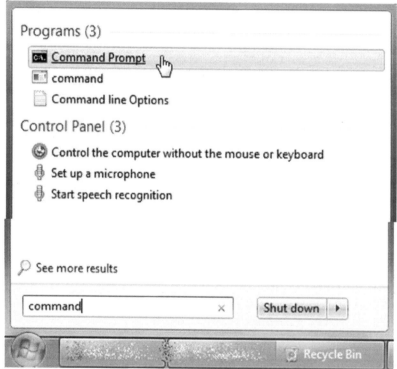

Figure: Start the Windows command prompt

In the now open command prompt window, type IFCONFIG /DISPLAYDNS (see screenshot). A list of cached DNS entries and the corresponding domain names will be displayed. These entries remain on your device even after applying all the earlier techniques in this book, illustrating just how insidious some privacy risks can be.

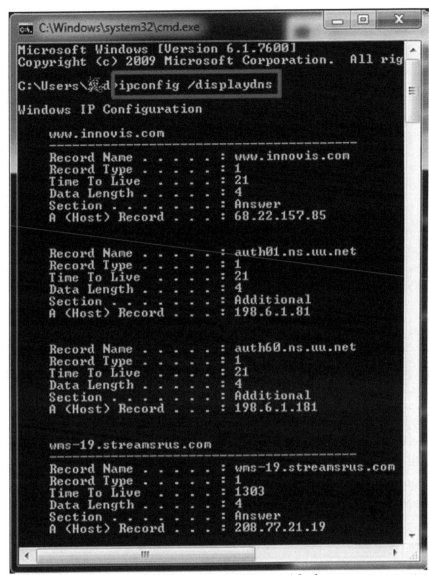

Figure: Listing the cached DNS entries on your system with the IPCONFIG /DISPLAYDNS command

You can manually *flush* (delete) these cached DNS entries in the same command prompt window by typing in IPCONFIG /FLUSHDNS (see screenshot).

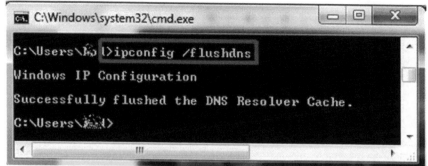

Figure: Running the IPCONFIG /FLUSHDNS command deletes the cached DNS entries

To double-check, run the IPCONFIG /DISPLAYDNS command again to confirm that the cached DNS entries are now gone.

Any good privacy cleaning app should rid your device of cached DNS entries and save you from this manual step. But you can also use these techniques to verify that your privacy cleaning app is getting rid of cached DNS entries.

Cleaning up after Leaky Apps, Compound Files and Private File Systems

The operating system and the apps on your device do many things in the background. Some apps leak data or leave lots of information behind in the form of metadata, autosave remnants or other file data which are sometimes referred to as *artifacts*. Other apps may keep recoverable copies of potentially sensitive data inside their own proprietary file systems or in file objects. Some apps also store most recently used items and other potentially sensitive information in their own configuration files (.INI) while other apps store them in the Registry.

Even if your sensitive items, downloads or documents and related apps are saved in an encrypted location (see chapter 15), one of your apps may, unknown to you, spill or leak data to a non-encrypted location where it can be discovered.

Top Tip - This spilling or leaking is a big enough problem that separate tools exists to address it. For example, see the www.sandboxie.com website for a detailed description of the problem and their solution for it (scroll down to 'How it Works').

Clearing the Windows Paging (Swap) File

When Window's memory (RAM) becomes full or Windows assigns an activity a low priority, it writes data to your storage media (for example, your hard drive) and uses this data as so-called *virtual memory*. This virtual memory is stored in a specially designated and protected file, often large, which is usually located at C:\PAGEFILE.SYS (or in older versions of Windows at C:\WINDOWS\WIN386.SWP). This file is called the *paging file* or sometimes the *swap file*, because Windows temporarily uses drive space for virtual memory in lieu of RAM. Windows also uses this file for *crash dumps* (saving a mass of data to it when Windows encounters a critical error such as the "blue screen of death" BSOD variety).

To see the virtual memory settings in Windows, type "advanced system settings" in the Start menu. When the system properties menu opens, under the 'Advanced' tab select the 'Performance Settings' button, then another 'Advanced' tab and then, under the heading 'Virtual memory', press the 'Change...' button (see screenshot).

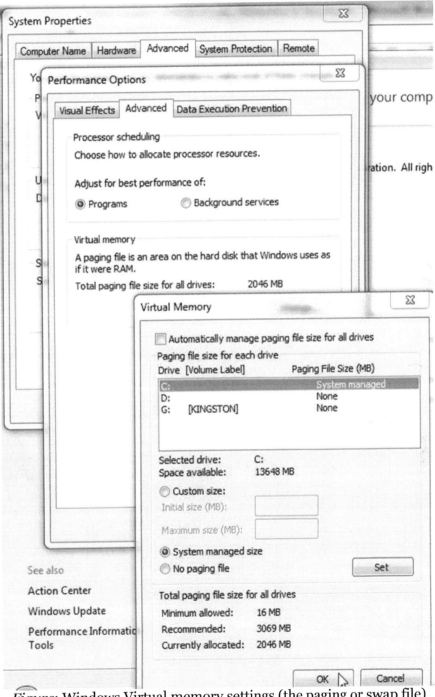

Figure: Windows Virtual memory settings (the paging or swap file)

The paging file can contain references to items, entire contents of items or parts of them even after you have deleted them. It could contain webmail or chat contents and even recent passphrases stored in memory. Because the paging file, like any deleted data, can be recovered and its contents examined, it poses both a privacy and security risk.

Unfortunately, the paging file *cannot* merely be selected and deleted as you would a normal file. The paging file is *locked* because it is almost always in use and so cannot be deleted easily.

Instead, you can set up your system to clear this paging file when your device shuts down. However, setting up your Windows device to clear the paging file will significantly increase the shutdown time. For that reason, it is recommended that you clear the paging file when the need arises or every now and then by changing the setting and enduring a few slow shutdowns before reverting the setting back.

! Warning ! - If you are not comfortable changing settings through the Windows Registry, please proceed with caution or enlist help because you could harm your device.

How to Edit the Registry to Clear the Paging File

Start the Registry Editor by entering "regedit" (no quotes) in your Windows Start menu (this was shown earlier a few pages back). Once in the Registry Editor, select from the menu *Edit > Find*.

Now search for the term "ClearPageFileAtShutdown" all as one word with *no* spaces and *without* the quotes (see screenshot).

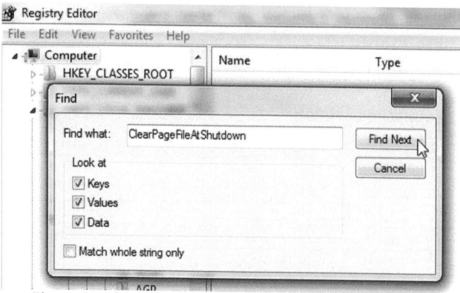

Figure: Searching for the clear paging file setting in the Registry

Registry Editor may take a moment to find it (shown below). The *Value data* should now be displayed (see screenshot); double-click on it.

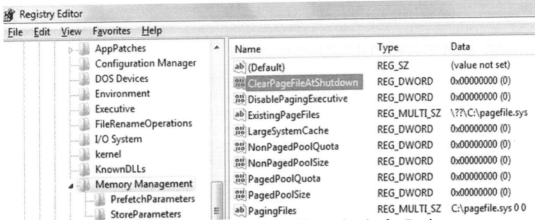

Figure: Locating the clear paging file setting in the Registry

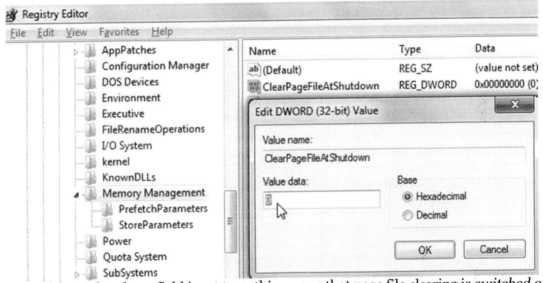

Figure: If the *Value data:* field is set to 0, this means that page file clearing is *switched off*

Change it from 0 to 1. This turns *on* the page file clearing at shut down (see screenshot).

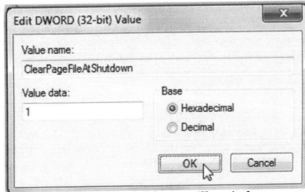

Figure: Setting the *Value data:* field to 1 will *switch on* page file clearing

Continue searching through the entire Registry for other instances of "ClearPageFileAtShutdown" values in case it appears multiple times. This might happen if you use multiple accounts on your device. To search for other instances, use *F3* to 'Find Again' in Registry Editor or go to the menu and select *Edit > Find Again*.

If you want to revert to *not* clearing the paging file at shutdown, follow the same steps as above but change the *Value data:* from 1 back to 0.

Top Tip - Of course, the increased amount of time it takes to shut down (of up to a few minutes) is not ideal. An alternative solution is to set up an encrypted or, better yet, hidden operating system because even the PAGEFILE.SYS paging file can be protected by using full disk encryption (see chapter 15).

About Forensic Software (Advanced Users)

Introduction

If an adversary is determined to examine your device for trace data, they could use specialized forensic software to thoroughly scan it for hidden trace information as well as long ago deleted items on your storage media.

All manner of devices, whether desktop computers, laptops, tablets, smartphones or removable storage media such as USB memory sticks, are routinely examined by forensic software experts hired for contractual, civil, employment or matrimonial disputes. Sometimes the expert is hired to access your device after hours, acquiring a copy of your storage media and examining it later off-site *without you ever knowing*.

Learning about how forensic snooping software works will help you to understand why a number of the techniques in this book are so important including clearing trace data, encryption (see chapter 15) and data wiping (see chapter 19).

How Forensic Software Experts Go About their Task

Generally speaking, the forensic software experts first create an exact physical duplicate of the device's storage media, called a *disk image* or *bitstream*. An exact physical duplicate means a bit-for-bit copy and therefore includes not only your original items and data files, but also all the trace data discussed earlier, including deleted files, Registry information, paging and hibernation files, memory dumps, temporary artifacts, hard drive indexes and even its file slack and bad clusters.

More About: *Clusters* - A *cluster* refers to the minimum amount of physical space on a storage media device allocated by an operating system. For example, a desktop computer's hard drive has millions of clusters.

Typically, the forensic software packages are as expensive as they are sophisticated. The packages most used by experts can cost in the *thousands of dollars* and require professional training on how to use them. The features of expert-level forensic software include disk image creation and the ability to perform powerful searches of internal, external and other storage media, and may also include capabilities such as file decryption, password cracking and steganography detection.

The leading forensic software applications include *EnCase* and *Forensic Recovery of Evidence Device* (aka *Fred*) - see http://www.cogipas.com/forensic-software/.

How to Affordably Examine Your Own Desktop or Laptop Computer

If you wish to get a taste of what it is like to poke around your own desktop computer or laptop to see what can be detected and perhaps recovered, you can try the app *Directory Snoop* (premium) http://www.cogipas.com/DirSnoop.

Directory Snoop may not be full-fledged forensic analysis software in the purist sense, but it is a powerful utility that lets you analyze your storage media at a detailed, technical level (right down to the cluster level). It might not be quite as powerful as the tools used by the professionals I mentioned above, but it is *affordable* and allows you to find and examine lots of hidden and trace data. Directory Snoop also gives you the ability to *purge* (delete) some of this trace data or recover it in the case of deleted items. This is a superb personal product. It is not free but you can use it free for a trial period before deciding whether to purchase a license.

To see how this tool can find sensitive trace information embedded in the clusters of hard drive storage media, see the in-depth illustration for advanced users in chapter 19.

* * *

For updates and additional information about getting rid of other kinds of trace information left behind on your devices, please visit http://www.cogipas.com/private-trace-information-on-devices/.

Chapter 19: Permanently Deleting (Wiping) Your Sensitive Items and Data

Introduction

Technologically savvy people know that when you delete an item on your device, it can be recovered (undeleted). It's not enough to simply delete your data, even if you regularly empty your Recycle Bin, as the deleted items are easily recoverable, even by amateurs, let alone by sophisticated snoops.

For example, after you delete an item in Windows, you can find it in the Recycle Bin and recover it very easily. This feature is provided in case you delete an item by accident. However, even after *emptying* the Recycle Bin and being prompted to confirm you want to "permanently delete" the item, it can still be recovered using widely-available and easy-to-use apps (discussed in the pages ahead).

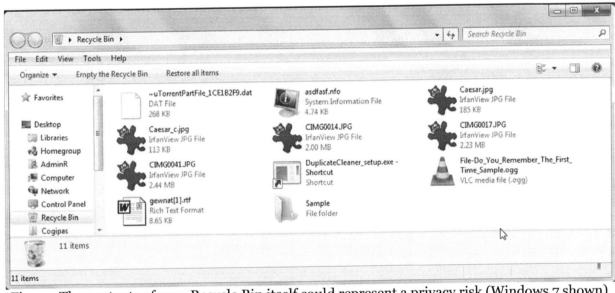

Figure: The contents of your Recycle Bin itself could represent a privacy risk (Windows 7 shown)

Don't make the mistake of thinking that merely deleting items is ever good enough. Storage devices are now so large that data and information from many years ago can still be recovered in perfect or good condition. Learn how to properly get rid of your sensitive information by *wiping* it. Also don't make the similar mistake of thinking that if you reformat the storage media the underlying data is gone for good.

Whether you try getting rid of an item by deleting it, renaming it, changing it or reformatting the volume on which it resides, the item can be recovered.

What Happens When You Delete an Item?

When you delete an item on your device, the operating system does not actually get rid of it. Properly getting rid of data would mean replacing (overwriting) every byte of space that an item takes up on the storage media, but this process takes precious time. To speed up performance, your device's operating system basically tells itself to ignore the item in future, something similar to crossing out an entry in a book's index. The operating system "forgets" the index entry for the old (deleted) item and releases the physical space on the storage media occupied by the old item for new items and data.

The former item is not actually deleted, but remains intact on the storage media. Eventually, the same space on which the old data resides may be over-written as new items and data are saved to the storage media. However, given the ever increasing size of storage media, it could be a long time, if ever, before this storage space is over-written. So items and data that you thought were deleted long ago could be discovered and undeleted, often fully intact.

For example, when you empty the Recycle Bin in Windows, all that happens is that the relevant entry for the deleted item(s) in the storage media's *index* is modified. Windows simply replaces the first byte of the entry in the index, ignoring the entry in future. This frees up space on your storage media for new data that was previously being used by the deleted data. Modified index entries appear as shown in the screenshot below. The individual index entries are called *directory entries* and the index itself is sometimes referred to as the *Master File Index* or *Master File Table* (MFT). Directory entries and the MFT are sources of device privacy risks and are discussed in more detail later in this chapter.

Using undelete apps, you can see what deleted items look like on a storage media's master index (MFT) and how easy it is to recover them (see screenshots for two different apps). Note that only the first character of the item's name in the index is deleted (shown by a '?' and 'x' respectively).

1st Cluster ▽	DOS Alias
45379	?XCLUDED.TXT
(45322)	?MAILT~1.TXT
2402	?__LA~1.TXT
(0)	?HOPPI~1.TXT
(0)	?MAILT~1.TXT

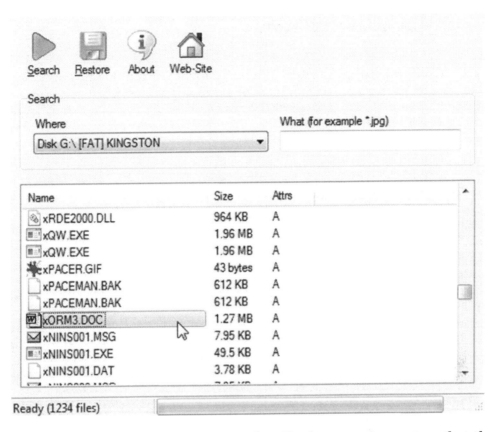

To recap: deleting an item on your device merely tells the operating system that the physical space the item was previously occupying on the storage media is now available for new data to be saved to it. The old data remains intact, until it is overwritten (if ever) with new data, and thus remains at risk of recovery (being undeleted).

Using a Shredder for Your Digital Items

People will take great care and time to delete sensitive *paper* files. You should apply exactly the same logic to your digital information too. If you want to get rid of sensitive digital items for good shred them, just as you would paper files. The equivalent concept to paper shredding for data is referred to as *wiping*.

At a minimum, you should *wipe* (as opposed to merely delete) any sensitive items and data on your devices. The difference is that wiped data has been deleted *and* the storage space it was occupying overwritten many times with other random data to ensure that the original item cannot be recovered.

Recommended Wiping Apps and Tools

I recommend the following apps and tools for permanently deleting items and data from your storage media, so that they are unrecoverable. For these same reasons, always exercise care when wiping items because you won't be able to recover them.

Wiping Apps

Privacy Eraser Free http://www.cogipas.com/pef will not examine your storage media at the same level of detail as premium apps, but it has a lot of powerful features for a free app. In addition to a host of trace data removal features, Privacy Eraser Free also has a built-in file shredder and drive wiping utilities. The free version accommodates single-pass overwriting, while its premium version *Privacy Eraser Pro* ¢ http://www.cogipas.com/pep can accommodate wiping methods from 1 to 35 passes.

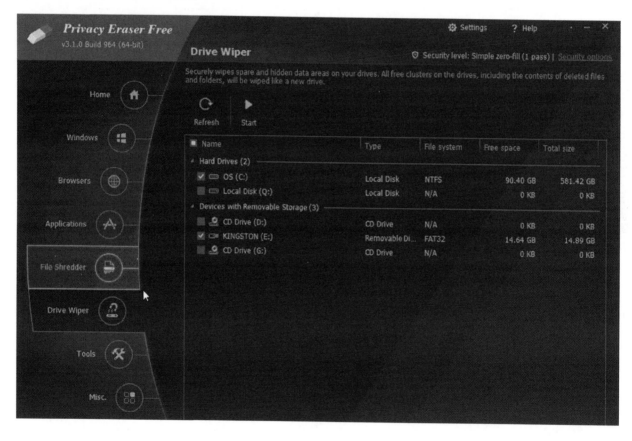

Directory Snoop (premium) http://www.cogipas.com/DirSnoop is a great app that allows you to snoop around your Windows storage media device's at a detailed, *cluster level*. This is a superb product that allows you to wipe specific items as well as to *wipe free space* on your storage media generally (discussed in the pages ahead). Directory Snoop also lets you browse master file indexes of storage media, which means it is a good app for confirming that items have been properly wiped. This access to master indexes allows you to *purge* the names of old, previously deleted items and folders (called *empty directory entries*, also discussed later in this chapter). Finally, Directory Snoop can be used as a general file recovery (undelete) tool. The app is free to try for 30 days.

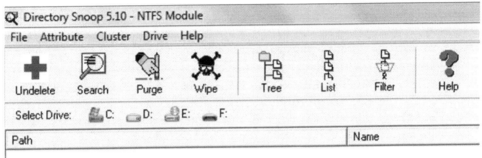

Figure: A partial screenshot of the Directory Snoop app

File Recovery (Undelete) Apps

These apps can be used to recover "merely" deleted items on your device. Of course, you can also use them to verify that your wiping methods have worked properly and that your wiped items are beyond recovery.

SoftPerfect File Recovery (free) https://www.softperfect.com/products/filerecovery/ (scroll down) is a simple and hassle-free file recovery tool. It requires no installation and can be installed to and run from a portable USB memory stick, making it quick and handy.

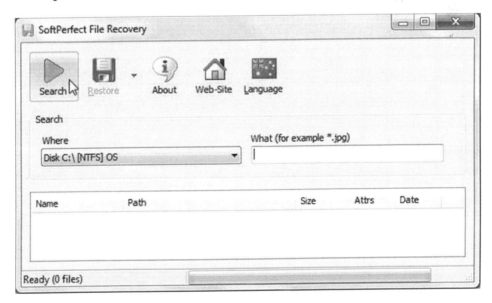

As mentioned earlier, in addition to enabling you to snoop around your storage media at a cluster level, *Directory Snoop* (premium) http://www.cogipas.com/DirSnoop also easily and effectively recovers deleted items (provided they haven't been wiped). It is free to use for 30 days.

Sensitive Data can also be Recovered from Your Hard Drive's File Slack

Another privacy risk, other than from your deleted items, is from old items and data remaining in your storage media's *slack space*.

Recall that the minimum amount of physical space allocated by the operating system for a storage device is called a *cluster*. Depending on its size, a storage device is divided into many millions of clusters. Each cluster is the smallest physical space allocated on the storage media for saving data to it and, for Windows, is set to a minimum size of 4k. Older storage media devices may have minimum cluster sizes of 16k which results in more wasted storage space. Any part of a cluster that is not fully used by the data saved to it is called *slack space* or *file slack*.

This slack is the space between the logical and physical ends of a file. The *logical size* of a file is the exact digital size of a file in bytes as reported by your operating system. The *physical size* of a file is the amount of space it physically occupies on the storage media, an amount of space that is usually larger and cannot be smaller than the logical size.

If you think about it, the minimum possible *physical* size occupied by a file on storage media will always be one cluster, even if the file is empty and has a logical size of 0 bytes. An empty text file is a good example of such a file; it has a file name and so will have a directory entry in the storage media's master file index, but the file itself has no actual contents.

Regardless of how small or large an item, file slack almost always results because the item will not completely fill the full space of the cluster(s) allocated to it. The *logical* end of the data comes before the *physical* end of the cluster – leaving the remaining portion of the last cluster filled with remnants of previously deleted items and data.

The bottom line of all this is that these remnants of previous data found in your storage media's slack space – in its nooks and crannies - may include your sensitive data that you thought was deleted long ago. This old (deleted) data residing in the slack space can also be recovered by snoops.

Top Tip - Think of clusters like empty buckets and your storage media device being made up of millions of them. If the volume of water you wish to store (or at least the last bucket worth) is less than the volume of a whole bucket, the last bucket will always have some empty space at the top; this space between the top of the water and the top of the bucket is the slack. Except instead of the empty space being filled with air, it's filled with your old data.

Recall from chapter 18 that forensic analysis software can easily recover deleted files, sometimes including items from *years* ago. This is often possible because the software examines and recovers the data residing in storage devices' unused clusters.

In addition to wiping individual items or a group of items you select, a good wiping app should also allow you to wipe the *free space* on a storage media device (the space on the storage device on which there is no active data). A *wipe free space* feature fills and overwrites *all* the empty space on a storage device. Wiping the free space of a storage device ensures that any old, previously deleted items cannot be recovered from it.

How to Fully and Entirely Wipe the Contents of Storage Media

Hopefully, you are not throwing out with your regular trash the hard drives, USB memory sticks, SD cards, CD/DVD-ROMs and Blu-Rays you want to get rid of. Not only is this bad for the environment, but it is potentially disastrous for your privacy. If a *dumpster diving* identity thief (see *More About* box) only needs a few bank statements from your garbage to make your life miserable, imagine the potential damage they could do with storage media filled with gigabytes of your personal information and data. Similarly, hopefully you are also not donating or selling your old storage media until properly eliminating the risk of data recovery.

More About: *Dumpster Diving* - A dumpster diving identity thief is an identity thief that looks through your curbside garbage for documents containing personal information such as bank or credit card statements.

As a rule, you should always *wipe* the entire contents of hard drives, USB memory sticks and SD cards before you throw them out or sell or donate them to friends, family or third parties.

Recommended Drive Wiping Apps

WipeDrive Home ¢ (premium) http://www.cogipas.com/WipeDrive is a US Department of Defense (DoD) approved app for securely wiping the entire contents of hard drives and external storage media devices. WipeDrive supports all hard drive sizes and formats, and uses military grade wiping technology to completely and permanently delete data, making it impossible to recover even by the most sophisticated of snoops. It is great for when you want to sell, donate or otherwise dispose of your storage media devices. You can also use it to start "fresh" if a storage media device has been ruined by particularly nasty and hard-to-get-rid-of malware.

For CD, DVD and Blu-Ray disks some experts advocate "nuking" them for a short time in a microwave oven, but understandably not everyone is comfortable with this method. It should be adequate (and can be fun) to smash these disks to bits with a hammer after having first wrapped them in an old dishcloth to make sure that no fragments get into your eyes or make a mess.

In appropriate circumstances, for example in a *business environment*, storage media containing sensitive customer data can be securely destroyed with specialized equipment. Permanently deleting digital data on hard drives, USB memory sticks and SD cards can be done with *degaussers*, see ¢ http://goo.gl/wzL1xO. CD, DVD and Blu-Ray disks can be physically destroyed with *disk shredders*, see ¢ http://goo.gl/DFotim.

What Even Wiping (Sometimes) Leaves Behind: Directory Entries (Advanced Users)

! Warning ! - The rest of this chapter is rather technical, so if you find the materials getting a bit complicated, feel free to jump ahead to the *Recapping the Lessons Learned* section at the end.

Introduction

As we have seen, wiping items and free storage space is the best way to make sure that your data stays unrecoverable. However, I am about to demonstrate using forensic analysis techniques that even when you properly wipe an item (or folder), its original name remains intact on your storage device's master file index or master file table (MFT), representing a residual privacy risk.

Recall that filenames and folder names indexed in a storage media device are called *directory entries*. The index entries of old (deleted) files and folders are called *empty* directory entries. While wiping will securely delete the *contents* of items and folders, the names of the old (now wiped) filenames and folder names may remain recoverable from the storage media's master index.

For example, although an adversary would not be able to recover and view the *contents* of a document you wiped called 'Love Letter to Co-Worker' or an image you wiped called 'Evidence of Director's Fraud and Wrong-Doing', the adversary would be able to recover these filenames and that alone could already tell them plenty.

Why Directory Entries Remain

In Windows, the master file indexing system treats filenames and folder names the same as items themselves. This means that when you delete, move, rename or even wipe an item, its old index entry (its filename) remains in the master table. The original name of an item or a folder will remain in its original location in the master index and with its original name but now with its first character struck out, as explained earlier.

So, even if you renamed either of the fictional items above to 'Sales Report' or if you thought you were well protected by faithfully getting rid of them by deleting them, wiping them for good or by moving them to another storage device or even an encrypted container (see chapter 15), the original item name could still be found among the empty directory entries on your storage media device's master index. Yikes!

You can see this for yourself by performing the upcoming test. After deleting, moving, renaming or even after wiping items and folders, you can still find their original names as directory entries in the storage device's master index.

You may have dozens, hundreds or even thousands of sensitive old filenames and folder names on your device. To eliminate the risk posed by these old filenames and folder names (the empty directory entries), the wiping app you use should include the option of eliminating them, a process called *purging empty directory entries*.

Top Tip - If you are following best practice and are rigorous about performing all of your private or sensitive activities from an *encrypted drive* or, better yet, an *encrypted operating system* (see chapter 15), the recoverability of old filenames and folder names will be much less of a risk. This is because once your encrypted drive or operating system is dismounted (re-encrypted), its master file index will be part of the encrypted data that is impenetrable without the passphrase.

Risks from Temporary Files and Filenames

The risk of recoverable old filenames and folder names can remain a concern for temporary items *no matter what methods you use*. For example, you download an archive of zipped items to a separate, perhaps even encrypted, storage media device. You unzip the archive and click on a few of the items to sample the contents, but unknown to you, those items you sampled (depending on your zip app's settings) may have been temporarily saved to and opened from a non-encrypted location on your device, such as `C:\WINDOWS\TEMP` for Windows desktop or laptop devices. Other apps or autosave type features may also use temporary locations. This means you must discover and purge the deleted item names (purge the empty directory entries) from these temporary locations as well.

Top Tip - If you initially download sensitive items to a non-encrypted storage location, even if only temporarily until you move them to an encrypted location, you will need to purge the entries of these filenames from the original storage device's master index.

Hopefully by now and certainly with the in-depth demonstration that follows you will understand how important it can be for you to purge empty directory entries from your system, even if you carefully use privacy cleaning and encryption apps.

Getting Right Down to the Cluster Level of Your Drives

Taking this further, let's analyze a desktop computer's hard drive with *forensic software* to see what sensitive information is embedded in the drive's clusters. We will use an app to search a drive's contents for a text string that represents potentially private or sensitive information.

For this demonstration I have used the affordable, quasi-forensic analysis app that I recommend earlier, Directory Snoop. Adversaries using full-fledged forensic analysis software (which is much more powerful and expensive) would turn up more information and more easily too.

In the next series of screenshots, I search a hard drive for the text string "steamy" and find traces of a document named, HOT STEAMY LOVE LETTER.DOC.

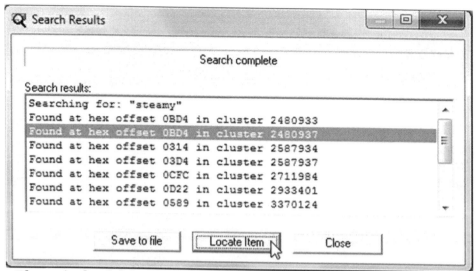

Figure: The entire hard drive is searched for the term "steamy" and generates some hits

 After the app's search is complete, you can select each search hit to see what it found. Depending on the app, you can note the cluster number for any search hit and view the data. In the screenshot below, you will see that the information in and around cluster 2480937 of the drive indicates that a document entitled HOT STEAMY LOVE LETTER.DOC once existed.

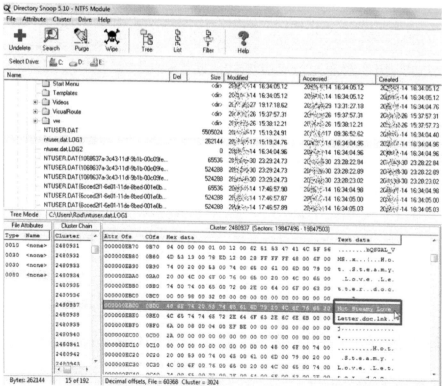

Figure: The search results are displayed at a detailed cluster level

In this case, the information is contained in a cluster used by the file NTUSER.DAT which forms part of the Windows Registry database. Similarly revealing information could just as easily have turned up in *unused clusters*, including from long ago deleted items and data. As discussed earlier, such trace information can also result from temporary or autosave files, RAM dumps, and as remnants from the Windows paging or hibernation files.

Top Tip - For these reasons, it is good to wipe a storage media device's free space *after* you have *purged empty directory entries* from its master index. This will better ensure that you get rid of the names (directory entries) of previously deleted, moved, renamed, and even wiped items and folders.

Detailed Example of How to Permanently Delete Files by Wiping Items *and* Purging Directory Entries (Advanced Users)

Because this example is long, detailed and relies heavily on images, it has been placed on the book's companion website at http://www.cogipas.com/detailed-example-permanently-delete-files/.

Using a practical example, I demonstrate the concepts explained in this chapter. For the demonstration, I saved and *then deleted* on a USB memory stick a video clip named STRIPPED.WMV. This item could just as easily represent a document about a medical condition you have, your personal budget, your diary, items from your erotica stash, a confidential company report or whatever else you consider private.

Then I use a file recovery (undelete) app to confirm that the now deleted video is easily found and recovered. In other words, by deleting the file "normally" I show that it can be easily *un*deleted.

Next, I again save the video clip to a USB stick, but this time I properly delete the video with a wiping app. This should make the deleted video beyond recovery by conventional undelete apps. To check this, I use the same file recovery (undelete) app to confirm whether the wiping has truly worked.

After confirming that the wiped video clip cannot be undeleted, I then move on to purging its old file name from the storage media's master index. I do this to address the risk of empty directory entries.

Finally, for ultimate privacy, I wipe the USB memory stick's *free space* using multiple passes to ensure that no trace of the video exists. By doing this, even sophisticated adversaries using the best forensic software that money can buy would not be able to detect the former existence of the video on the storage media.

For the tutorial in full, please see http://www.cogipas.com/detailed-example-permanently-delete-files/

* * *

Recapping the Lessons Learned

This chapter covered why and how to delete data beyond recovery and leave no trace that the files even existed in the first place. The concepts were reinforced with concrete, step-by-step demonstrations.

To recap, the best way to protect your devices from privacy breaches is a combination of the following:

- wipe (rather than merely delete) any items you wish to truly delete permanently

- purge empty directory entries from your storage media devices' master indexes to get rid of the old (deleted) names of items and folders that were deleted, moved, renamed or wiped

- wipe the free space on your storage devices to further eliminate the risk of previously deleted items being detected or recovered

- from chapters 11 and 18 you will appreciate the importance of using a privacy cleaning app to clear trace data from your device

- from chapter 15, you will recognize the benefits of embracing on-the-fly full disk encryption

* * *

For updates and additional information about permanently deleting (wiping) your sensitive items and data, please visit http://www.cogipas.com/permanently-deleting-wiping-items-data/.

Chapter 20: Privacy at your Workplace or your Small Office / Home Office

Introduction

If you are an employee, the safest approach for how to conduct yourself at work is on the assumption that you have no reasonable expectation of privacy. The "legal" answer is more complicated than that, but that's the general rule I recommend you follow. This means conducting yourself on the basis that your employer may be entitled to record and monitor everything you do as an employee, including at home or after hours when using any equipment, facilities or Internet access your employer provides. In some circumstances, employers record and monitor employees pursuant to the legitimate goals of increasing employee productivity, protecting against workplace harassment lawsuits, and preventing the disclosure of confidential information or trade secrets.

Don't Be Stupid at Work

Email, social media and chat are especially prone to gaffes at work and can attract disciplinary measures since these informal means of communication may cause you to be overly candid, casual or careless.

Top Tip - As a rule, when at work do not include anything in messages that you would *not* want your employer or boss to see.

When it comes to the workplace, I recommend that you simply follow your employer's policies, period. Even if you delete a message or undo an action that you regretted, it is sure to be saved somewhere on your employer's servers or back-up systems and may, depending on your employer's archiving practices, be retrievable for a long time.

"NSFW" and Personal Web Browsing at Work

NSFW is an acronym for 'Not Safe for Work' which you may have seen in the subject lines of online articles and posts. It is often used to designate content that you would be well advised *not* to access at work. In fact, it is best not to pursue any personal online activities while at work. Some of the techniques in this book are more difficult if not impossible to apply in the workplace because you are usually prevented from installing any apps on workplace devices. Nonetheless, if for whatever reason you are compelled to pursue personal online activities at work, there are some ways to curb the risks.

If your web browser isn't blocked from doing so, you can use a web proxy that scrambles or masks the *addresses* of the websites you visit. This way, your employer's logs and detection methods will display website addresses that are different from those you are actually visiting. For example, using such a web proxy to visit http://www.cogipas.com would instead show up in your employer's logs as something like
https://proxyone.net/browse.php?u=6ooFgWHwVTr9RvlufEpHlfSx&b

Good choices are https://proxyone.net/ and https://www.hidemyass.com/proxy (scroll down to the bottom of the page). Experiment with the advanced options to encrypt the URL, allow cookies, etc.

However, some employer's monitor the actual *contents* of the webpages you visit, for example, by taking screenshots of what you are doing at certain time intervals, so even this method is far from fool-proof.

If possible, perform any personal web browsing in private mode. Refer to chapter 11 for the detailed instructions on how to do this. *However*, in many workplace environments the ability to change any browser settings, including browsing in private mode, is often disabled. In fact, most workplaces allow little if any control over the settings and preferences of apps installed on workplace devices; instead, the settings are migrated corporate-wide pursuant to centrally established IT policies.

If your access rights at work are limited in this way you will also not be able to download and install privacy cleaning apps, although some utilities can be downloaded and installed at home to a USB memory stick, and then run at work. Good choices for *portable* versions of privacy cleaning apps you can run from a USB memory stick include *BleachBit* (free) http://bleachbit.sourceforge.net/, *Privacy Eraser Free* http://www.cogipas.com/pef and its premium counterpart *Privacy Eraser Pro* ¢ http://www.cogipas.com/pep.

However, even having gone through all this trouble, it may not be a great help if your workplace is logging, backing-up and examining employee activity.

You'll note from all the "however" and "if" qualifiers above that achieving privacy at work for your personal online activities is very difficult. That's why I recommend that you simply don't try.

Device Security at Work

It is also important to protect your devices at work, primarily your desktop and laptop computers, by following these tips.

When away from your desktop or laptop computer, even for only a few moments, *lock* it. This was discussed in chapter 9. In summary, invoke the lock by holding down the *Windows key* (it may look like a clover leaf on your keyboard) and the *L key*. Or you can press the key combination of *Ctrl+Alt+Del* and then select *Lock this computer* from the menu that appears. It only takes a minute for a rogue colleague, adversary or passerby to snoop your device, send a damaging message from your accounts, sabotage important work, or read, copy or delete information.

In addition to locking your devices when you step away, consider *physically* locking your laptop computer at times. Most laptops have a *security slot* which allows you to secure your laptop much the same way you would your bicycle. Laptops are too easy for thieves to walk away with. Having your work laptop stolen at the coffee shop could get you in heaps of trouble. See http://www.cogipas.com/laptop-lock for an example of a laptop lock that attaches to the universal security slot found on 99% of laptops. You probably didn't even realize you had a security slot on your laptop. Take a look.

If you are paranoid or if you work with particularly poisonous or competitive colleagues, you could also periodically check the physical ports on your desktop computer to ensure that no *keylogging* devices (see chapter 7) have been connected, whether by your employer, a competitor or a rogue colleague.

The Privacy Risks Posed by Printers and Copiers

Be aware that printers and modern photocopiers pose privacy risks too. Would you believe that a physical printout can be traced back to you?

Consider this example: a whistle-blowing employee sends an "anonymous" letter to the auditing department in order to expose some wrong-doing. Could the exposed senior management use the original letter to somehow track it back to the source, subjecting the whistle-blower to retaliation or worse? The answer is, yes, it is entirely possible.

How Print-Outs Can Be Traced

Unknown to most people, many major brands of printers leave a unique fingerprint on each printed page they produce. The fingerprint is in the form of too-small-to-see yellow *microdots* that are secretly placed on each printed page. This marker signifies the printer's unique serial number and, in some cases, the print-out's timestamp. No one seems to know for sure, but there is much speculation that the printer manufacturers implemented this feature under pressure from certain government agencies.

Of course, in a workplace setting this means that it is relatively easy to trace a printout back to a printer and then, from cross-referencing the printer's activity logs, to the actual person who printed it. Even in a private capacity, a printout made at home with the telltale dots could be traced back to you in combination with any warranty information you registered with the manufacturer.

Which Printers have Tracking Dots?

To see whether your workplace or home printers use tracking dots (sometimes called *forensic watermarking*), check the comprehensive list maintained by the Electronic Frontier Foundation (EFF) via http://www.cogipas.com/printer-tracking-dots.

Unfortunately, there is no practical way of disabling the tracking dots feature. Therefore, if you anticipate printing sensitive documents that you wouldn't want coming back to haunt you, either steer clear of printers on EFF's list or buy a used printer that you will *not* register for warranty purposes. In the workplace you are stuck with your assigned printer so simply do not print anything at work that you wouldn't want traced back to you.

Photocopiers also Carry Risks

Photocopiers represent an entirely different kind of risk. Most modern photocopiers contain a hard drive that temporarily stores copier jobs. Unfortunately, all the privacy risks about storage media outlined earlier apply to the hard drives in copiers too: the data is recoverable from the storage devices in copiers.

It is no wonder that identity thieves are very interested in copier hard drives. If you ever used a copier to copy your financial records, medical information or any other sensitive personal information, it may be sitting on a copier hard drive somewhere just waiting to be recovered; a treasure trove of information for identity thieves, snoops and adversaries.

Worse, the multifunction copiers that also act as faxes, scanners and printers, may store those jobs on their internal drive too. Yikes!

How to Protect Yourself

As an employee, you can avoid using workplace equipment to copy, fax and scan your personal records. You can also encourage your employer to adopt policies to wipe or physically destroy the drives of decommissioned copiers. If you own the copier as part of your business, arrange to have the decommissioned copier's hard drive properly *wiped* or physically destroyed (see chapter 19).

Small Office / Home Office (SOHO) Considerations

Small office and home offices (SOHO for short) are especially vulnerable to Internet privacy and security risks as they often rely on 24/7 high-speed Internet access but without the same sort of safeguards that a big company can implement. This lack of scale and funds makes SOHOs a target for hackers. SOHOs may also keep on site much financial and personal data (customer and client data) as part of their operations.

Security and Privacy Strategies for SOHOs

Here are some steps that small office and home office entrepreneurs can take to reduce the risks of privacy and security breaches affecting their business operations. These SOHO-specific tips are cross-referenced to materials in the book where you will find the detailed information.

- Although easy to overlook or take for granted, using *strong passphrases* that are hard for hackers to crack is probably the most important strategy you should employ for your business. Your online merchant accounts are only as secure as the passphrases you use for them. Using strong passphrases is a fundamental aspect of your business' IT security strategy. Passphrases should be *at least* 8 characters long (but the longer the better) and be a mix of character types (uppercase, lowercase and numeric) and even symbols (! – +), if supported. If you have trouble coming up with your own good passphrases and keeping track of them, there are plenty of tools to help. See chapter 3.

- Keep the operating systems and malware apps up-to-date on all of your devices. This is your best protection against viruses, worms, Trojans, rootkits and other malware that could infect your business systems. This can be as simple as making sure that the *automatic updates* feature for your operating system and apps is activated on all your devices. See chapter 5.

- It is also paramount that SOHOs set up their *wireless network* correctly. You should spend some time reading the instruction manual for your wireless networking router no matter how boring that sounds. It is important to take steps to minimize the threat of someone using your Internet connection without your knowledge. Otherwise, it could be taken over, monitored or used to launch attacks on other victims. In particular, change the default password, disable SSID broadcasting and use MAC codes. See chapter 8.

- SOHOs can gain much leverage from *social media*, but be careful what information you share on social networking sites and do not advertise your absence. Inadvertently, you could be advertising a golden opportunity to thieves, corporate spies or adversaries to access your business premises while you are away. Also make sure not to post any information which could help hackers answer 'forgotten password' request questions for your accounts. See chapter 6.

- Use a *web anonymizing service* such as a web proxy, Tor or a VPN when you want to mask your IP address, for example, when checking out your competitors or conducting market research. See chapters 12 and 13.

- Use easy, yet powerful *encryption technology* to lock down your business data (especially on laptops which are often the target of thieves). Encryption apps will keep your digital business records safe, whether from determined hackers or inadvertent disclosure in the case of theft or loss. Encryption might sound complex and expensive, but the apps are now easy to use and, if not free for commercial activities, rather inexpensive in relation to the protection they offer your business. See chapter 15.

- Make sure to *permanently wipe* items and data, rather than merely delete them, especially when disposing of hard drives, USB memory sticks or SD cards. Because deleted data and files can be easily recovered, you should properly and permanently delete sensitive digital information by wiping it. See chapter 19.

- If necessary, keep tabs on any suspect IT use by your employees perhaps using monitoring software. However, you should *always* seek formal legal advice before taking such a step to make sure that you are on safe ground.

On a final note, don't be discouraged as you don't have to go overboard with the extent of your efforts. Some common sense and diligence on your part will go a long way to protecting the business that you worked so hard to establish and grow.

* * *

For updates and additional information about privacy at your workplace or your small office / home office, please visit http://www.cogipas.com/workplace-soho/.

PART III - ANNEXES OF SPECIAL INTEREST

These materials are a little different in that they serve to reinforce and sum up the earlier contents, so rather than appearing as chapters, I present them as Annexes to the book.

~ ~ ~

Annex A: Online Privacy Checks You Should Do Right Now (Quick Privacy Audit)

Check your online privacy with these handy resources. The results will give you just a small glimpse into how online tracking and profiling works. These resources are grouped thematically and are all free.

Top Tip - There are plenty of online resources you can visit to check up on the level of your online privacy. However, you should only use *reputable* resources as you often need to provide some information (for example, your email address) or to use a social login (SSO) (for example, allowing the resource to link to your Facebook profile).

General Tracking

EFF's Panopticlick https://panopticlick.eff.org/ determines if your browser configuration is rare or unique and thereby whether you are easy to track with device fingerprinting techniques

MyPermissions http://mypermissions.org/ shows you which websites and online apps have access to your information, helping shed light on your privacy settings

StayInvisible http://www.stayinvisible.com/ tests to see what tracking methods work on your browser

What's Public?

Do a general web search of your name in your favorite search engine. If you get too many results, narrow the search by putting your name in double quotes "firstname lastname" and perhaps adding your city or some other detail about yourself. To be notified about future matching information showing up online, set up an automatic alert such as Google Alert https://www.google.com/alerts.

Search your name and/or telephone number in any number of free databases to see the information about you that might already be widely available:

- *Zabasearch* http://www.zabasearch.com/
- *Spokeo* http://www.spokeo.com/
- *US Search* http://www.ussearch.com/
- *Intelius* http://www.intelius.com/

Search your most recently shared photos of yourself at a *reverse image search* site such as *TinEye* https://www.tineye.com/ or *Google Image Search* https://images.google.com/ to see where on the web your photos may be resurfacing

Google (& YouTube)

Account History https://www.google.com/settings/accounthistory collects in one place your activities across Google's wide array of services including

- what you searched https://history.google.com/history/
- even the places where you have been https://maps.google.com/locationhistory/b/0

YouTube's history features include what you have watched https://www.youtube.com/feed/history as well as what you have searched https://www.youtube.com/my_search_history

Email

MIT's *Immersion* https://immersion.media.mit.edu/ analyzes the metadata found in your email often revealing a detailed description of your personal and professional interactions

Sites such as *PwnedList Monitoring* https://pwnedlist.com/ and *Hacknotifier* https://www.hacknotifier.com/ let you check if your email address has been compromised appearing in publicly available hacked databases

Facebook

Activity Log https://www.facebook.com/me/allactivity shows all your recent Facebook activity

Apply Magic Sauce http://applymagicsauce.com/ analyzes your personality based solely on your Facebook likes, giving a small glimpse into how online trackers and profilers may be using the same information

Your Facebook *Likes* https://www.facebook.com/me/likes can tell a lot about you (most people keep all their likes public but there is no reason to, especially if you would rather keep some of your likes secret)

Profile Watch http://www.profilewatch.org/ examines your Facebook page and assigns you a privacy score out of 10. Go to the site and, after declining a solicitation that pops up, under 'Advanced Start', paste your Facebook profile page URL into the form.

Wolfram Alpha's *analytics tool for Facebook* http://www.wolframalpha.com/facebook/ (signup required) maps your online relationships

Torrent File-sharing

ScanEye http://www.pobralem.pl/ demonstrates how easily snoops can monitor your torrent file-sharing activities by your IP address

Usenet Newsgroups

Search for your name in decades worth of Usenet messages archived at Google Groups https://groups.google.com/. As with the web search above, if you get too many results, narrow the search by putting your name in double quotes "firstname lastname" and perhaps adding your city or some other detail about yourself.

* * *

For updates and additional information about checking your online privacy, please visit http://www.cogipas.com/online-privacy-checks-right-now/.

Annex B: Device Privacy Checks You Should Do Right Now (How to Snoop on Yourself Doing a Quick Trace Data Audit)

Introduction

In addition to being tracked and profiled *online*, you also have to worry about *offline* snoops, what anyone with or gaining access to your devices might be able to find out about you and your activities.

Here are some *basic* device snooping techniques you can try on your own devices. Spend a few minutes poking around your devices to see what snoops might be able to find. Note that these are only basic techniques. A sophisticated adversary using, for example, powerful forensic analysis software (see chapter 18), would be able to probe much deeper into your device.

Performing these checks helps you to gauge how privately you are going about your activities and the extent to which trace data remains on your devices.

The steps below tend to get more technical as you move along, so stop at your own comfort level or enlist the help of a technically-inclined friend if you need some assistance.

Top Tip - Though I don't advocate it, these techniques can also be used as a way to check any suspicions you may have about whether your spouse, partner, children or anyone else may be up to inappropriate behavior on a device. For example, whether they may be: indulging in pornography; accessing hateful, sexist or racist materials; engaging in cyber-cheating or cyber-flirting; downloading copyright infringing (pirated) materials; or engaging in other kinds of potentially inappropriate activities.

Deleted Items

One of the quickest and easiest checks you can perform is to see if your device's Recycle Bin (or Trash) contains any hints of private or sensitive items. Unless the Recycle Bin has been *emptied*, its contents are easily accessed and can provide plenty of clues about the activities you have been up to on your device.

In Windows, simply select the Recycle Bin icon on the desktop to see what items have been recently deleted.

If an item's filename alone doesn't sufficiently satisfy your curiosity, you can right-click on an item and select *Restore* to un-delete it. When doing so, take note of the item's displayed *original location* as this is the folder in which the undeleted item will reappear. This folder might also contain other items or clues about the item and related activities.

Figure: Undeleting some seemingly suspicious items from the Windows Recycle Bin

Most Recently Used Items

As mentioned in chapters 11 and 18, most operating systems, including Windows, retain records of items you most recently accessed on your device as a way for you to quickly access them again. However, these records can also reveal private and sensitive activities.

Look for the most recently used items on your device. In Windows generally, click on the *Start menu* and select the 'Recent Items' fly out (see screenshot). You will see a list of the items you most recently accessed on your device.

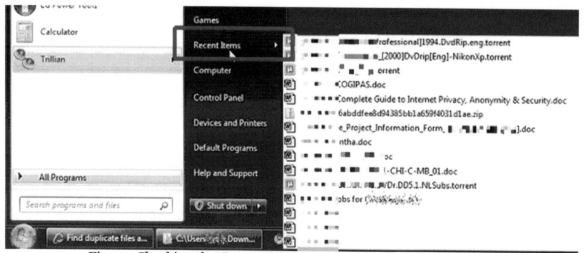

Figure: Checking the *Recent Items* accessed on a Windows device

For individual apps, from media players to word processors, check if they have a recent items feature. This can usually be found under or near the *File* and *Open* menu items.

In either case, selecting an item from the list will open it unless it has been deleted, moved, renamed, encrypted or saved to a different location or device. Even in these cases, sometimes the filenames of items alone may reveal plenty about your activities.

Web Browser History

Look at your web browser app's records of the websites you have visited. Specific instructions vary for each browser but look for menu items or icons called *History*.

In the Chrome web browser for Windows, you access this information from the following menu choices: Customize and control (the three horizontal lines icon at the upper-right, ≡) > *History* menu item. You can also access the History directly in Chrome with the keystroke shortcut *Ctrl+H*.

Unless these records have been cleared, the browser will display a detailed list of all the websites you have visited, sometimes going back a very long time. Scroll through the list of sites to see what it contains and select a link (if its name or description is unclear) to revisit the destination webpage and investigate further.

Downloads Folder and History

Look in your device's *Downloads* destination folder(s). In Windows, select the Start menu and select the *Downloads* item or type "downloads" to access the main downloads folder. Or you can use Windows Explorer and look for the Downloads folder(s).

Your web browser also keeps records of what you download from the web; look for a Downloads menu item. In the Chrome web browser, select the Customize and control icon (the three horizontal lines at the upper-right, ≡) and then *Downloads*. You can also access the Downloads records directly in Chrome with the keystroke shortcut *Ctrl+J*. If the records have not been cleared, you will see a list of the items you downloaded.

Web Browser Bookmarks

If someone checked the bookmarks saved in your web browser what would they find? These are amongst the easiest and potentially most personal records on your device. In the Chrome web browser, bookmarks are quickly accessible from the Customize and control icon (≡) and then selecting the *Bookmarks* fly-out menu. You can also access them directly in Chrome by pressing *Ctrl+Shift+O* which presents them together with a handy search feature.

233

Web Browser Autocomplete

Most web browsers have an *autocomplete* feature for the search bar. If the feature has not been disabled or its hidden records cleared, your browser retains past searches you conducted and websites you visited to help you re-search or re-visit them more easily. Though intended as a convenience, it can also be a way for a snoop to detect your past web searches and browsing.

For example, if you start to enter "cogipas" in your web browser's search bar, it will display any terms searched or websites visited that match the letters as you type them in (see screenshot).

Figure: Chrome's Autocomplete is meant to save you time but reveals past web searches and browsing

Of course, the same holds true if you enter the word "bankruptcy", "illness", "depression", "flirt", "sex", "porn", "divorce" or any other terms you wish to check. You can experiment with different words, terms or parts of them. If it was previously entered into the web browser's search bar or matches a website recently visited, the browser bar will display the full search or URL (see screenshot).

Figure: Unless the browser's autocomplete feature has been disabled or its records cleared, it can be used to reveal your past web searches and browsing

You can even enter a single letter or a couple letters of the alphabet at a time and check the displayed list of matching searched terms or visited websites. This is more time consuming, but a more comprehensive way to check the autocomplete's records. In contrast with a web browser's History, most web browser's do *not* let you see a list of the Autocomplete records.

Web Browser Cookies

Cookies can also provide snoops with clues about your activities. Check to see what your cookies may reveal. In the Chrome web browser, you access this information from the following menu choices: *Customize and control* menu button (the three horizontal lines at the upper-right, ≡) > *Settings* > *show advanced settings...* (near the bottom). On the displayed page look for the *Privacy* heading and select the button *Content Settings....* Then select the button *All cookies and site data....*

You will usually see a long list of cookies, some of which will correlate to websites you've been visiting.

Detecting Deleted Items with a File Recovery (Undelete) App

Many free and easy-to-use file recovery (undelete) apps are available that can detect the names of deleted items and sometimes recover the items fully intact. By deleted items, this time I mean items that have been *emptied* from the Recycle Bin (or Trash).

Many of these apps are free and can be installed to and used from a USB stick, leaving no obvious traces behind on the device scanned. This is an ideal way for a snoop to check your device without you ever knowing about it. Use such an app to see what deleted terms it detects on your device (see screenshot).

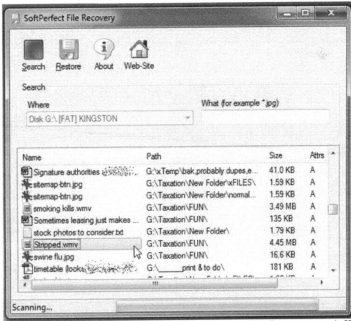

Figure: An easy-to-use and free file recovery (undelete) app finds a potentially suspicious deleted video called STRIPPED.WMV

Searching Item Names

Though it can take a bit of time depending on the size of your storage media, it is easy to search for a certain term in the names of all the items on a device. In Windows, select the Start menu and type "computer" in the Search box. Select *Computer* from the list or you can select the *My Computer* icon on your desktop.

A file Explorer window will open and in the upper-right corner (see screenshot) you can enter a search term or file type to initiate a search across your entire device. There are two main strategies you can use and you can always try both.

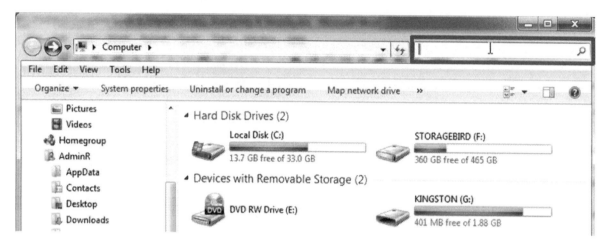

Search strategy #1: Adding a search filter by the kind (type) of items you are searching for such as pictures, movies, music, documents, etc. (see screenshot). This strategy may give you lots of wrong hits (sometimes called *false positives*), but it ensures that your search is wide and, for example, that you detect items that were carefully named (or renamed) so that they wouldn't stand out.

Search strategy #2: Using terms common to the subject matter or topic you wish to search for such as financial information, personal documents, medical information, erotica, media downloads, etc. This calls for a bit of judgment because you have to think of and enter in the search box some terms that are relevant to what you are searching for.

Whichever strategy you use, you will be presented with a list of your search results (it may be very long and have taken some time!). Simply scroll down the list and investigate (open) any items of interest, continuing this process and performing additional searches until your curiosity has been satisfied.

Manually Searching the Registry (Advanced Users)

This search technique looks for a term (keyword) in the "guts" of your Windows device including its app settings, the names and folder locations of recent downloads and temporary items, as well as many other often *hidden* sources of data and trace records.

Recall that the Registry is a large database of technical data and information used by Windows and your apps. Using the Registry Editor, you can search for specific strings (keywords) related to any downloads, items or activities you would rather keep private.

This technique is somewhat similar to the one above about searching item names and it too may generate many false positives. However, it can also discover items you deleted, renamed, moved, encrypted or even wiped.

Advanced users can check the Windows *Registry* by typing "regedit" in the Windows Start menu (see screenshot). The look and feel of the Registry Editor is similar to Windows Explorer.

! Warning ! - You can harm the operation of your device if you delete or change items in the Registry, so please make sure you use only the *Edit > Find* command from the menu to view entries, *never delete or do anything else in the Registry for this exercise.*

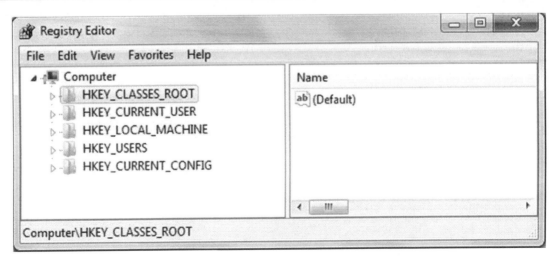

From Registry Editor's menu choose *Edit > Find* (or *Ctrl+F* on your keyboard). Now type your search term in the dialogue box and select OK or Find Next (see screenshot). Unlike searching for file items, you can only look for one keyword at a time in Registry Editor so do not enter multiple words or you will not get any results. The Registry is a large database, so the search may take a while.

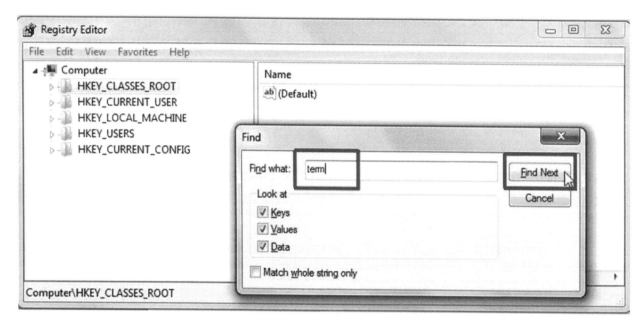

You can keep searching through the Registry for this same search term by choosing *Edit > Find Again* from the menu (or pressing *F3* on your keyboard). Keep going until you reach the end of the Registry.

Make sure the hits are true positives as some words can occur by accident because there are large amounts of raw data in the Registry. Sometimes search hits are not what you first think they are, so check them carefully.

When you get hits using this method, you *cannot* open the underlying item by selecting or double-clicking it. Rather, when you find items that match your search term in the Registry this means that these items may once have existed on, been downloaded to, viewed on, accessed by, or saved to the device. However, you can often recognize a clear pattern of activity from recurring hits.

Even if the Registry does not contain matches of what you were searching for, this may simply mean that you have been applying the techniques in this book superbly, for example, by using trace data removal and encryption apps to safeguard your digital items, information and data.

* * *

For updates and additional information about checking your device privacy, please visit http://www.cogipas.com/checking-your-device-privacy/.

Annex C: Quick and Practical Checklist for Protecting your Internet Privacy, Anonymity and Security

Putting it All Together

It's impossible to briefly encapsulate a book of hundreds of printed pages, but that shouldn't stop me from trying. Use the summary below as a refresher or as a comprehensive checklist, adopting as many of the recommended techniques, apps and services below as you can. Follow these guidelines to *maximize* your privacy, anonymity and security.

More About: Links to Other Sites (and the ¢ sign) - For full transparency, please note that some of my links to external websites contain affiliate links (indicated by a cents sign, ¢). This means that if you ultimately buy the relevant app or service, I will earn a benefit (usually a small commission or the chance at one) at no cost whatsoever to you as it's the sellers that pay any commissions, not you. You can be sure that I would never highlight apps or services that I don't personally believe in as that would undermine the hard work I put into this book and all my related efforts. You can read more here, http://www.cogipas.com/about-links-to-other-sites/.

The Basics (Achieving Security)

- Construct strong passphrases. To keep track of all your passwords and to automatically generate good passphrases use a trusted password management app. Also enable any double-authentication features offered for your accounts such as Google https://www.google.com/landing/2step/ and Facebook (Settings > Security > Login Approvals) http://www.cogipas.com/eb8c.

    → see chapter 3 and use an app such as *LastPass* ¢ (free) http://www.cogipas.com/lastpass or *RoboForm* ¢ (premium) http://www.cogipas.com/roboform

- Keep your operating system up-to-date (whether automatically or manually) and use anti-malware apps, perhaps choosing from many excellent free ones, to prevent *viruses, worms, Trojans, rootkits, spyware, adware, email/web bugs* and other *malware*. Pause and reflect before selecting *links or attachments* - whether received via email, social media, torrent file-sharing, chatting, or Usenet newsgroups - even when received from trusted sources.

> → see chapter 5 and use anti-malware apps such as *AVG Anti-Virus* (free)
> http://free.avg.com/ or *Kaspersky Internet Security 2015* ¢ (premium)
> http://www.cogipas.com/premium-anti-malware

- Properly configure your wireless Internet connection to thwart hackers and mischievous neighbors from stealing, sniffing or hijacking your Internet connection. Don't access any password protected accounts or conduct any sensitive web browsing over public Wi-Fi *hotspots* unless using secure end-to-end protection. When shopping online look for a secure connection (https, noting the 's') and trust your instincts. If something online seems too good to be true, it probably is.

> → see chapter 8 and use a tool specifically geared for protecting you when using public Wi-Fi hotspots such as *HotSpotShield* (free with ads)
> http://www.hotspotshield.com/ or its premium *Elite* version ¢
> http://www.cogipas.com/hotspotshield

- Always lock and password protect your devices. Also consider using accounts or profiles with limited privileges, especially for web browsing, to limit the harm hackers and drive-by download malware attacks can inflict.

> → see chapter 9

- Protect your *children* by taking an interest in their online activities and by mentoring them to ensure that they do not engage in *inappropriate behavior* on the Internet or become victims of online bullies, trolls or predators.

> → see chapter 10 and use proven monitoring apps such as *Family Cyber Alert* ¢
> (premium) http://www.cogipas.com/family-cyber-alert-app and *Spector Pro*
> (premium) http://www.spectorsoft.com/products/SpectorPro_Windows/

Intermediate (Enhancing Privacy)

- Be careful what information you share on *social media*, keep your circles of friends tight and avoid using social logins (SSO). Be careful and cautious providing *personal information* to anyone, but especially to strangers or unknown websites, and provide only the bare minimum or even fake details.

> → see chapter 6 and frequently check your Facebook *Activity Log*
> https://www.facebook.com/me/allactivity and use plugins that block tracking such
> as *Facebook Disconnect* (free) https://disconnect.me/disconnect

- Use proven web browser plugins to *block tracking cookies* and prevent *third party tracking elements* from monitoring your online activities and from building invasive profiles about.

    → see chapter 4 and use free anti-tracking browser plugins such as *HTTPS Everywhere* https://www.eff.org/https-everywhere, *Ghostery* https://www.ghostery.com/ and *AdBlockPlus* https://adblockplus.org/

- Use your web browser's *private mode* especially for any sensitive browsing (using Chrome's *Incognito*, Firefox's *Private Browsing*, Internet Explorer's *InPrivate* or Safari's *Private Browsing*). Browsing in private mode disables tracking cookies and also prevents plenty of trace information such as browsing and search histories from being saved on your device.

    → see chapter 11

- For sign-ups and subscriptions, use disposable *temporary email* to keep your personal email address private, especially when signing up to unknown or obscure sites or services.

    → see chapter 14 and use reliable services such as *Mailinator* (free) http://mailinator.com/, *MailExpire* (free) http://www.mailexpire.com/ and *Guerrilla Email* (free) https://www.guerrillamail.com/

Advanced (Reaching Anonymity)

- *Hide your true IP address* from snoops using a trusted and well-established *web anonymizing service* whether a proxy, the Onion Router (Tor) or a premium VPN service.

    → see chapters 12 and 13 and use free web anonymizing services such as *Tor Project* https://www.torproject.org/ or *HotspotShield* (with ads) http://www.hotspotshield.com/

    → For ultimate anonymity, use a *VPN service* such as *Private Internet Access* ¢ (premium) http://www.cogipas.com/pia or *PureVPN* ¢ (premium) http://www.cogipas.com/purevpn which offer better overall protection and are more versatile. For example, in addition to encrypting your Internet connection end-to-end, these VPNs also let you choose the location of the exit gateways, access streaming television webcasts or other geographically restricted content, and mask your IP address for other activities too such as torrent file-sharing (see below)

- Use a *mass downloading app* ideally in conjunction with a web anonymizing service to download dozens or hundreds of items at a time and to grab embedded or streaming videos and audio from websites.

  → see chapter 12 and use apps such as *HTTrack Website Copier* (free) http://www.httrack.com/ and *Internet Download Manager* ¢ (premium) http://www.cogipas.com/idm

- Use powerful *encryption apps* to hide and protect the information, data and downloads on your devices, whether from inadvertent disclosure (for example, through loss or theft) or from determined adversaries.

  → see chapter 15 and use trusted apps such as *DiskCryptor* (free) https://diskcryptor.net/wiki/Main_Page, *VeraCrypt* (free) http://sourceforge.net/projects/veracrypt/ or *BestCrypt* (premium) http://www.jetico.com/encryption-bestcrypt/

- In addition to understanding the privacy and security risks of *torrent file-sharing*, use an *anonymizing service* especially tailored for torrenting.

  → see chapter 16 and use a torrent app such as *μTorrent* (free) http://www.utorrent.com/ or *Vuze* (free) http://www.vuze.com/

  → protect yourself from "unfriendly" connections while torrenting with *PeerBlock* (free) http://www.peerblock.com/ and consider enhancing your defenses with additional blacklists from *I-BlockList* (most are free) http://www.iblocklist.com/

  → for ultimate torrent file-sharing anonymity, choose a VPN service that caters to torrent users *and* has a strong privacy policy such as *Private Internet Access* ¢ (premium) http://www.cogipas.com/pia

- Be aware that your access to *Usenet newsgroups* is likely censored. Also know that everything you post to Usenet will be archived forever and could be traced back to you unless you take certain precautions.

  → see chapter 17 and use a reputable Usenet provider that gives you full uncensored access to all available newsgroups and respects your privacy with a no logging policy such as *Newshosting* ¢ (free trial & premium) http://www.cogipas.com/newshosting or *UsenetServer* ¢ (free trial & premium) http://www.cogipas.com/UsenetServer

- Use *privacy cleaning apps*, especially after any sensitive activities, to clear the traces of information left behind on your device by its web browser, operating system and apps.

→ see chapter 18 and use proven apps such as *BleachBit* (free) http://bleachbit.sourceforge.net/, *Privacy Eraser Free* (free) http://www.cogipas.com/pef and *Privacy Eraser Pro* ¢ (premium) http://www.cogipas.com/pep

- Understand that *deleted items* on your devices can be easily recovered by snoops. Securely and permanently delete items by *wiping* them. Also don't forget to *wipe free space* (empty storage) and to *purge empty directory entries* (old file and folder names) left behind on your storage media.

  → see chapter 19 and use apps such as *Privacy Eraser Pro* ¢ (premium) http://www.cogipas.com/pep and *Directory Snoop* (premium) http://www.briggsoft.com/dsnoop.htm

Last Thoughts

- Periodically conduct a privacy check or an "audit" of your online privacy and of your devices to confirm that you are exercising good privacy practices.

  → see Annexes A and B

- Keep learning and don't forget to have fun. The landscape for Internet privacy, anonymity and security is changing all the time and probably not for the better. However, you should look upon the Internet, not just as a source of risks, but as a great source of information and enjoyment. Just keep your head up and watch your step.

* * *

For updates and additional information about this quick and practical checklist for protecting your Internet privacy, anonymity and security, please visit http://www.cogipas.com/privacy-protection/.

A Final Word

Congratulations! You've made it through the book.

You now have all the knowledge you need to protect your privacy, stay secure and be anonymous online. Although the risks are real, you should try not to be paranoid about them.

* * *

I hope that you enjoyed this book. I put a lot of hard work into it and I am very proud of the end result. Please consider providing a review. Even taking just 10 seconds to assign a star-rating and to add a few words would be greatly appreciated as this gives me valuable feedback. Thanks!

- to leave a review on *Amazon USA*, please visit via http://www.cogipas.com/Amazon-USA
- to leave a review on *Amazon UK*, please visit via http://www.cogipas.com/Amazon-UK
- to leave a review on any other site, such as *Goodreads*, please visit via http://www.cogipas.com/review-book

~ ~ ~

The End

61739141R00145

Made in the USA
Lexington, KY
18 March 2017